THE SKIN GAME

612?

THE SKIN GAME

The International Beauty Business Brutally Exposed

Gerald McKnight

SIDGWICK & JACKSON
LONDON

First published in Great Britain in 1989 by Sidgwick & Jackson Limited

Copyright © 1989 by Gerald McKnight

ISBN 0-283-99668-4

Typeset by Hewer Text Composition Services, Edinburgh
Printed in Great Britain by Billing & Sons, Worcester
for Sidgwick & Jackson Limited
1 Tavistock Chambers, Bloomsbury Way
London WC1A 2SG

Contents

Acknowledgements

My thanks, firstly, to my editor Susan Hill for entrusting me with what was, for a man, a daunting commission. It has revealed some of the roots of human folly and allowed me to see our weaknesses and insecurities in a more compassionate light; perhaps, also, to wonder a little at some of the harsh quirks of nature.

My gratitude goes to many others who guided me through the complex and often mysterious hinterland of the cosmetics industry. I am especially indebted to Dr Albert Kligman and his wife in Philadelphia; to 'Sam' Sugiyama of Shiseido in London, to his distinguished colleagues in Tokyo and their redoubtable Dr Ozawa in Yokohama; to Dr Earle W. Brauer of Revlon, New Jersey; to Jacques Courtin Clarins, Pierre Dinant and Dominique Lapierre in Paris; to Ted Clarke in Grasse; and to the Société Lautier, also in Grasse.

In and around London, I offer my special thanks to Ross Young, publisher of COSMOPOLITAN; Buddy Wedderburn; and Pippa Lacey, editor of *SPC*; also to my old colleague Gordon MacKenzie of the *Daily Mail*; Robin Vincent of Clarins Paris; Leslie Kenton; Steve McIvor of BUAV; Ken Green of Revlon; John Terry; Nikki Smith; Myra Sims; Margaret Allen; Maureen Barry; Wendy Baker; Joanne Glasbey of *Time Out*; Sally Gilbert; Anne-Marie Haas; Stephanie Roberts; Felicity Hone of the London College of Fashion; Anthony Edwards of *Harpers*; Marion Kelly of CTPA; Paul Rossiter; Desmond Elliot; Dr David Thom of Unilever; Dr Leslie Gardiner and Dr Dev Basra of Harley Street; Dr Stuart Ungar; Mr Peter K. B. Davis; and others too numerous to mention.

In New York and the USA, I can only single out those most valuable to the work, but there were many more who helped. First, Mimi Wise, whose selfless researching steered me clear of many traps; also Betty York, for her unstinting encouragement and advice;

Amelia Bassin, who proved as enchanting to meet as she was enlightening; John Ledes, who became a generous colleague of the road; Stanley Kohlenberg, for wise counsel; and James Lee, for the use of his apartment.

Lee Israel, too, was materially most helpful. So were Morris Herstein, who gave valuable advice and encouragement; the indomitable Susan Rich, Leslie Fain, Steve Mannheimer, Hazel Bishop, Annette Green, Mark Rosen, Bobbie Long and Dr James Reardon. Corinne Sharpe, Nick Ludington, Tony Marshall, Mary Potter and Dawne Arden were among many friends who suffered my travellers' tales if not gladly, then at least with encouraging warmth.

I thank them all, and gratefully acknowledge permission to use excerpts from *Consumer Reports*, February 1988, on page 1 (Copyright 1988 by Consumer's Union of United States, Inc., Mount Vernon, N.Y.10553).

Gerald McKnight
1989

Foreword

Scowling like a nervous prince, Dr Tatsuo Ozawa was ushered into the laboratory ante-room in Yokohama by a bevy of white-coated assistants. I found myself face to face with the man whom many believe to be the world's most forward-thinking cosmetics scientist alive. As director of research and development at Japan's biggest cosmetics skin care company, Shiseido, Ozawa is respected as a visionary leader among the most advanced in his field. I had come to Japan to learn how and why it is that the realistic Western world allows itself to be lulled into spending billions on lipsticks, creams, scents and skin care lotions, at prices which in many cases multiply by ten the true value of their ingredients. If anybody could answer those questions, it was Dr Ozawa.

In London, Paris, New York and the South of France I had tried in vain to discover the reason. Now, at the fountain-head, I earnestly hoped for enlightenment. Did Dr Ozawa believe that dreams – the hopes and aspirations of millions upon millions of women to become more alluring, more beautiful, to banish the signs and wrinkles of age – could justify the profits of such prestigious cosmetics corporations as Estée Lauder, Revlon, L'Oréal and his own Shiseido? Was it morally right to charge so much for so little?

At first sight it was hard to imagine Dr Ozawa advising women on anything to do with glamour and beauty. A lean, dark man in his mid-fifties, he wore a withdrawn expression that suggested lofty insularity. Here, unquestionably, was a man to whom all visitors were an intrusion, a waste of valuable time. Yet Ozawa had agreed to share his secrets with me. I had been told that his theories and predictions were as exciting as any to be found in the scientific inner world of cosmetics, and I wanted to hear them.

'The present dramatic progress in science and technology,' he had forecast, 'is about to usher in a new era of human civilization. It will bring cosmetics closer to medical products.'

What, I asked, made him think so?

The dark eyes gleamed. The answer, when it came, was enigmatic. 'Beauty and health,' Ozawa told me, 'will develop in a completely separate manner, clearly distinct from pharmaceuticals. The extension of man's lifespan is already on our scientific horizon. It will increasingly require the help of cosmetics.'

Using a blackboard to demonstrate the chemistry involved, Dr Ozawa produced a serious of equations and formulae that would have baffled Einstein.

His firm belief, I knew, was that our generation was likely to be the last to regard the biblical three score years and ten as the limit of life. But how did cosmetics come into this?

'In tomorrow's world, man will probably live to be a hundred and fifty,' he said.

I began to see. The great man's theory sprang from the belief that this longevity can only be achieved by replacing worn-out parts of the body, and by helping us to age less quickly. Thus cosmetics, including plastic surgery, would have to play a vital part in disguising these physical changes.

After all, who would want to live on for an additional half century as an aged and infirm relic? As Ozawa explained, the really big change in lifespan which is now in the sights of more than one branch of science must inevitably increase the role of what he calls 'human science'. Therefore it has to include cosmetics. He links the future of his profession, of all their beautifying creams and anti-ageing products, with the rapidly approaching advances in atomic physics, biotechnology, computerization, data storage, electronics, fine chemistry and genetic engineering. All of these, he points out, are working towards the same goal of extending our lifetimes.

In short, Dr Ozawa envisages a future in which cosmetics, including the after-care and provision of spare parts for our ageing bodies, will become a commonplace necessity, a major contribution to an extended lifespan. 'If we are to live longer, the need to hold on to our youth will become essential,' he argues persuasively. Only cosmetics, he believes, can provide the means to do so. Thus even the enormous outlay of $50 million a year on his vast and superbly equipped laboratory is fully justified in his eyes. He sees his own function, and the work of the enthusiastic young team of scientists and technologists under him, as part of an urgent drive towards a better, fuller and considerably longer life for coming generations.

Meanwhile, of course, we must pay what many think are exorbitant prices for his products, in order to fund the enormously expensive research going on in Yokohama and elsewhere. I heard the same argument repeated in Revlon's New Jersey plant, in the Paris experimental centre of Clarins – indeed in every one of the large cosmetics companies I visited. They all ask us to invest in the future – more correctly *their* future, for the cosmetics business is highly competitive – whenever we buy their goods.

At a time when many of the world's major skin care companies – including Shiseido – are facing a crisis, when regulatory bodies in the United States and other countries are seriously questioning their 'miracle' and anti-ageing claims, Dr Ozawa's predictions may seem wildly optimistic. If some of the charges stick, many of the present 'wrinkle removers' and 'age eliminators' will either have to be tested, licensed and sold only on prescription as drugs, or be withdrawn.

But he insists that the present distinction between cosmetics and drugs will have to be eased. Until then, he agrees, the cosmetics manufacturers will sail under the threat. The promises they make of reducing age and the signs of age; of replacing dying cells in our bodies and eliminating unwanted fat; of restoring hair growth and making the ugly attractive, are too cost-effective to drop.

But with pressure mounting on the major companies to alter their rules, to accept that some of their products are or should be listed and tested as drugs, the whole vast, enormously valuable beauty industry is at a crucial stage. I left Japan more than ever determined to find out what lay hidden beneath its glossy exterior, and whether – as many believe – the promise of its seductive fruits is little more than a costly illusion.

1

LONDON PRIDE

In London I asked Dr Ozawa's co-director, 'Sam' Sugiyama, to tell me what value cosmetics provide for the money we spend on them. What, in the opinion of this sophisticated, affable and intelligent ex-chemist, could explain the tyranny that keeps a world of Englishwomen paying ten times the actual cost of the ingredients in their make-up and skin care for his company's goods? Why, for instance, should such an apparently simple substance as Shiseido's Bio-Performance Cream – sold in Harrods, Selfridges and other major British stores since early 1988 – cost £36 for a mere 40 millilitres, which is to say £27 an ounce?

Could he also explain to me the price structure of an ordinary designer lipstick? A recent survey in America discovered that some brands of the oily, coloured wax that all lipsticks are made of would cost more than $150 an ounce to buy, yet cost the manfacturer only *ten cents of every dollar the consumer spends on it*.

Since American women spend more than half a billion dollars a year on the stuff, that is an awful lot of dimes. And Revlon, one of the biggest in the lipstick trade, has so far managed to market 148 different lipstick colours, including forty-one shades of pink.

Whichever way you look at the cosmetic jungle, I put it to Sugiyama, the costs seem outrageous. And frequently the customer is paying for little more than a famous name. In the same *Consumer Reports* test on a panel of American women, fifty per cent of samples of a lipstick by Chanel (costing $14.50 for .08 ounces, or $181.25 per ounce), were taken out of their elegant, expensive tubes and swapped with the contents of a regular drugstore brand, Flame 'N Glow (only $2.26 for .12 ounces, or $18.83 per ounce). The women had no idea which was which, and many of them found that they preferred the cheap lipstick to the one costing ten times as much.

In Britain, a 1988 poll commissioned by *Cosmopolitan* magazine into the buying and user habits of women under 35 revealed that only 6% of those questioned admitted to using no make-up at all on their faces. In the younger age groups those who used it did so, on average, less than five days a week. Use of make-up began at the age of fifteen, mainly with eye colouring, shadow and liner. Mascara, lipstick, and blusher followed in descending order of popularity.

Less than a third of the women had begun with foundation, still fewer with face powder. The poll found that use of these products increased later in life. Over three quarters of the women said they spent five minutes or more applying their make-up, while a sizeable few – one in four – admitted devoting over ten minutes to the task.

Among the youngest, the majority gave 'creative enjoyment and fun' as their main reason for using the stuff, while only just over a quarter said they wore it to impress a man, or men in general (this jumped remarkably, however, in the late teens when nearly half the women questioned admitted that this was their chief motivation).

Significantly more than half of all age groups insisted that high-priced make-up is no better than cheaper brands, with 60% declaring that 'all you're paying for with high priced products is their glossy image'.

For in spite of all the millions spent on packaging, hype and promotion, the poll showed that modestly priced products sold by High Street chemists, particularly Boots No 7, lead by a long way with the younger British woman. The fancy goods so enticingly marketed by Estée Lauder, Revlon, and Clinique are bought by only three in every hundred.

According to another survey carried out in the United States last year, the average woman owns seven lipsticks, of which only 2.6 are frequently used. The same woman will probably invest in twelve eye shadows, but only use about five of them. Sticks and pencils in her possession can, says the report, 'be counted in dozens'.

So what, in Sam Sugiyama's astute and experienced eyes, can excuse such hyper-inflation in the marketplace? Other than the lure of packaging and hype and a billion dollar promotional budget – which, again, add to the cost of the goods? Is not Shiseido's expansion into one after another European country, and into others in the Far East (seen as the next big market area, with China coming on stream in the '90s), simply adding to the cost of its products? Are they not forcing their way, however elegantly and attractively, onto the British public?

'I totally disagree,' he said. 'If our products cost a lot, then that is because of what we put in them. Our biotechnology has succeeded in extracting hyaluronic acid by fermentation, and do you know how much that costs? It is only obtainable from chickens' combs. One gram – smaller than my little fingernail – will cost over £50. A kilo is over £7000. No, this industry is so tough that there is no real chance of overcharging, or undercharging. You have to be very, very smart to survive.'

Survival, I pointed out, hardly seems a pressing problem for his Japanese giant of a corporation, whose Yokohama laboratory covers an area the size of London's Middlesex Hospital. And which, along with the luxury suites of offices in all parts of the world, has been built entirely out of profits made by selling dreams.

Not that Sugiyama accepts for one minute that that is what he and his colleagues are doing. Twenty years ago Shiseido began expanding into Europe. First came Italy, then Holland, Belgium, France and West Germany. And now Britain. Why so long in getting here? I asked as we talked in his comfortable office in Mayfair's Cork Street. Was this a sign of British maturity, of the English proving less easily persuaded to share in the dreams, or was it an indication of their insular conservatism?

Queen Elizabeth II, as he must have read, will use no other skin care creams and lotions than the Cyclax products she has always used. The company, which no longer makes cosmetics for the general public, reportedly continues to supply her. Like the long-established Patou fragrance, Joy, with which she perfumes her morning bath, and the occasional dab of Penhaligon's Bluebell she puts behind her ears, the Queen sticks to old favourites. Cyclax proudly claims that, on the day she was married in 1947, she wore their Balmoral Pink lipstick. And reports say that she has worn it ever since. So changing the habits of British women like her could well have exhausted Sugiyama and his researchers. Was that why we were so low on his list?

'No, it's because you made it so difficult,' he said. 'We do not believe in expansion for its own sake, and we had to wait until we could find the right people here. Also, because we had to do our homework.' Three years was spent researching into British women's skins, Sugiyama explained. What he and his technologists learned in that time was that English ladies' peaches-and-cream complexions are not all that they seem to be. 'Very interesting,' he said. 'We did find some ethnic differences which were not expected. And, of course, we had to ensure that our products would suit the British ladies, though it cost us a fortune to do so.'

With the help of a professor of dermatology from the University of Wales, Professor Ronald Marks, Sugiyama and his team also learned that British women's skins age far faster than many others. 'For instance, they have these beautiful ivory complexions. A very nice texture. And with unusually small pores. But their skins deteriorate very rapidly after a certain age. Faster than American, French or Japanese women's.

'Another interesting feature is that their sebum secretion rate is very high – three times as high as that of the American women we tested, and probably twice what our women have in Japan.' Sugiyama has found no explanation for this curiosity, and is investigating what appears to be a contradictory situation.

In make-up, though, British women barely rated. 'Walk along Oxford Street and you probably only see one woman in ten wearing proper make-up,' he said, 'whereas the French like heavy make-up. And the majority of Englishwomen don't worry about the quality of their moisturizers. They buy them from the Body Shop or Boots. But on the other hand they are very fragrance-orientated.'

Had his researches revealed why any of this happens? Why British women wrinkle sooner, despite their fine-textured skins and ivory complexions?

Sugiyama looked thoughtfully at his own flawlessly white hands. 'It is all to do with gravity and mother sea,' he said. 'When the earth was born, every living creature, including man, was in water. In the sea. And after perhaps fifteen million years of evolution, there are still ingredients in the "mother sea" – the placenta liquid in our mothers' wombs – which are good for us in a way we do not fully understand. We are studying that now.

'The real cause of ageing, of our skins losing their elasticity, is the pull of the earth, which you don't get in the Dead Sea, or in the womb, or in outer space.' He laughed. 'So if you want to avoid ageing, you must live in space. There is no other way to avoid getting wrinkles, once you are out of the womb.'

No answer to my question, perhaps. But a clue to why cosmetics cost so much, and need so much money spent on them to reach our consciousness and to maintain their position in the multi-billion dollar industry.

In September 1988, Shiseido ranked third in the world, with $2.7 billion sales. Ahead of them was the huge French company, L'Oréal, dealing primarily with hair products and scent, with $4.1 billion. Then came Britain's Unilever, just pipping Shiseido with $2.8 billion (following their recent acquisition of Chesebrough-Ponds, which has given the British firm a huge hold on the lower end of the market). Close on Shiseido's tail comes Avon, the great American cosmetics giant, built on direct selling. Then Revlon, followed by Proctor & Gamble and the indefatigable Estée Lauder.

How, I wanted to know, would any of these measure up to close scrutiny? And who were the men (with few exceptions, the industry is male-dominated) who were emptying our pockets at such great profits to themselves?

In 1909 a Mrs Elizabeth Hubbard persuaded Florence Nightingale Graham, a young Canadian woman of Scottish-Cornish parentage, to partner her in opening an entirely new Fifth Avenue beauty salon in New York. Borrowed money was being used to finance what was then a risky commercial venture. But the new employee was to become known the world over as Elizabeth Arden, and since that historic day the beauty jungle has been growing steadily in wealth and power.

Today, it is vast. It revels in profit margins of well over 50 per cent from a turnover of close on $20 billion worldwide, of which fragrances share half and half with make-up and skin care. But since Helena Rubinstein and Elizabeth Arden died, and their one charismatic successor and rival, Charles Revson of Revlon succumbed to cancer, the industry has – with the honourable exception of Estée Lauder – lacked major entrepreneurial personalities.

Today's cosmetics tsars are less noticeably stamped with the individuality and chutzpa of those early go-getters. But that is not to say that they lack the shrewdness and cunning to run the shop as well as any of them – there are certainly no paupers among them. Wall Street analysts Goldman Sachs assess those at the top in America as being among the highest earners in the land. According to surveys, many are drawing down salaries and perks of close to – in some cases well above – a million dollars a year. For these men, the world of cosmetics is a gilded playground.

Take a fictitious case, which could happen any day . . . At 12.45 Robin Vincent, British managing director of the French company,

Clarins Paris, is steering his boss towards a corner table in a fashionable London restaurant. Jacques Courtin Clarins, head of an empire of skin care products that is now among the top ten in the world, is seldom seen in this city: he does not speak the language and is not crazy about the food. It must be something special that has brought him to London today.

Courtin Clarins is here, surely, to discuss the electrifying news he has just received in Paris, not through the BBC World Service or the local media, but on one of the cosmetics industry's many grapevines. It is a rumour that Estée Lauder in New York is about to launch a new and remarkable product on the already super-saturated fragrance market. Word has filtered through to M. Clarins that Leonard Lauder and his ambitious wife Evelyn – who jointly run the still privately owned company pioneered and built to one of the world's top three by Leonard's mother – are about to plunge more money on this launch than ever before. More millions will be spent on world TV, press and promotional advertising, on bottling and packaging and hustling than at any time in Lauder's long history.

Still more significant and disturbing, to M. Clarins, is the name of the top film and television soap opera beauty whose name is to be used on the product. Faultlessly in shape, despite five decades of hard living, the star is to be the gold and platinum image-booster for the fragrance. It will bear her name, with all its immense sales potential.

Not only is an expensive, prestige fragrance being born. There is also an accompanying range of skin cleansers, moisturizing creams, make-up and every other species of beautifying embellishment favoured by women since the days of ancient Egypt. At a time when Clarins Paris has just absorbed the great Paris couturier house of Lanvin, with its competing perfume range, this piece of intelligence is as welcome as a badly cooked Yorkshire pudding.

Only one thing can be done. A rival launch must be put in hand at once to counter the threat. Clarins Paris must create, perfect and market an equally new and wonderful product to add to their existing 57-plus varieties of creams, potions, powders and fragrances.

Having decided this, the chairman has wasted no time. As the head waiter seats him beside Robin Vincent, and their two heads bend towards one another over the white napery, there is no doubt at all about the importance and urgency of his visit. Jacques Courtin

6

Clarins and his London manager have more to talk about than the food.

In Paris, meanwhile, it is raining. Had the anxious skin care magnate but known it, one of the chief threats coming from the new scent is emerging literally on his doorstep. In the Rue Raspail, running off the Avenue Victor Hugo in the outlying Paris district of Levallois-Perret, Pierre Dinant, leading designer of bottles and packages for prestige perfume houses, is already at work on its design. It is he, according to the scenario of this fictional story, who has been chosen to create the wrapping and the *flacon* (in France, one must never call it a *bouteille*) for Lauder's new fragrance. Through half-round, gold-framed spectacles, Dinant is eyeing an iridescent model made of hand-chiselled and drilled plastic. The top is magically sexy and gem-encrusted, like a Tiffany lamp.

Satisfied, M. Dinant takes a quick look at the wet street. The day does not tempt him even to venture across the road for a sandwich. Sweeping back two tassels of shoulder-length blond hair, he shrugs. When did a missed lunch ever tear Pierre Dinant away from a new project? The *flacon* ordered by Lauder will be daringly original. And ready on time, of course.

Simultaneously, six thousand miles away, a fourth member of the imagined cast is becoming involved in the drama. Through the one-way darkened windows of his stretch limo, Ronald Perelman, president and chairman of Revlon International, is gazing gloomily out at an early morning haze wrapping Manhattan's skyscrapers. A wedding veil – or a shroud?

The news that his company is facing immediate competition from Lauder has only just reached him through the car's radio telephone. With his own company's equally 'most expensive launch ever' of a new prestige fragrance about to take place, this is terrible news.

He has personally assured his board that there is no need to worry about competition. The French, he has told them, led the world into fragrances half a century ago. But a new age has dawned. America – and, thanks to the genius of its late founder, Charles Revson (super-charged by Perelman's own considerable business acumen), Revlon itself – is now at the head of the game. Perelman's highly paid, expert team of researchers under Revlon's top chemist, Dr Earle W. Brauer (the only dermatologist working in the industry

7

who is certified by his professional board) have been working on the new product for months. If any other cosmetics house should attempt to bring out a rival product, then Perelman and the Revlon millions will soon whip them back through the market fence.

None the less, he has to admit to himself, this is unwelcome news. Who could have guessed that the shrewd Leonard Lauder – with his mother still cautioning him, between the incessant social engagements which now fill her life, to 'sell, sell, sell' – could have loosed such a body blow at his plans? And without anyone in his company getting an advance whiff of it?

So tight is the Lauder family clan, so discreetly held its balance sheets and accounts, that not even Revlon's chairman and chief executive had known that he would be facing this rival in the same ring, in the same bout, and for the same prize. At this very moment, Lauder's salesmen will be calling on the same offices as his people, the key centres of the cosmetics buyers and directors of every store group in the country. Not to mention the international marketplace, from New York's top flagship outlets to the smallest international chain.

The new fragrance will be in direct competition, challenging his incentive structure, his price positions and his mark-ups. No doubt some of his best counsellors and sales assistants will be lured to the Lauder stands in the valued sites of prestige stores' cosmetics areas – defined by the trade as 'real estate'.

Perelman's one consolation is that it takes more than genius to produce anything as dazzlingly beautiful and complex as a new quality fragrance. Those layouts he approved at yesterday's final meetings were . . . what was the word? Scintillating! Yes, they were. And his sales and marketing people are predicting well over two thousand 'doors' (each store has a known number, all hotly fought for and promised in advance – in exchange for 'break' deals, which guarantee the store free inclusion and prominent mention in launch advertising). Just for starters.

All this, in our fictional story just as it would be in real life, has been meticulously costed and planned. Revlon's exclusive opening campaign will be staged in Bloomingdales, Macys and Saks, representing the top prestige areas of New York. But now, with the intruder on his heels, who knows what the chairman can rely on?

Perhaps others are also on the starting line? What about Jim Preston, president of Avon Products? Since his company's take-over of Giorgio, he has become a massive threat to the top of the market. Avon's huge direct-selling operation has crossed the tracks into the élite area with astonishing ease. Companies like Lauder (along with its satellites Clinique and Prescriptives), Revlon and the few others with long-term claims to exclusive territory are having to make room for this door-to-door outsider and its multi-million dollar invasion.

The cosmetics business is played like an unending hand of poker. Everyone gambles with enormous stakes on catching a fickle, elusive but seduceable consumer public which, though it may spend billions in the first year on a new product, can equally refuse even to put the stuff on their dressing tables. But if one player puts up, the others must follow or drop out of the skin game altogether.

And Perelman cannot be sure that Jim Preston is not ready with yet another 'brand-new' fragrance. Indeed, it would be unlike the Avon chief not to do his damnedest to snatch some of the lustre from Revlon's and Lauder's launches. There may be others, too.

In Paris there is L'Oréal, giant parent of America's Cosmair corporation. This, the greatest of all hair preparation makers, is also the merchant of Lancôme, of Paloma Picasso and other famous fragrances. With Shiseido and Unilever, L'Oréal is currently in the world's top three. What Lindsay Owen-Jones, L'Oréal's president, is planning, and what the leading Japanese companies – Yoshio Ohno of Shiseido, Kanebo, Pola and the others – have hidden up their kimono sleeves, Perelman can only guess.

Shiseido has quietly been establishing itself in the markets of the West for several years. Won't that brilliant dermatologist of theirs, Dr Ozawa, right at this moment be dreaming up something in his vast, high-tech laboratory in Yokohama?

In the cosmetics industry, as the chairman of Revlon knows only too well, there is one quality that counts for more than money. In its influence, it counts for more even than brains. Illusion, backed by entrepreneurial flair, is the essential element. In the past it has brought wealth to the industry, and Ron Perelman is putting his faith in it now. Without it, as he knows, all Revlon's research and development facilities, the expensive testing and developing plants set up to justify ever further-reaching claims, would be worthless. It is the company that has best understood the nature of illusion, and best expressed and marketed it, that will win the hard, competitive struggle that our fictional story has exemplified.

2

THE PECKING ORDER

The rulers of the world of cosmetics take themselves and their business very seriously indeed. They are among the most sensitive of any of the men running the world's major commercial undertakings. Some seem to be afraid of any inquiry at all into their business. They either express numb horror at the suggestion that they should show their hands, or give such grudging, guarded interviews that it becomes difficult to believe they have nothing to hide.

Today the giants have to be financial heavyweights where their forerunners were merely opportunists and entrepreneurs. Leonard Lauder, who runs the business created by his mother, now in her eighties, is credited by his promotion department with a fine nose for detecting the different 'notes' and essential ingredients of a fragrance. This may be a useful asset, but nowadays few if any of the big company executives need to be involved in the actual creation of their products.

Ronald Perelman, who sits in Charles Revson's chair in the General Motors building on Fifth Avenue in New York, would indeed prefer to be known as a shrewd, billionaire businessman rather than as a cosmetics tsar. He shuns personal publicity as fiercely as Estée Lauder courts it from café society and the fashionable press. Perelman is sometimes offensive to reporters who approach him too closely, or to those who try to take unflattering pictures of his TV star and ex-gossip columnist wife, Claudia Cohen.

In the year that Perelman took over Revlon, David Blum, researching a story on the new tycoon chairman for *New York* magazine, described a memorably unpleasant brush with the Revlon chief outside a Broadway theatre. During the fracas, in which Blum says Perelman gave his, Blum's, wife a fairly sharp shove, Perelman allegedly displayed a persona far from the smooth, cool image of his firm. When the reporter objected to his wife being

10

pushed aside, Perelman demanded his identity 'in a threatening manner', says Blum. The impression left on the reporter was of a man who not only disliked media interference in his private life, but who actually believed that he had the power to control what the press said about him.

This hardly seems to be an exaggeration. A recent profile complained that 'the couple's life is public only to the extent that columnists are permitted to bubble about their parties. Further liberties are darkly discouraged.' As many other celebrities have found, this kind of behaviour is not a way to get good, or even fair, treatment from some sections of the press. Perelman's haughty refusal to supply their needs has led to some of the more virulent American gossip writers and reporters using him and his wife as soft targets for barbs and gibes:

> Perelman is known at Revlon for his omnipresent plainclothes security guard; for leaving half-finished meetings; for being abrasive with his secretaries. Ronald, in short, is the very model of a modern tycoon.

So writer Peter Hood described the Revlon chairman in *Spy* magazine's February 1988 issue. Hood also quoted 'a social observer who knows the Perelmans' – a source whom one could accurately describe as unimpeachable – telling the writer that

> they [the Perelmans] have a lot of hangers-on who do things. In those circles, nobody is friends anyhow – they're all using each other for cosmetic reasons, to give the idea of a powerful, intimate circle.

In the Revlon offices it was possible to confirm at least that Nancy Tuck Gardiner, former beauty editor of *Town and Country*, is employed by the company, and that she works closely with her secretive chairman. But nothing I was told about her boss, or about the Revlon company and its subsidiaries, Max Factor, Almay and Halston, could confirm these unpleasant reports.

The *Spy* story, which was outrageously offensive to both Ronald and Claudia Perelman, was on the streets as we talked. In an editorial prologue, the magazine had referred to their 1985 marriage as 'a boon to everyone concerned. It takes two unpleasant people out of circulation.' Nancy Gardiner's view of her chairman was, as might be imagined, very different.

Suffice to say that their marriage and what the magazine called Ron Perelman's 'crazy but successful attempt to buy Revlon when Revlon absolutely did not want to be bought' both happened in 1985. Previously, Ronald Perelman had been no closer to cosmetics than the odour of after-shave, cigar smoke and aspirin in the boardrooms into which his corporate raids had taken him.

Suddenly he was one of the biggest players in the skin game, a billionaire chief executive of a multi-billion dollar combine of nail varnish, make-up, skin care, lipstick and fragrances renowned all over the world. It may explain why, as Peter Hood had heard rumoured, that Ronald and Claudia had chosen the fragrance of Revlon's relaunched, $130-an-ounce perfume Intimate together.

Perelman, who grew up in Philadelphia, had acquired Bachelor and Master of Science degrees before entering his father's business. Reportedly he had attended board meetings of the company, Belmont Industries, since the age of eleven. He had left in 1978 to start his own business, and in the same year bought 40 per cent of a jewellery distributor, Cohen-Hatfield, for $2 million.

As one report says: 'Seven years and half a dozen companies later, he would offer to buy Revlon for almost $2 *billion*. He had perfected the new way to make money: find an undervalued company, buy it with junk bond financing, sell the inessential product lines to recoup most of the purchase price, and return the core to profitability.' What this naïve assessment overlooks is the skill it takes to achieve this successfully. Perelman may be a publicity-shy tycoon, but he is also a dynamic and industrious chairman who, if Nancy Tuck Gardiner's faith is not to be shattered, will make a significant and formidable mark at Revlon and in the industry as a whole.

Welshman Lindsay Owen-Jones is an even newer new boy. The former managing director and chief executive of L'Oréal in France only took over as president late in 1987, but his hand is strong. He carries as many aces as Revlon, Lauder, Shiseido or any of the other majors.

'While Revlon was built on marketing savvy,' reported *Forbes* magazine in March 1984, 'L'Oréal's roots are in research.' Eugène Schueller, an obscure French chemist, had established L'Oréal in 1907 to sell his invention, hair colouring. At night in his small Paris apartment he made and bottled the stuff, calling on hairdressing salons by day to sell as many bottles as he could fill. Schueller established a reputation for care and proficiency, and still today L'Oréal's cosmetology laboratory at Clichy, outside Paris, is said to be the largest in the world, employing more than a thousand researchers. In 1984 the company was spending 3.3 per cent of cosmetic sales (turnover) on research, double that spent by Revlon and triple that of Avon, according to *Forbes*.

In 1988, when Britain's trade press was calling L'Oréal 'the biggest and most successful cosmetics company in the world', forty-three-year-old Owen-Jones was showing himself to be as firm a believer in the value of persistent research as the man he succeeded, François Dalle. 'Our secret is knowing how to develop brands from France and to create them worldwide,' he told Fiona Walsh of the London *Sunday Telegraph* last spring. 'Acquisitions are a very expensive way of building a business.'

Curiously, the new president must have forgotten L'Oréal's successful take-over of Warner Communications' cosmetics business – for $146 million – in January 1984. It was this that, according to *Forbes*, 'gave the company some of the fastest-growing fragrance names in the United States, Ralph Lauren and Gloria Vanderbilt', and set it on course for world leadership. It also signalled the end of François Dalle's legendary feud with Michael Bergerac of Revlon. Bergerac had taken over from Charles Revson after the founder's death. Dalle, so it was widely believed, resented what he saw as Bergerac's deliberate 'playing up of his Frenchness' to compete with L'Oréal's authentic Gallic flavour. He made the Warner acquisition in order to break Revlon's and Estée Lauder's hold on the US department stores, where L'Oréal operated through its Cosmair subsidiary. Whatever Owen-Jones says now, however much he claims that acquisitions are not methods that L'Oréal uses, he – as Dalle's chief executive – must have enjoyed the valuable uplift that his predecessor's take-over of Warner gave to the company.

Leonard Allan Lauder finds no difficulty in taking an extremely tolerant, one could almost say humanitarian, view of his role in life. His companies, as cosmetics consultant Allan G. Mottus reported in 1987, account for 38 per cent of the US cosmetic market – that is to say for well over a billion dollars – in overall turnover.

Devoutly religious, in New York he pays dutiful observance to his

Jewish faith. On High Holy Days he is known to desert his office for his rabbinical temple, where he and his wife Evelyn are active participants.

In this regard, though in few others, he differs – according to Estée's perceptive biographer, Lee Israel – from his mother. She, apparently, has been too busy to devote herself as he has done to religion. Lee Israel writes that Estée (she was born Josephine Esther Mentzer) has been noticeably absent from many holy occasions attended by her son. Bruised by Estée Lauder's notoriously sharp, pushy elbows, there are those who believe that her only true religion is trade. But it probably does not much matter what this ageing cosmetics queen does these days. Estée won her throne by hard selling and cool cheek. She had the audacity and the drive to push her products hard enough to achieve international acclaim. Admired and envied by some of the toughest people in the business, she says she has no head for heights, which is a commercial paradox. To climb to where she has got to, she had to force her way from obscurity to social eminence.

Israel infuriated her by recounting in her unauthorized book how Estée once surprised the Duke and Duchess of Windsor by appearing beside them at a Florida railway station as they were about to board a train. Holding the Duchess's arm, Estée was pictured by a photographer in well-publicised affinity with the distinguished couple. In 1988 she persuaded Raisa Gorbachev to visit her showroom. The question is, will Estée now describe herself as one of the Gorbachevs' close friends, as she did with the Windsors?

Once barred by the élitism of the Palm Beach Everglades Club, she showed equal courage, and unlimited sauce by getting herself invited to lunch there. Her equally daunting hostess was officially reprimanded by the committee and lost her tennis privileges, following a complaint by a scandalized member. Estée may have been simply trying to demonstrate the logic of Groucho Marx's refusal to join 'any club that would have me as a member'. But in her case nobody had asked her to join, and nobody did.

It did not stop her tidal-wave business success. Mrs Lauder's hunger for social prominence, for almost regal recognition, may have failed to win her a coronet or a guaranteed place in blue-blood society, but her drive, her uncanny use of touch, feel and smell in seducing a world of lesser women, have enthroned her in cosmetics. She is the last of the genuine personalities to become its queen.

When Estée Lauder learned that the biography of her was being diligently researched and written by Lee Israel, she did two things in a hurry. She dictated her own far less revealing auto-biographical work, and – through third parties – tried to suppress Ms Israel.

But Lee Israel, who had already written a number of prize-winning biographies, was not to be halted. The incident, dis-creditable as it may seem to Mrs Lauder's reputation as a generous and fair-minded person, was accepted by her peers in the indus-try as perfectly justifiable. Indeed, there are few toes inside those hand-made English leather shoes that can stand even the slightest pressure on them from the outside world.

Dreamland, it becomes clear to anyone trying to enter it, must never be tinged with doubt; still worse, with the harsh truth that some of its products are unbelievably overpriced, a few of its practices risky and many of its miracle claims unsupportable. We are asked to accept, therefore, that its inmates believe in their dreams as implicitly as Henry Ford believed in his Model T. That is hard to do. The most powerful and important of the dream merchants make their own rules. What they say and do, and the money they commit to launches of new products, are the sinews and fibres of a great industry. If we include related lines such as toilet soaps and some household products like air fresheners (containing the same basic fragrances as scent), that industry would have more money rattling through its tills than General Motors.

Yet no one can sensibly deny the therapeutic value of cosmetics. Indeed, future historians will be able to record that we spent more on them than on curative medicines, and for perfectly sound reasons. What of the woman who ends her life in a gas oven because her husband has left her, insisting that she has 'lost her looks'? Or of the man who is made redundant when over fifty, and knows it is due to his thinning hair and thickening waistline? Or of the working woman who comes home tired and dirty to cook the supper every night for her critical family? Do they not all deserve whatever help cosmetics can give them?

Whatever sins the leaders of the beauty business may have com-mitted, nobody can deny their belief that what they are doing is ultimately good for humanity. In persuading us to part with billions for their products, the moguls of make-up and skin care, of anti-ageing and beautifying, genuinely believe they are doing us a service. The question is, how fair are the business practices involved? How ethical is it for the dream merchants to trade on our susceptibilities?

3

THERAPY OR THEFT?

'We all know there isn't anything that'll make you look younger.' Anthea Disney, the forty-three-year-old British editor of the American self-help women's magazine *Self*, looks light years away from needing anything in the way of anti-ageing magic. But she hears and listens to the problems of the women who read her journal. She knows when they are being ripped off. 'We're all the same,' she says. 'We go on paying for what promises to rejuvenate – because maybe, just maybe, it'll keep us from looking quite as old as we feel.' And how old a woman over forty feels, she says, is sadly and irreversibly laid down by the hormonal changes going on in her body.

'Of course, she's dying to be the girl she was, young, nubile and beautiful,' Myra Sims, a leading London skin specialist, confirmed for me. 'She wants to retain, at whatever cost in rigid diets and expensive lotions, potions and treatments, what she has been accustomed to all her life. She can't believe what's happening to her. Why now? Why to her? She's still a young woman, vital, able, athletically capable and full of – if not the joys of spring – certainly the yearnings of girlhood made firmer and surer by maturity.'

The basic question is this: can anything – including cosmetics – banish those blues for her? Can the miracles promised in the full-page ads of the glossy magazines, telling her that Estée Lauder's Eyzone Repair Gel will rebuild her skin's appearance 'from inside out', ever be realized? With the claims that the same company's Future Perfect (as developed 'for the space program') will make an 'actual improvement' in the lines and wrinkles and smoothness of her face, convincingly make her feel younger and more attractive?

These are the most potent psychological issues facing the cosmetics manufacturers today, and have been since Cleopatra bathed in asses' milk. A woman's pitiful need to beat the clock at whatever price works incessantly for the cosmetics companies, no matter what they put in their pots and bottles. Their most valuable commercial asset is human gullibility. It is why the cosmetics giants without exception spend more of their turnover on advertising than do any other group of similarly financed business houses in the world.

When you buy a £5 prestige lipstick, you are paying perhaps 25 per cent – £1.25 – for this vital 'hype'. For the advertising and PR puffery needed to market it successfully. The balance, according to one experienced cosmetics analyst, reads something like this:

	£ p
Stores' profit	1.00
Maker's profit	75
Container	40
Packaging	20
Research and development	30
Overheads	35
Incentives (gifts etc)	25
	4.50

The remaining 50p is what you pay for the blend of waxy fat, pigs intestines and coloured oil inside.

Penny Chorlton dug up an interesting fact when researching her book *Cover Up*, published by Grapevine in 1988. She discovered that major lipstick manufacturers sell to their staffs at rock-bottom prices, and still make a small profit on the actual costs. Charles of the Ritz, she says, charges its employees only 25p for lipsticks selling in the shops for £7; the same for nail varnish costing over £5; and 50p for sparkling rainbow eye shadow palettes which sell for £9.

The manufacturers well know that the gratification and fulfilment a woman gets from using their make-up and skin treatment comes largely from self-delusion. It is the art of the possible. But by telling her in their seductive glossy ads that the economically unjustifiable sum she has had to lay out will, in fact, make her feel and look better, they answer a secret cry in her heart. And it can come true, as the ads predict. She will look younger, if only for a few hours or days. Miraculously, she *does* feel better. She *has* temporarily lost those unsightly wrinkles. Like Cinderella, she can dance in magically restored beauty – at least until the clock strikes midnight. The tired, grey, real world recedes during those few hours. And the cost? Well, in the words of the old song: 'Who can bargain over paradise?' The feeling that it's all happening, that mystically, magically she is being transformed, made more desirable, is worth any money. Economic reality stands no chance against it.

Tell her that cosmetics may be moving along a dangerous causeway between drugs and caring. She already knows that, and it does not deter her. Her instinct is to risk whatever harm may come from them. Anything, she thinks, is better than the terror of being left, stranded and unaided, alone with her ageing self.

When a woman passes over the threshold which divides her life, when she can no longer bear children and must accept that she has ceased to be the girl she was, who can blame her if she seeks refuge in illusion? She does not have to be told that there is no going back, no fountain of eternal youth. You cannot stop her dreaming.

Nor can you shield her eyes from those glossy, enticing magazine ads, all pointing the way to supreme, unmarked beauty. Of course it's absurd, but then dreams are not built of blocks of hard sense and practical experience. They are what she needs, desperately, to make up for what is lost, what she can no longer be. If their tempting lures can bring these wonders even a shade closer to her life, who cares if they are demonstrably overdone?

'Women are stuffing money down a rathole,' declares Edie Coulson, an athletic, fifty-year-old London tennis player. 'What they should do is get off their backsides and do some healthy exercise. Eat and drink less, and live active lives, instead of sitting around looking in their mirrors and counting the lines and grey hairs. *Of course* there's no need for them to pay fortunes for all that muck they put on their faces and bodies! They're all the same, overpriced garbage!'

She has a friend who is convinced that using Elizabeth Arden's Visible Difference Gentle Scrub has done wonders in removing her dead surface skin, because of its 'dermabrasion' content. 'Of course it has!' Coulson says. 'Probably because it contains finely ground apricot stones! A good rough flannel rubbed over the skin would have the same effect. Any ordinary chemist's cream at a tenth of the price [Elizabeth Arden's is £11 for 100 millilitres] would do every bit as much good.'

Well, would it? That is the crucial issue. Visible or otherwise, there is a true difference between the therapy of dreams and charging ten times the worth of a product. If the fat cats of the beauty jungle are

19

merely exploiting human vanity and the problems of women's ageing as bait to entice their victims, then the whole beauty industry is little more than a massive con. Are women – and an increasing band of men – being duped to pay far more than the worth of the product by the dazzling hype, the sexy bottles and jars, the sensual feel and smell of the stuff? Psychologically therapeutic cosmetics may be, but the jaded lady who buys a beautifully packaged dream, with an intrinsic value of less than a tenth of what she spends on it, is falling for a sweetly disguised form of commercial robbery. Would she be better off without it? That too is worth asking.

Only one man is universally known to hold an entirely unbiased and unvarnished opinion on the issue, backed by extensive knowledge of both sides of the question: the medical and the cosmetic. Dr Albert Kligman, of the University of Pennsylvania School of Medicine in Philadelphia, is a notorious gamekeeper who stalks the preserves of the beauty industry with keen eyes for any poachers and trespassers. He wants no part in the ripping off of desperate women in search of youth and beauty.

Kligman is the *enfant terrible* of the skin game, and his criticisms can sting like a scorpion. He has frequently denounced the wilder claims and assertions of those who try to exploit the millions of cosmetics users. His trenchant comments and clear-sighted opinions about the effectiveness of anti-ageing and beautifying products are renowned for their candour.

And nobody knows better than he does whether or not the dream is worth the candle. He is intimately connected with the world of cosmetics, and knows all there is to know about skin disorders and what can and cannot be done to alleviate them. Since he invited me to come and talk to him in January 1988 in his busy laboratory-office in Philadelphia, Professor Kligman has advanced towards a new and, as far as I know, unique $2 million Chair of Investigative Dermatology. The paradox – especially in view of some of Kligman's criticisms of the Estée Lauder company – is that Leonard Lauder ('after a long lapse', as Kligman told me) has subscribed a tenth of the cost of his chair, $200,000, to the Philadelphia faculty.

Yet this man continues outspokenly to condemn all misleading and unscientific cosmetics labels, press statements, packaging and hype wherever he finds them. An embattled idealist, Kligman has demonstrated an almost boyish belief in scientific principles while working largely for and in the cosmetics industry. Withal, he remains uncorrupted by its false, often double standards.

His work on the scientific aspects is widely respected, but that does not stop the industry from holding its breath every time he makes a statement to the press or public. A scientific Mark Twain, this engaging, down-to-earth man simply does not know how to lie. It is no matter to him that his utterances can prick balloons which have cost fortunes to inflate. In August 1987 Professor Kligman was quoted in a magazine warning that: 'In the industry today, fakery is replacing puffery . . . a consumer and FDA [America's Food and Drug Administration] crackdown is inevitable and damaging to credibility.' That, I was about to learn, is still the opinion he holds today.

The irony of Lauder's sponsorship of his chair is not lost on those who know how deeply the Lauder organization, and Estée Lauder herself, resent such criticism. It was Leonard Lauder who, in 1985, gave a keynote speech to an audience of women intending to become entrepreneurs in cosmetics and elsewhere. The multi-millionaire president told them then that 'fantasizing, projecting yourself into a successful situation, is the most powerful means there is of achieving personal goals.' He could hardly have been thinking then of Albert Kligman.

Lauder, like his counterparts elsewhere in the industry, plainly believes in puffery; Kligman, equally certainly, does not. 'It's got the hell out of proportion,' he told me while his dermatologist ('I'm a mouse doctor') wife, Lorraine, was next door testing a product to make hair grow on bald mice. 'When they make a claim of anti-ageing, of the stuff having deep biological effects, then they have to be stopped. It's pure bunkum!'

In almost the same breath he insisted that he is not in any way against the use, or the underlying principle, of cosmetics. 'I think a world without them would be infinitely tragic,' he explained. 'You're talking to a man who has a great respect for women, and I hate to see them taken in by these ridiculous claims. The prime function of skin is to insulate us from our environment. Skin is our packaging. It is only by its means that we keep the mechanism in, and the rest the hell out!'

The way women are lured into buying products that seem to do things he believes are impossible plainly disgusts him. 'I was in London when Dr Christiaan Barnard's Glycel stuff – supposed to

21

regenerate or replace dead cells – was on sale in Harrods. Nice, courteous Englishwomen were hitting each other over the head with umbrellas to get to the counter. How do you like that? The whole thing was a fake, a complete fake, and had to be withdrawn. But they couldn't get enough of it!'

Tirelessly, he keeps pointing out that many of the molecules in extravagantly claimed new products simply cannot function as their backers and makers say they do, because it is physically impossible for them to get deep enough into the skin to make any lasting difference to wrinkles. The same applies to the removal of lines and wrinkles, or the permanent prevention of the ageing of cells. The hope of anything achieving such beneficent effects is, he says, 'actually zero'.

This does not mean that skin cannot be helped by certain cosmetic products. If our inner bodies can benefit from exercise, massage and a healthy diet, so too can our outer coverings, our skins. So does this basically mean that age is a negotiable factor? I asked Kligman.

'Topical photo-ageing – caused by ultraviolet rays of the sun and other factors – is definitely negotiable,' he explained carefully. 'But intrinsic, chronological ageing is going to happen without our being able to stop it. There is nothing to stop that.'

The dream, then, that a large part of the vast $20 billion-a-year industry is trying to sell us just isn't true? By keeping 'our face in a jar by the door', as the Beatles' Eleanor Rigby did, we cannot obliterate from our faces the dryness, the sagginess and the criss-cross network of lines worn by use and time?

Dr Kligman shook his head. 'There are no miracles,' he said. 'We all age.'

Well, so we do. But some age more quickly and noticeably than others. It is the hope that they will be able to beat the clock that sends women in their millions into the shops and stores to buy expensive prestige creams and lotions. It is the inspiration of the dream – marketed with such infinitely persuasive promotion and publicity, packaging and display, by the giants of the industry. It is also the inspiration governing their huge and profitable scientific, pharmaceutical and chemical industry suppliers – the companies that provide the cosmetics industry with many of the ever more complex and seemingly miraculous ingredients for its products.

Morris Herstein is a leading figure among these companies. A self-styled American 'pseudo-scientist' with close on thirty years' experience in both pharmaceuticals and cosmetics, Herstein works in New York for the French cosmetics wholesalers Laboratoires Sérobiologiques. It is the largest supplier in the world of certain ingredients to the skin game. Its products, and Herstein's research capabilities, provide exactly the right measure of touch, feel and smell to the lipsticks, the face creams and the anti-ageing miracle treatments they sell. 'You can no longer sell hope in a bottle,' he says. 'Today you must have serious claims, serious chemical testing. And, of course, serious consumer acceptance of the product.'

As much a realist as Albert Kligman is an idealist, Herstein refuses to accept the professor's conviction that the industry is too dependent on creating illusion. 'You can't do it today,' he told me firmly. 'It's just not practical to package something and say, "This is hope." And that's it. Because people are not going to pay the money these things cost today – whether prestige or mass brands – unless they can really see and feel a benefit. It can't be just psychological any more. It has to be real, something they can see when they look in a mirror. Unfortunately, many people don't recognize that cosmetics today is a very serious industry – and that includes some of our government agencies.'

Herstein's specialized work in skin care has shaped his view that the technology of pharmaceuticals has been responsible for many of today's cosmetics advances. 'For instance, look at liposomes, which are being marketed as a new cosmetic by half a dozen companies. That product has been under investigation in the pharmaceutical industry for over twenty-five years. What are liposomes? Basically, and in technical jargon, they are bi-lave membrane encapsulations that allow you to entrap an active principle and carry it to a specific site. What we call a "target reaction".'

The boon of this to cosmetics, he says, comes from the use of liposomes as a form of 'train' to ferry other, believed curative, particles to predetermined 'targets' in the body. 'It goes exactly where it wants to go, stops, then releases the ingredient. Like a delivery. It works either internally or on the skin surface, topically. Or by injection even. You can target these things to go into the dermis with them, or if you want to release it only in the epidermis you can put the brakes on. So, depending on how you design its function, and what you do with it, it'll go as far as you want.'

Herstein does not deny that this – in his view, an obvious and valuable advance down the road of effective cosmetic use – is in direct conflict with the view of the FDA, which insists that any ingredient capable of such penetration must be altering the body 'physiologically'. Hence it is a drug, says the FDA, and should be tested and treated as one.

'No,' says Herstein. 'I think the industry as a whole has done an excellent job of policing itself for safety, and the FDA is only saying, "Look, we're concerned about what you're *saying*, not what you're doing." It is a dictionary problem, a lexicon problem, a question of vocabulary. They're not asking, "Do you have proof?"'

Are they not? Kligman's forecast of an FDA crackdown has already begun. In 1987 the Agency demanded retraction of anti-ageing and other 'miracle' claims from many of the business's leaders. In letters sent to twenty-three of the top cosmetics companies under review, each specific complaint was spelt out. If it could be proved that the product acted only on the upper layers of the skin, there would be no case against it. All along, the FDA had insisted that where drugs were used in cosmetics they must be registered and controlled. Herstein's bland belief that they would merely be content with a change of wording in the ads and labelling falls a long way short of the official standpoint.

'Yes, I know,' Morris Herstein said when I reminded him of the seemingly devastating effects these official objections might have on the industry. 'The FDA has always had this dilemma. Anything that affects the body's function is a drug in their eyes. It's ridiculous – a bar of soap and a washcloth have a physiological effect on the body's function. The mere rubbing of the skin with a washcloth will increase cell renewal. Does this make a washcloth, or a piece of pumice, or a bar of soap a drug?'

Pseudo-scientist Herstein's personal career in cosmetics began with Revlon in 1960 when Charles Revson was alive. 'This was the beginning of the boom, and the way I saw it then was that, as an industry, it was 80 per cent art and 20 per cent science. But I've watched it grow, and today I'd say the equation has shifted, until it is now almost totally the reverse.' The biggest change he saw happening began in the early eighties. 'We were then able to see and measure things that had been impossible before. It came about when the technology of the space programme was made available, when we were allowed to use their sophisticated analysis techniques, the biotechnological advances which allowed us to see things at the cellular level. Before that we had had to touch and feel.'

Today he believes there is an entirely new and revolutionary way of ensuring that cosmetics do what women want them to do. 'Now we can get very precise measurements. We can use monochrome antibodies as traces to quantify things. With these advances in computers to supplement our analyses we can be better detectives.' Indeed computers, Herstein feels, are the most important new key to the advances taking cosmetics into the next century. 'There's very important research being done in universities to use genetic engineering to reprogramme the cells in our bodies. So that even in the case of natural biological ageing, which today we can do nothing about, I do believe that it may one day be possible to manipulate the whole process. Just as we have done by creating life in a test tube.'

That, surely, would have to involve the use of drugs, would it not?

'Yes, clearly it would. But that doesn't mean that it should not be available to the public. The important thing is that cosmetics companies and their suppliers are among the very few industries addressing these problems, and perhaps the only ones with the resources to do it successfully.

'And we're doing it in a very important way. Progress has been made. You see, the skin is like a computer chip. It has a fantastic memory, and we are now at the stage of manipulating this to overcome some of the problems. The cosmetics industry is saying "OK, how can we neutralize these natural phenomena in the body and thereby combat the ageing process?" Before too long, they'll come up with an answer.'

It is certainly a cosy theory. Jam tomorrow, and jam yesterday. And if we have to pay enormously inflated prices for products that still lack this wonder magic – stuff that can no more make us look thirty when we're fifty than soap can make a black skin white – then must we tell ourselves that it is in a good cause?

The big players in the skin game are putting many of their surplus millions into research and development. In Yokohama, where I was the guest of the vast Shiseido company; at Revlon's New Jersey plant which I was courteously shown over by their eminent scientific director, Dr Earle W. Brauer; and in the Paris suburb where Jacques Courtin Clarins houses his highly efficient research laboratory, I verified the scale of these immense process factories. It is enormous.

The nagging, perhaps uncharitable, doubt persists, however. Are they being maintained to perfect, and make more effective, the products sold to us? Or are they an important, highly expensive tool in the competitive war between the leaders of the industry, for which ultimately we consumers have to pay?

As more and more products come on to the market, the race to find a pathway heading at least in the general direction of the legendary fountain of youth grows hotter every year. Competition to be the first with each new and better-selling product has never been fiercer.

And of course it would be ingenuous to imagine that it is only our health and security that are in the minds of the white-coated scientists and their assistants at work in these expensively appointed laboratories. The men at the top of the industry that employs them want results. They clamour for new magic, fresh breakthroughs to thrust on to the market with ever more engaging claims. It is this, as much as any other tangible reason, that explains why the goods cost so much and why the laboratories are so busy.

Stephen Manheimer runs a company supplying vital – some say the most expensive – ingredients of an increasing number of cosmetics products; fragrances. His and Morris Herstein's views hardly sound as if they are talking about the same planet, let alone the same industry. Yet the two men operate in the same city, New York.

'I'd say the cost of the essences we sell, which are the raw materials of many of the famous perfume names we supply, constitute between 1 and 10 per cent of what people pay for the stuff in the stores,' Manheimer told me.

Doesn't that suggest that the companies which buy and use his products are charging an outrageous mark-up, even allowing for the cost of the necessary hype and packaging? Can he explain how it can be justified?

'No. We agree. We do think the products are far too expensive – the fine fragrances, that is. But that's because the companies are giving away umbrellas and suchlike gifts to boost sales. As far as costs go, it seems to me the industry's no different from high fashion. They're both selling dreams.'

Manheimer continued, 'When a woman buys an Oscar de la Renta dress, costing only $50 to make, and pays $5000 for it, does that make any sense? I certainly do think that if we could get down to, say, $100

26

to $125 an ounce for fragrances it would be better for the industry, but that's only my opinion. It's not my job to tell them what to charge.'

Or anyone else's. To dare to cut the prices of these exotic products, with their aristocratic and often titled continental names and badges of rank, would sabotage a carefully fostered mystique. In times of acute financial distress, such as another Black Friday on Wall Street, women at the prestige end of the market actually buy more cosmetics, I was assured. The threat of war and rationing seems to depress only the cheaper brands.

Social historians put this down to an atavistic fear among the wealthy. A panic terror might catch them without their favourite creams and perfumes. On the day of the Cuba crisis in 1962, for instance, when nuclear confrontation seemed almost inevitable, Harrods in London and Bloomingdales in New York both reported lively business on their cosmetics floors.

Even in normal times, the market forces that apply to these luxury products work in a diametrically opposite way from those that apply to necessities. To price a beautifully wrapped and packaged product advertised in fashionable magazines at less than the cost of solid gold or platinum would, I was repeatedly assured, actually *lose* sales among the sensitive élite. 'To tamper with the price structure,' an experienced cosmetics marketing executive told me, 'would be suicidal at the prestige end and disastrous in the middle range.'

And not everyone even believes it would be commercially viable. Mark Rosen, a top design executive with Elizabeth Arden (now owned by British Unilever) and a regular spokesman for the industry, told me he believes the price structure is fully justified. He has very definite ideas on pricing and refuses to accept the idea of any reductions.

'A certain price gives credibility,' he said. 'But the belief that perfume costing $50 is really only worth 50 cents is totally inaccurate. It's overlooking what goes into marketing the product – the advertising, the development, the research and the packaging. All right, advertising costs a lot of money – but advertising today is essential.'

Whether it is as essential to Rosen's customers as it is to his company is a moot point. But there is no doubt that, when a product offers what a woman truly and urgently wants – when it can sincerely promote a cure for the signs of ageing on her face and body, or suggest that it will add refinement and glamour – then in the upper end of the market a fancifully high cost will seldom deter wealthy women from buying it. For them, it seems, price ceases to be a priority once they can be convinced – by hype, by advertising and by subtle intriguing at a social level ('The princess was noticeably fragrant in . . .') – that the product is something that will either give them status, or actually do them some good.

Whether cosmetics prices should be democratically controlled, in the same way that the price of drugs is controlled and as some people believe should happen, is an issue that futurists like Dr Ozawa in Japan would have strong views about. Advertising is prohibited, for prescribed drugs. Where would that leave the cosmetics business?

Already there is faint but perceptible writing on their designer walls. It foretells an approaching conflict of mammoth proportions between the captains of the beauty industry and a subsidiary of one of the largest of America's pharmaceutical giants, Johnson & Johnson. It concerns a product which has been whispered about, recommended, discussed and dramatized during 1987 and 1988 – a substance called Retin A, that really reduces the signs and wrinkles of ageing.

It is now approaching the marketplace with messianic force: new, about-to-be-licensed and seemingly effective. Behind Retin A are the experience and wisdom of the man whom cosmetics people know to be the most humane and reliable member of their community, Professor Albert Kligman; the same man whom I listened to in Philadelphia deploring the 'puffery and fakery' of present anti-ageing products.

Kligman invented Retin A. In its original form, it was a cure for acne. He then discovered that it had other properties, and has approved its manufacture by Johnsons once a licence for its use as a drug has been granted. From all that I can gather, his product is likely to change the whole face and geography of the beauty jungle. Only a cure for acne it may be, but the fear among the big cats who rule that jungle is that it is going to knock spots off more than one of their expensively hyped and ballyhooed products.

4

KLIGMAN'S MIRACLE

The human skin is a complex organ. Like a pneumatic tyre with an inner and outer tube it consists of two basic layers, but with the tougher one on the inside. On top is the epidermis, which can be drier or moister according to age, genetic type and previous exposure to pollution and other harmful effects of the atmosphere. These, as we now know to our cost, can include dangerous ultraviolet rays from the sun.

It is this porous epidermal layer that can be puffed up, penetrated and moistened by creams and lotions containing water and oil. Cosmetic moistening and barrier creams and cleansers act only at this superficial level. Directly below, but still within the epidermis, is a spongy barrier that is constantly creating fresh cells in its lower depths. These push their way to the surface to take the place of old cells nearing the end of their life-cycle. As the old cells die they exfoliate, dropping away and floating off like dead leaves. Alternatively we remove them by rubbing with a flannel, or by cosmetic abrasives and other techniques. The greyish household dust lying on bedroom wardrobes and picture frames contains the detritus of these spent cells.

Further down still lies the dermis, which is entirely unreceptive. It allows no oil or water – the basic ingredients of all skin care emulsions – or indeed any substance other than acids (which can burn and force their way through) to get past it. This protective barrier prevents foreign bodies from entering our bloodstream from the outside, and is the safeguard that the FDA and all serious scientific authorities are intent on defending against unwarranted invasion.

There are two ways in which this twin-layered skin can age. The outer layer, the epidermis, is at the mercy of our way of life, or of the atmosphere we live in. Ageing here is called 'topical', and can be caused prematurely. It is largely brought on by unhealthy exposure

29

to fuel gases, frostbite, illness and harmful toxicity. Additionally, the epidermis can be subject to 'photo-ageing'. This is the effect of dangerous doses of sunburn and ultraviolet rays directed at us by the sun, once these have penetrated the protective ozone layer around the earth.

Natural ageing, on the other hand, is going on all the time. It begins on the day we are born and continues until we die. Every cell in our body has a pre-programmed lifespan, after which it must be replaced by a fresh cell made by our constantly regenerating body. Other than by the untried and ethically sensitive science of genetic engineering – the reprogramming of our body mechanisms by cellular surgery – no way is known of altering the timing of this cellular clock.

So when we talk of preventing ageing, when cosmetics offer us the illusion of 'anti-ageing' – of putting the clock back – we are really only dealing with the *signs* of age, not age itself. Most of us know this and are happy to pay exorbitant prices for products that will do away with those alone. All they do, in the main, is temporarily puff up the epidermal layers of the outer skin with moisture – water suspended in an oily emulsion. Thus, for a short time, we do see a satisfying smoothing out of the lines.

But what Professor Kligman is saying, with considerable confidence, is that there is now a way to banish many of the signs of ageing completely. Not only to smooth them away for a few hours, but to remove and make them invisible for longer; perhaps permanently. His revolutionary discovery that Retin A will get down to and act on the dermis, where ageing and constant movement of the skin have set up furrow-like corrugations, is now under test. If the effects he claims for it are proved, he believes it will reduce and eliminate many of the problems. Previously only acids would penetrate, causing injury and inflammation.

If Retin A can effectively and harmlessly reduce the distortions in the dermis, then the wrinkles will indeed be erased. But since this will constitute a physiological change in the body's structure, and any product that can do this must be listed as a drug, it will threaten the hitherto unlicensed freedom of the cosmetics companies to claim that their products – the ones they market with claims that they do exactly the same thing – must also be drugs.

Either their claims of anti-ageing must be withdrawn, or they too will have to register their products as drugs. Either Kligman's Retin

A will be refused a listing as a new drug, effective in the care and treatment of skin, or the big cosmetics companies must be prepared to submit their miracle substances for rigorous tests. Licensing them as such would restrict most of the current anti-ageing substances to medical prescription only.

The terrifying prospect of what this would cost the companies is currently involving many of them in a savage battle with their erstwhile colleague and counsellor, the renowned heir to the Leonard Lauder Chair of Investigative Dermatology in Philadelphia. It is one that could change the whole nature of beauty jungle life.

It was hard to believe that all this furore had been caused by the affable, unaffected Professor Albert Kligman; that this small, grey-haired doctor is the discoverer of what may be the hottest product since monkey glands. On the day in 1988 we sat talking in the office where the anti-ageing properties of his acne formula had first come to his notice, it seemed as likely as balancing an angel on a pin. On these scales and workbenches the vitamins, esters, acids and emollient creams had fused together in the proportions needed to create a substance with which Dr Kligman has given mature women hope.

In the considered opinion of at least one senior authority, Annette Green, the executive director of the American Fragrance Foundation, 'Retin A works!' But there are others, like John Ledes who edits the influential newsletter *Cosmetic World*, who maintain that it sets up unpleasant and even malignant reactions. There are many also who try to belittle its claims, since it – or its predecessor – has been on chemists' shelves for years in its original role as a cure for acne.

'Retin A,' Professor Kligman told me in his self-deprecating way, 'just happens – more or less fortuitously – to have the capacity to remedy some of the things that take place in ageing.' If that is so, then it 'just happens' to be the breakthrough that the entire cosmetics industry has been seeking for generations. Should the tests that Retin A is currently undergoing, in the expectation of it being officially accepted for prescribed use as a drug, support this, then it will rank among the modern wonders of the scientific world.

Even before the result of these tests is known, Kligman's formula, his published reports on Retin A's effect on the dermis layer of the skin – 'A mechanism,' he says, '*not* caused by inflammation' – has spun the cosmetics trade on its axis and started a wave of excited anticipation among women. Since they first heard of it, those whose

31

mirrors tell them that the unlined skins of youth are no longer attainable have been hounding their doctors and dermatologists for prescriptions to obtain the product from drugstores and chemists.

From the beauty jungle has come a rumble more of fear than of fury. In an editorial in spring 1988, Ledes accused Kligman and his commercial backers, Johnson & Johnson, of breaking every cardinal rule in the skin game. By submitting an application to the US Food and Drug Administration requesting formal approval to market the substance *as a drug*, they had exposed the cosmetics companies who were making similar claims to invidious and embarrassing comparison.

Everything the cosmetics giants had been painfully and expensively arguing with the FDA was thereby threatened. If Kligman could admit that such effects on the skin were only possible by the use and action of a *drug*, where did it leave their argument that anti-ageing was a strictly *cosmetic* process? Where did they stand if Retin A really did do what they themselves had been claiming for their over-priced products (with no such proofs of official acceptance)? And if, once licensed, Retin A was to be sold on prescription only by chemists, and at normal drug prices, then what would happen to the whole future position of cosmetics in the anti-ageing campaign?

It was a tense and bitter moment for the big cats of the industry. Typically, they looked for ways to repel this unwarranted invasion of their territory. The first necessity was to hit back, if possible to discredit Kligman's damaging claims. If Retin A really was not as good as Kligman claimed it to be, then they had nothing to worry about.

But it was. Glumly, their technical reports confirmed that it worked successfully in the majority of cases. Scientific publication in the *Journal of the American Medical Association* put on record the positive results obtained in a clinical study. The report, published in January 1988, gave unarguable support to Kligman's discovery.

John Ledes, however, was not to be silenced. He circulated an attack on Retin A, claiming it was 'old hat, a substance that had been around for years'. It could do nothing that cosmetics products had not been doing, he wrote.

Kligman's backers no doubt found it hard to suppress their smiles. Shares in Johnson & Johnson had leaped $3 at the news that Retin A was coming successfully through its tests. It was being rumoured that these would take up to two years to complete, but already the Johnson plant in New Jersey, Ortho Pharmaceutical corporation, where Retin A was being made, was working to capacity.

Its inventor's rewards were less evident. Dr Kligman has decided to donate his royalties from the patent to his department in the university. Reportedly set to yield 3 per cent of the cost of every tube sold, his generosity seems likely to make it the most profitable university in the country.

Was Ledes wrong? Had he gone too far in his 25 January editorial in *Cosmetic World*, in which he flatly stated:

Vitamin A ester has been used in cosmetics for almost the entire period of the existence of the FDA. The Retinalic Acid which is J & J's patent is a first cousin and an acid. When the Vitamin A ester metabolizes in the skin, it becomes an acid. While the FDA seeks to prevent cosmetics companies from telling the truth about their Vitamin A ester, it will allow J & J's drug-qualified acid to make such a claim. In simple English, the FDA . . . is censoring the truth. The cosmetics companies have been thrown to the wolves by their toiletries and pharmaceutical colleagues.

Professor Kligman's expression as we discussed this attack was tolerant, even understanding. He seemed less disturbed than an entomologist bothered by a wasp at a picnic. 'No, he is a little bit mixed up,' he said. 'It is true that if you use vitamin A in alcohol some portion of it will be converted to retinalic acid. But Retin A is not retinalic acid. And, as I say, only some portion of the vitamin A will be converted when it enters the skin.'

He was careful, I noted, not to say what happens to the rest of it. Presumably that is where the magic of Retin A lies. 'It is an acid,' Kligman agreed, 'but not that acid. I think it is a real advance, and I've published on it. But since I'm the discoverer, if you want unbiased views you'll have to talk to someone else . . . However,' he added mischievously, 'if you ask me, does it contain properties of anti-ageing? . . .' – he was weighing his words like a golfer who has just sunk a hole in one and is asked to say how he did it – 'then all I can tell you is, yes, it does.'

For anything more concrete than that, the world must wait for the FDA test results and findings which, in time, will almost certainly list Retin A as a licensed drug – for the treatment of both ageing and acne (though Kligman hints that the two substances may not

33

be identical). Only then will it be possible to see if this truly is the magic breakthrough that the professor has been keeping locked away in secret files in his office, and if the rumours that caused such a lucrative run on Johnson & Johnson's shares were based on fact.

A cure for ageing is the hidden card, perhaps the ace to beat all aces, that the industry has been having nightmares about for five or more years, ever since the race to find it began. And Retin A – according to those like Annette Green who share the inner secrets of the business – could very well sweep the board when it is approved for prescriptive use.

Even now there is no ethical objection to doctors and dermatologists prescribing Retin A. It is up to the patient whether or not he or she uses it as an anti-acne treatment or for wrinkle reduction. In at least one case known to me, the physician claims to be getting good results by mixing it with a moisturizing cream. This, he thinks, will be less likely to cause any initial adverse reaction. And so far, he says, it has proved remarkably successful.

There are also cosmetics experts well prepared to accept Kligman's claims. Stanley Kohlenberg, the recently retired head of Sanofi Products, told me he is wholly optimistic about Retin A. 'Once it's listed for marketing, J & J will be able to make genuine claims, to show that real improvement takes place in 60 to 70 per cent, or whatever it is, of the patients. They'll show that it not only does work, despite the period of reddening and peeling and abrasion, but that it clearly is a drug and not a cosmetic.' If it poses a major threat to his colleagues in the beauty business, Kohlenberg says they have only themselves to blame. 'If they make drug claims without being drugs, that's their problem,' he says.

Even as a drug, Retin A shows every prospect of leaving the cosmetics companies' over-hyped anti-ageing products standing on the shelves. America's only board-certified dermatologist operating a cosmetics factory and research facility, Dr Earle Brauer of the Revlon corporation, told me: 'It's true. It's absolutely no figment. And although our company has marketed, is marketing, and is about to market many products with anti-ageing claims, we are among those threatened by it. Because, let me safely say, for anything like it [Retin A] to be made available *in cosmetic form* by a company like ours, it has got to take us not less than fifteen years!'

By which time, if Retin A is as good as Albert Kligman and his backers believe, there may be no demand for anything more. This is the main cause of the nightmares disturbing the industry's dreams at this moment. However desperately their PR people try to suppress talk of 'cosmetics at the crossroads', of 'a Retin A crisis', the fear of what Kligman has locked in his desk and patented (so that no copies can be made in the customary way of the cosmetics marketplace) grows no less with time. Indeed, the frightening knowledge of what could happen in a year or so, if and when the magic breakthrough is confirmed and Kligman's discovery launched as a safe and tested cure for the signs of ageing, as well as for the removal of topical blemishes caused to the skin by sun and pollution, is causing wide-spread anger and alarm among the manufacturers. As America's most forthright cosmetics observer, Amelia Bassin, told me, 'My instinct, when I first saw the "before and after" pictures on TV, was to rush to my doctor and get a prescription. The news stories were so positive. So, yes, I do think it will damage the industry, and for quite a while.'

Bassin's initial impulsive reaction is not what the cosmetics business want to hear, or what its shareholders enjoy reading in her columns. But it does justify Professor Kligman's caveat on Retin A: when the product is applied to skins of a certain texture and sensitivity, 'there can be a nasty reaction.' Many women, less well informed than Bassin, will want to try it out. She told me: 'A friend of mine who used to be beauty editor of *Vogue* used a product that had Retin A in it. She suffered terribly. Her skin got all itchy and scaly, which I assume is what it does to cure acne. I'd say women with sensitive skins should be very careful.'

A London beauty editor who asked to be nameless shared this negative view. But she said she had little expectation that it will prevent a tidal wave of women deluging their doctors with requests for prescriptions when the drug comes on the market in the near future. 'Reputedly, it works,' she told me. 'But I can assure you it *does* peel the skin. I know, because I used it for a whole year to test it out, and my face peeled all the time. I don't think people really need that sort of thing.'

She may not, but the smile on Albert Kligman's face and the high price of Johnson & Johnson's shares seem to be telling another story. The company feels confident of a huge boom in sales of their product. A spokesman told me: 'If the price of removing wrinkles – perhaps not permanently, but certainly for a far longer period of time than has ever before been possible – is a slight, or even a heavy, peeling off of outer skin, I doubt if it will deter many of the women who fear the loss of their youthful looks more than most things in life.'

Meanwhile Amelia Bassin's caution has become a popular chant among frightened experts. Veteran American cosmetics expert Hazel Bishop, whose name is on a once-famous product of her own and who teaches as Revlon lecturer at the New York Fashion Institute of Technology, believes firmly that neither Retin A nor anything else can eradicate wrinkles or iron out lines permanently. She too has heard of the drug's less than pleasant side-effects. 'There are certain problems with it,' she told me. 'But I don't agree that it is a drug in the full sense. It has a biological effect, but that doesn't mean that it is not a cosmetic. There should not be this distinction between cosmetics and drugs where a product doesn't alter the skin.'

None of the cosmetics kings would hesitate to say amen to that. It is the whole basis of their costly battle to legitimize what Kligman calls their 'puffery and fakery'. As their champion, campaigning journalist John Ledes is doing all he can to limit the damage. A US army veteran of World War II, he gives an impression of still being engaged in fighting the Battle of Midway from his cluttered command-post of an office. Ledes has been in the forefront of the crisis since the first indication of it reached him. To him, the way Kligman and his backers have joined the enemy (by applying for drug licence, and hence admitting that it is a drug) is little short of renegade. But he dismisses Kligman's claims.

'Retin A, when you put it on your skin, metabolizes,' he insists. 'It becomes acid. But it's the same bloody thing, unmetabolized, that has existed for fifty to seventy years. Now we in the industry are making claims that some of our products are anti-ageing, or whatever the claim is, and they are taking the position that it is now a drug – something that has gone on for fifty years! Of course it works, and you can prove it. It always has. But it's no more a drug than it ever was.'

Ledes also knows, as well as any of the 'miracle' manufacturers, that anti-ageing techniques, even Retin A, can never offer a permanent remedy against what Charles Dickens in *Little Dorrit* called 'the wrinkles traced by the mind'. As Ledes argues forcibly, 'When you say something "permanently works" . . . look, the child that comes out of the womb is ageing. No one stops ageing. You can reduce the rate of ageing, that's all. And that rate differs with everyone – it's like a fingerprint. But you can't stop it dead. Nobody lives for ever.'

'Many of the changes that you call ageing,' Professor Kligman had explained, 'are in fact not programmed. They represent cumulative injury from external effects. You cannot define anything as an intrinsic aspect of ageing unless it occurs in all individuals independently of time.

'So, for example, the female menopause really is ageing. No woman of sixty is going to lay eggs. You can't get over that. But most of what you see in my face, and your face, has nothing to do with ageing. It is age-related, but it is largely due to sunlight, ski-ing, what's in the air. What is commonly called ageing is in fact injury from the environment.'

He raised a white-coated arm. 'If you look at your skin under here,' Kligman pointed to the underside of his upper arm, close to the armpit, 'you'll get some idea of how trivial are the changes that take place in skin due to age alone. In that area, your body has never been exposed to the damaging effects of sun and atmospheric pollution.'

He is currently studying a group of Buddhist priests in Japan who have never exposed themselves to direct sunlight. 'Some of them,' he said, 'are ninety years old, and you'd put them down as forty. I'm not saying that people don't age – I'm saying that the common idea of ageing is wrong.'

Professor Kligman has also learned to respect the body's own mechanism for slowing down the ageing process. I had asked if injecting fresh cells into an ageing body would prevent the ravages of time from becoming so sadly noticeable. He did not think so.

'You don't have to do that, you see. Because the supplies exist. There are sufficient numbers of cells already there – dumb cells, we call them. They are just sitting there, from God knows how long, in a reserve pool.' When you cut yourself, he explained, or suffer a skin burn, these reserve cells step in and do the job of replacement. 'And while they're standing by, waiting, the changes that take place in their metabolism are very, very small. They're not functioning – they're outside the cell cycle, just waiting to be called on to produce more cells. So we don't need to do any of that injecting of new cells. There are enough reserves in our skin to last for 250 years!'

But the cosmetics companies are claiming that some of their skin

37

care products contain ingredients which replicate cells, are they not?

Kligman, who has used Retin A on himself and looks far younger than his seventy-three years, chuckled drily. 'The use of collagen, oestrogen, DNA and enzymes . . . that's all complete bunkum! Even if collagen did get in – which it doesn't – there's not the slightest reason to believe that it would be kneaded into the fabric, absorbed and catabolized.'

More soberly, he added, 'No, what this all means is that people are far more frightened and alarmed by the loss of their appearance than by the loss of time, by the actual approach of death. Young people, of course, don't really believe they're going to die anyway. That's so far off. But at the first wrinkle, the first sign of ageing, many women think, "Well, we're over the hill now."

'In Western culture – and that's everywhere – women in particular are supposed to stay eternally young, beautiful, sexy, vigorous and healthy. And that's not possible. So they just disappear. You don't find them reading the news or presenting shows on television. They're not sought after in Hollywood. I think it's a cruel business.'

Professor Kligman has both love and compassion in his heart for these sufferers. His first wife died after only nine months of their life together. Happily remarried, he is now dedicating his life's work to helping women as much as he and his skills can. He will do anything possible in his speciality to offset the hardships of disfigurement and loss of attraction through age.

But if his dismissal of hope-and-dream claims upsets the industry he has most to do with, the cosmetics industry, this does not mean he is against cosmetics. 'You're talking to a man who thinks that to go along without cosmetics would be tragic,' he assured me. 'I absolutely agree that they do a wonderful service. But why can't the companies just say, "We make good, lasting cosmetics, camouflage, whatever" and leave it at that? If they did that I'd be all for it. Absolutely.' But, as he says, they don't. 'They have to get into gremlins. Why do they do that? They are providing a fantastic service, yet they have to go beyond the bounds of reason and truth.'

By so doing they are breaking, in Professor Kligman's view, the barriers of honest commerce and leading consumers into the land of puffery and hype. It distresses him to have to argue this point with scientific colleagues who see cosmetics as an arena in which beauty is at the mercy of money-grubbing beasts.

'Some of my colleagues', he admitted, 'tell me, "Women are so dumb! How can they buy all that grease and stuff? Educated women, who've been to Radcliffe and Cambridge and Oxford and the Sorbonne – what gets into them? Why do they go to Bloomingdales and pay $250 for that hokum?" '

He tells them why. Professor Albert Kligman is too great a respecter of women not to know that cosmetics are necessary to women's – and increasingly men's – self-esteem. They are vital to their spiritual and physical wellbeing, and even to the love of their fellow beings. If the price to be paid for entering dreamland is high, it can never be more than its worth in this regard. But Albert Kligman has seen the terrible deserts of despair and self-doubt that less fortunate mortals are prone to find themselves in. It is only he and others like him who can truly assess the value of the comfort provided by the life-giving oases of cosmetics.

5

BEAUTY'S BEASTS

In the American TV series *Hill Street Blues*, the lovable desk sergeant with a heart as big as Manhattan growled, 'Don't get me started, or I'll tell you what I think of what that scum out there do to animals!' Regrettably, few of the players of the skin game would care to echo those words, or the sentiment behind them. Nasty things, they would say, have to be done to rabbits and mice and guinea pigs, so that the stuff we smear on our faces, the lipsticks we suck in with food and cigarette smoke, the eyeliner pencils and paints that touch some of the tenderest parts of our bodies, are safe as the houses we (and our pampered pets) live in.

Only the animal rights movements, vociferating and proliferating throughout the world, as well as the warriors of Greenpeace and a growing band of courageous drum-beaters in America and Europe campaigning on behalf of 'ethical treatment' for animals, keep up a violent protest against the sacrifice of these small creatures in the name of 'mere' cosmetics. Are they right to do so?

To face this question squarely needs a strong stomach. Even reading about the inspection of prison cages, the sound of the screams which rise from them, the sight of mice paralysed with fear and bunnies with dilated and suppurating eyes from constant drips of stinging poison, is not for the queasy. It does not sit well with a romp on the downs with Rover, or the hamster or guinea pig brought home to delight a small child on its birthday.

Nor, of course, would an in-depth survey of butchers' slaughter-houses, species-culling, or the agricultural necessity of emasculating millions of male meat-producing animals for our tables make it easier for mankind to enjoy his or her steak tartare. The question then is, how necessary are the tests and experiments which daily kill and mutilate countless hundreds of tiny animals, to the point where one would ordinarily regard their condition as unpardonable, if not actually criminal? Do the test abattoirs – for the most part well out of earshot and sight of the expensive, sanitized laboratories and research faculties of the big companies – reveal a vital need for the work? Is animal testing, which is both costly and unpleasant for those doing it, indispensable and vital for our safety? If it is not, then the continuing (though diminishing, under pressure from the anti-cruelty lobbies) trade in these experimental horrors shames us all. What may be excusable on behalf of foodstuffs and medicines should never be tolerated for the profit of the beauty business. Nor, if other means could be found, should it be an acceptable excuse to say that these were carried out in the name of 'safety' (as is the case in the majority of the ingredients of today's forty thousand and more existing brands of cosmetics, sold as 'tested for allergic reaction' and other claims).

There is no law, in Britain or the United States, that specifically requires an ingredient of a cosmetic product to have been tested on *animals*. All that is required, under the legal safety Acts of both countries, is that the product must have undergone 'reliable' tests for safety. Human beings and laboratory specimens could equally well have been used as guinea pigs, though it is said by the British Research Defence Society that humans 'present a number of disadvantages . . . because people vary so much'. Apparently animals do not.

So, how vital *is* animal testing? How necessary to human safety is this revolting, and eventually lethal (after every last possible use of the animal has been squeezed out of its tortured body) activity? The main and most compelling argument for its continuation seems to be that it is being done on our, and our children's, behalf. But can no other way be found to protect us equally well from whatever dangers exist?

In my experience, nobody has put the cosmetics companies' answer to this better than Dr Earle Brauer of Revlon. As one of the most scientific and humane experts in the industry, and one who cares deeply about the techniques for ensuring safety in cosmetics, Dr Brauer has a right to be listened to with respect and understanding.

It is his job, as the dermatologist in charge of what he claims is 'probably the largest cosmetic research facility, housing only pure cosmetic research, that exists in the world', to see that nothing in the very least harmful to human life and health leaves his plant under the Revlon label. This is not just a question of taking care that no toxic, or otherwise harmful, substance is used in the production of Revlon's huge cosmetics range. It has to take account of what happens, or could happen, to the product *after* it leaves the factory at Edison, New Jersey.

We were in Dr Brauer's impressive microbiology facility at the research plant when he explained this to me with considerable passion. 'If there is a secret in what we do, it's right here – the means by which we preserve our products from the onslaughts of society. Have you ever considered how we make them safe from the woman who opens the jar up, then doesn't put the top back on – leaving everything in the air to get into it?' He looked mildly shocked. 'How do I know, when she puts her finger in the jar, where that finger was three seconds before she put it in? Her children open it up. They cough into it. They let the cap slide under the bed, where the cat can lick it. Then somebody grabs it and puts it back on the jar. *What is all that doing to our product?*'

It is a fair point. If it was wine, or food, it would have to be clearly marked with a warning that it must only be kept for so long – for a scientifically predetermined shelf life – and under certain conditions of temperature. As a result, no caring housewife leaves tops off food jars, or exposes opened tins and bottles to the air for an undue length of time.

But restrictions of that kind cannot be put on lipsticks, or colour compacts or brushes – the items that lie in handbags, purses and pockets for weeks and months on end. To do so would make them unmarketable. No woman would want, as Dr Brauer says, 'to keep her face cream in the refrigerator'. Eleanor Rigby's casual behaviour is common to most, if not all. Nor can he tell women to wash their hands before using his carefully prepared products. Dreamland does not follow the same rules as the real world, and cosmetics are *expected* to be clean and free from injurious substances.

So when the average woman thinks at all about the risks, it is more likely to be in terms of 'What will it do to me?' and seldom, if ever, 'What will I do to it?' Brauer's department, he explained, exists to protect her from both.

'When a product is under test with us as part of our research and development routine,' he began, 'it has already been formulated with preservatives against organisms that we know are indigenous to our users. We deliberately seed these organisms into the product, in which the preservatives have already been built in, to test if they are effective.'

We were standing behind a bench on which dozens of marked samples were being examined under elaborate microscopes linked to computers. Brauer told me, 'What you're seeing here is only a minute part of a very long process. We sample the product over a twenty-one week period to see what, if anything, we can grow back. If we see that the organisms are quickly falling down to nothing, as a result of the preservatives, we've got ourselves a good product. But if this slowly goes up, and stays up, then we don't have a product at all.'

All that work wasted! Dr Brauer was speaking, surely, no less than the truth when he told me: 'We can't ship any product with our name on it if it is going to contain a measure of organisms that could cause trouble to society. That work is done here by the people in this department, and it is their responsibility to ensure that it never happens.'

How? At Revlon, New Jersey, no animal blood is allowed to stain their hands. Dr Brauer assured me, 'We don't have an animal testing facility in this building. Where necessary, we are obliged to use these – but under the strictest possible control measures.' He paused, then continued with great emphasis, 'But I don't want you to leave here with any misconception. I am not saying that we do *not* test on animals. Because we do.' The tests take place, as he said, 'in outside facilities'. And only – he repeated this with even firmer conviction – *where absolutely necessary.*

Animal rights has taught Revlon and others that their public image – and internal costs – are improved by using animals as little as possible. 'They've taught us a lot,' Brauer admitted. 'And we respect them. For one thing, we discovered that we don't have to be quite so elaborate in the volume of our testing. We have reduced it greatly.'

On 1 July 1986, Revlon gave up their facility for animal testing altogether. 'We reduced the use of animals to such a degree,' Brauer explained, 'that it was no longer economically feasible to do it. And that was entirely due to the animal rights groups. They are the ones that pushed us into this, for which we thank them.'

Earle Brauer is an obviously sincere man who would prefer to forego all cruelty to animals on behalf of cosmetics – or for any other reason. There is no reason to doubt what he says. Yet what he does not say is that animal testing has not been carried out on most if not all of the ingredients in the Revlon range of cosmetics.

And nothing he could show me was capable of obliterating the nauseating memory of a film made secretly in 1986 at an American animal testing laboratory servicing the cosmetics companies. It was shot by Leslie Fain, a young researcher and animal lover who worked at the plant undercover. She told me she had originally taken a job there with no intention of spying. Only when she saw so much that appalled her did she, at some risk, decide to use an amateur film camera, which she hid under her lab coat, to shoot scenes of the suffering animals.

Fain said she was as much appalled by the brutalizing and dehumanizing effect the work had on some of her colleagues as she was by the cruelty inflicted on the animals in her care. 'The people I worked with, thirty-five or so young men and women, didn't give a damn about the animals. When a rabbit screamed in agony, they'd slap it and tell it to shut up. I had to listen to them cutting into the brains of rabbits, killing a hundred at a time. It was a status symbol to have the most blood on your white coat.'

She stayed at the plant for eighteen months. 'Largely because I was afraid of what some of the people working there with me would do to the animals. One guy was a real sadist. He enjoyed castrating hamsters and shaving all the hair off their backs to see if various products we were testing would grow it back. The male hamster has a flank organ, like a little spot. Once the animal is castrated, hair won't grow back in this area. They used this model for either baldness or beard growth. I could hardly believe it, but they were trying to formulate an after-shave that would also make hair grow – to promote the sale of razor blades!'

Leslie Fain managed to record many of the worst effects of the tests, including the notorious Draize eye irritation experiment. In this, shampoo is dripped on to the retina of a trapped rabbit's eye until it swells, discolours and finally oozes pus.

Other scenes she captured show rats and guinea pigs undergoing force-feeding with creams and other products. Watching scenes of the trapped beasts with feeding tubes forced down their throats while the stuff was unendingly pumped into them until their stomachs and organs came close to exploding was something I shall not lightly forget.

During a test known as the LD50 test (in which 50 per cent of the animals must die to prove the safety of the material) Fain witnessed mass sacrifice of animals which had outlived their usefulness, or failed to survive the LD50. If this, as she believes, stands for 'Lingering Death', it could not be more aptly named.

Leslie Fain's unnerving film provides the first convincing evidence of these tests, since the people who carry them out will never willingly let reporters or unofficial investigators view their work. As a direct result of it, she told me, the US Department of Agriculture carried out a thorough investigation of the plant in Rockville, Maryland, where she made the film, and sent the company a warning letter. Whether as a result of the film or not, a year later they closed this animal testing facility down.

I was given a video copy of Leslie Fain's film by Susan Rich of the Washington-based PETA (People for the Ethical Treatment of Animals). Earlier, Steve McIvor of the British Union for the Abolition of Vivisection (BUAV) had discussed it with me in London. McIvor's view was that it represented only one drop in the animal bloodbath currently overflowing on behalf of our cosmetic 'safety'.

'There were roughly 260,000 animal experiments a month done for a wide variety of purposes in British laboratories in 1988,' he said. 'Those are Home Office figures. No one gives information on tests, of course, so it is difficult to see what is going on. But we have a list of the companies doing contact testing (i.e. the deliberate application of questionably harmful substances to captive animals). Their sole interest is money.'

Susan Rich was able to be more explicit about the number of American companies using animal-tested products in cosmetics. 'All of them, unfortunately, do. Either they test on animals themselves, or they pay an independent laboratory to do it for them. That's how they hide, because if one of the majors, say Proctor & Gamble, is doing tests, we can get government reports on them under our Freedom of Information Act. That is, via the Department of Agriculture. But if the company doesn't do it themselves, then we don't know.'

Despite Dr Brauer's assertion, Rich says Revlon has had to defend itself more than once in the courts in cases where animal testing has been cited. 'There have been many successful actions against the big cosmetics companies,' she told me. 'In 1974 a woman complained to the FDA that a hair shampoo had set up eye irritation. The agency ran their own series of Draize tests on the product, but the judge

45

ruled that the agency had failed to prove that Draize test results were applicable to humans.'

Three years later, according to Rich, a woman in Tennessee sued over a skin cream which had set up an allergic reaction on her face. 'She was awarded $1.5 million, and there have been many other cases, too. But the cosmetics companies have a lot of economic clout and know how to manipulate the media, so these things seldom get much publicity. We've had examples of writers sympathetic to our movement who have written articles and had them killed by their editors. Our commercials, however innocuous, are often refused by the TV networks. No reason given. We have people power, they have the money – the classic battle.'

Yet there is evidence that Revlon is not the only one paying heed to growing public concern. More and more pressure is being put on the cosmetics giants to ban all unnecessary and cruel animal tests.

In Britain Steve McIvor has encouraging figures to show to the fourteen thousand or so subscribing members of BUAV. 'Home Office figures reveal that experiments have fallen in the last eight to ten years by about two million,' he told me. 'Last year, for example, there were just over three million. A few years ago we monitored it at five and a half million – quite a dramatic drop. And public awareness has helped. We've certainly had an impact, because previously nobody questioned it.'

In Washington Dr Ethel Thurston, one of the cruelty-free movement's chief supporters, talked proudly of the rising number of cosmetics companies, like Britain's rapidly expanding Body Shop chain, which claim they do not use any ingredient that has been animal tested. They are all pledged to use only 'cruelty-free' products. 'There are now over a hundred makers of excellent cosmetics which are not animal tested,' she told me. 'Why don't more people use those?'

This, however, involves a complicated definition of what is, or can be claimed to be, 'animal tested'. In order to market an ingredient for use in a cosmetic, companies like Henkel in Britain and the Société Lautier fragrance essence house in Grasse can satisfy the standards of safety regulations provided the materials used have not been tested for a specified period – at present five years. If animal tests have been run on the substance prior to that, there is no legal requirement for the company to say so.

The crucial issue is whether alternative methods could ensure the same degree of safety. The cosmetics industry has a proud record. Despite the obvious difficulties of Dr Brauer and others in sanitizing such intimate items as lipsticks and deodorizing cream, there have been remarkably few causes for complaint. No epidemic has ever been laid at the door of the cosmetics industry. There appears to be no evidence to prove that even the common cold or flu germs have been able to thrive and infect people via cosmetics.

Perhaps it would be better for the cruelty-free campaigners if they had. Professor Albert Kligman's characteristically outspoken view of the situation as it stands ('I don't have any objection to animal testing. I do it all the time') may be contradictory – he fought vainly for permission to use paid volunteer jail inmates as test human guinea pigs in place of animals. But it does not spare the protesters.

'My value system is such that I think cosmetics are an indispensable and important part of civilized life,' he told me. 'So in a sense I am a religious believer in them. And my personal view of the alternative people is similar to my view of the priesthood – they like to make a buck.'

Kligman openly condemns 'people in the alternative sphere' as suspect, whatever field they operate in. 'Jobs, philosophy, religion, whatever – I don't agree with them. Many are impostors. It's a good way to get money – go to Revlon and say "If you'll stop using animals and give us a million dollars, we'll search for alternatives and stop parading around your premises." I think that's a disgraceful form of pressure. But leaving that aside, there is no reason to cause a great deal of pain and injury to animals. That I agree.'

Where Kligman does not agree is that the accusations of Rich and McIvor and their supporters are valid in today's world. 'The Draize test has come under severe criticism, but that's all hokum. Nobody does those things any more. It's true the Draize did cause eyes to fall out, and blindness, but it doesn't happen any more. It's irrelevant. I mean, I don't test shampoos myself, but the way it's done is to start with a little concentration, go to a minimum toxic dose and then stop. I'm very much against making a rabbit suffer, because there's no need for it. When we do tests here using guinea pigs and mice, we are careful to cause the least possible amount of injury we can.'

Who can tell what that is, or what pain it causes? In the next room, Professor Kligman's 'mouse doctor' wife Lorraine was dissecting

47

the bodies of bald mice, presumably for microscopic analysis after absorbing or being injected with substances that could be toxic or harmful to humans.

She told me, 'I strongly feel that we need to have animal testing. There just are no *in vitro* systems (under which cell cultures are grown in the laboratory to simulate animal tissue used for testing) which can possibly mimic all the complex biology of the living organism. There are things we cannot do on humans, things we cannot duplicate.'

To the scientist, it poses an unanswerable dilemma. Nobody, certainly not any normal healthy person – though Leslie Fain's discovery of sadism cannot be ignored – wants to cause undue suffering in animals. Dr Brauer's words came back as I watched Lorraine Kligman's mice in their cages.

'If it was your two-year-old child who was on the floor screaming because of playing with your wife's cosmetics, getting some in the eye, and suffering possible blindness because the stuff had not been tested for safety, what are your interests at that point?' Brauer had asked me.

'As I see it,' he had said, 'there's only one. You want to know why the hell that stuff was allowed to be sold. Are you going to be happy if all we can tell you is, "we really don't know, Mr McKnight. It's just one of those things – we decided not to do any testing because we were being pressurized. I'm sorry, but we just don't have any information for you"?

'No, I believe it's my – and Revlon's – obligation that when the doctor calls to see your child there *is* an answer. Do we have that answer? We sure do.'

Yet Earle Brauer's words did not answer the critics of animal testing. In today's world, and until other equally effective means of protection are found, Lorraine Kligman's laboratory and vivisection would seem to him to be vital to the human race.

'I try to handle the animals as humanely, quote unquote, as possible,' the 'mouse doctor' told me. 'No doubt there have been abuses, but I think with the newer guidelines a lot of that has been eliminated. The newer tests are not quite as drastic as they were in the past. As far as I know even the Draize test for eye irritation is not quite as violent as it used to be.'

Not quite as violent, perhaps. But Earle Brauer admitted to me that Revlon had spent 'close on $2 million' vainly seeking an alternative. 'We have found methods that are promising,' he said, 'but they are only screening methods at this time. They help us to say of some products, "Well, this is one we needn't bother to put on an animal. It's no good." So they are helpful, though not a complete answer. Some day we may have the answer, but it's not available yet.

'I know the animal rights people say an alternative could take its place,' Kligman told me, 'and that some way with tissue culture could be used to predict irritancy just as well. In my view, that is an absolute lie. The whole argument, in my opinion, is a fake! It's a good game to play, and they get a lot of money for it.'

Yet he admits that a genuine case can be made by the protesters. 'There's no question but that there have been misdeeds in the past, and I don't hold anything against these people for what they are trying to do. But you'd have a hell of a time getting approval for anything uncontrolled in *this* university. They insist on how much space the animals must have, how much food. And, yes, there are people, doctors, who, every time they get a hare-brained idea, want to experiment, to make some animal suffer. Those shouldn't be allowed, I agree.'

Kligman accepts moral responsibility for everything he does to animals ('mainly putting on patch tests to study their irritation and resistance') because he believes that the millions who will use the cosmetic products he tests must be fully protected.

He also believes that far less animal testing is now carried out. 'I can tell you,' he said, 'that the number of animals, and the handling of animals, in the last five years has changed enormously. The original LD50 test, for example, has been contracted down to just a few animals, though the statisticians say you must use fifty. So, in this sense, the alternative movement – phoney and opportunistic though it is, in my view – can have a good effect.'

Kligman credits Britain in the last century with the origin of the protesters. 'Little old ladies worrying about bunny rabbits!' As a result, he has to admit, new and stricter controls are operating in Europe. A 1985 report of the EEC Scientific Committee on Cosmetology recommends animal tests only when there is a threat of 'human exposure to dermal toxicity [skin reaction] and carcinogenicity [cancer].'

Marion Kelly, Australian head of Britain's Cosmetics, Toiletries and Perfumery Association in London, told me that in practice she finds EEC rules on cosmetics are interpreted differently in each of the member countries. 'A number of the countries erect separate barriers. France has a number of them – for instance a required percentage of alcohol in any alcoholic preparation. Greece insists that producers must print the telephone number of the poison centre on their products. In Italy they finally bowed to EEC pressure and passed a law which is completely out of line with the rest of the Community.'

Kelly points out that Kligman's 'little old ladies' have less to worry about in Britain today. 'Only point five per cent of animals tested in the UK are for cosmetics. That's about 16,500. The biggest misconception is that animal testing is a routine production. It is not. Most of our companies do not know one end of an animal from the other. They don't do animal testing *per se*. In fact there is very little testing done here of actual finished product, because certain ingredients are by law prohibited for use in cosmetics in this country. And others are limited for use only at certain levels or with warning notices.'

To Steve McIvor, Susan Rich and their growing band of dedicated followers this is an evasion of the point at issue, since most cosmetics ingredients do still originally achieve acceptance as 'safe' by painful animal tests, whoever carries them out. In Shiseido's huge and super-efficient scientific research laboratory in Yokohama I was escorted, after working hours, through the locked doors of the animal testing department. I saw white rats, held by collars and 'restrainers', being force-fed with white cream. The oppressive death-charged atmosphere of the place left an uneasy impression of a slaughterhouse, an execution block. The Japanese scientist in charge told me, through an interpreter, that he did not believe that the work carried out in the cages and laboratories under his control was 'cruel'. I wondered how he could be so sure.

I also wondered how the other skin game players would answer the same question. And was there, in some of the growing number of mostly smaller cosmetics companies which have signed a 'cruelty-free' pledge, a better answer than any of them could give?

6

BODY SHOPPING

In 1976, in the small British seaside town of Littlehampton, a raven-haired young woman of Italian extraction, Anita Roddick, announced that she was going to open a shop between two back-street Brighton undertakers and call it the Body Shop. Oh no, she wasn't, she was told by the local authority. In official eyes the obvious connection with her dark-suited neighbours was neither funny nor seemly.

Roddick's shop was to be an establishment selling creams, potions and lotions. But not just another beauty parlour or make-up emporium. This, though it was to offer fragrant, nicely packaged face creams, moisturizers, cleansers, bath oils, hair treatments and eye colourings, was something entirely new. Almost homeopathic in its resistance to the lures and blandishments of the established cosmetics companies, the Body Shop was to be a daring first attempt by its proprietor to market her own brand of skin products and fragrances. These were, almost without exception, cruelty-free – never, so far as she knew, had they been tested on animals. They were also, for the most part, developed by her from natural ingredients such as seaweed, exotic fruit and vegetables.

The official objection might have stopped many budding entrepreneurs, but not Mrs Roddick. If she had taken this rebuff lying down, nobody outside the Sussex town might ever have heard of her again. But Anita Roddick was shrewd enough to turn the rejection to advantage. Presumably she had banked on the name, and its questionable poke of fun at the funeral parlours, to get her business talked about. The refusal, as she saw it, had handed a golden opportunity to her on a town hall plate.

'I disguised my voice,' she told an audience of businessmen and city tycoons at the Savoy Hotel lunch honouring her acceptance of the 1987 Business Enterprise Award, 'and phoned the local paper, the Brighton *Argus*. "Do you know?" I asked, "that there's this woman with two kids, and a husband who's abroad riding horses across South America, trying to open a tiny shop in a side street between two big, undertakers, and being told that she can't call it the Body Shop . . .?" '

No need to go further. The publicity the paper gave the story told all south-coast England that here was a brave little woman with a wicked sense of humour challenging the big powers and interests of the town. Embarrassed officials hastily reversed their decision and advised Anita Roddick that 'a fresh application by her would be favourably considered'. A licence was granted, and the public flocked in both to support her with their cash and to meet this female David whose single slingshot had slain the commercial Goliath.

'From that day,' she told her amused and admiring listeners at the lunch, 'we have never paid for a single advertisement!'

If the new company had been taken as seriously as it deserved, or even been noticed, by the financial world and commercial community which was later to honour its instigator with their highest plaudits and awards, a number of fortunes could no doubt have been made. For Mrs Roddick and her husband, George, it was perhaps as well that the control of the business and most of the equity remained in their hands. Only one far-seeing investor benefited from what has become one of the great success stories of the eighties. He was a Sussex garage owner, presumably a trusting friend, who matched the £4000 the Roddicks put into the business with a similar sum.

Today Body Shops, both franchised and Roddick-owned, are perfuming and enlivening streets across the United States, Europe and the Far East. There are, as their current brochure proudly declares, Body Shops in thirty-three countries, including Dubai and Denmark, the Arctic and Australia, Sweden and Singapore, Holland and Hong Kong. At the time of Anita Roddick's award 87 outlets reportedly offered her products in the UK, and a further 169 abroad. By March 1988 the influential British trade journal *Soap, Perfumery and Cosmetics (SPC)* had upped those figures to '93 in the UK and almost 200 overseas'. A formidable leap from the back streets of Brighton.

In the same issue *SPC* reported that Body Shop's pre-tax profits in the previous year had increased by 75 per cent to a total of £6 million. Newspapers labelled Roddick (said in a television interview that year to be worth £22 million, or $40 million) 'a child of the sixties', along with the Beatles and Carnaby Street hippies.

Everything she did, from refusing to sell goods that had caused death and suffering to animals, to setting up a Body Shop Boys' Town to assist young boys to develop their skills and find jobs, was based on a single-minded philosophy of 'caring'. Whether for the environment, or for the well-being of her staff and associates, it underpinned everything under her control.

Her stores were designed to attract. Shop fronts had been opened up invitingly, scent allowed to perfume sidewalks and pavements outside. Once inside, the customer or browser was greeted by enthusiastic, charmingly helpful (though never, in the Estée Lauder manner, pushy) salesgirls, who cheerfully made up pretty baskets of soaps, cosmetics and treatments in any chosen variety. The shops daringly displayed Mates, the brand name of airways tycoon and fellow 'carer' Richard Branson's condoms. Intended to help reduce the risk of AIDS among the young, they also emphasized Roddick's personal, deeply felt concern for society.

Even today, as Roddick moves into the competitive world of big-time beauty, her basic philosophy remains undaunted. What Jacques Courtin Clarins of Clarins, Lindsay Owen-Jones of L'Oréal, Ronald Perelman of Revlon, James Preston of Avon, Leonard Lauder of Estée Lauder and Yoshio Ohno of Shiseido are mutually and individually interested in – the ever more profitable expansion of their market share – holds no intrinsic attraction for her.

She was awarded an OBE by the Queen in 1988, and her prime interest, as she declares at every possible opportunity, lies in bettering the world she lives in. 'Why is altruism in business so suspect?' she asked Bank of England Governor Robin Leigh-Pemberton and his top tycoon guests at the Savoy lunch honouring her. 'What we have learned in Body Shop over the last ten to twelve years is that private greed never translates into public benefit. The corporate world is hung up on money, and the word "love" is never mentioned, certainly not in the corridors of business. But we have also learned that it is not money but the action to grow ideas that counts.'

In what should have sounded a warning siren in the ears of those who see themselves as monarchs of the territory, Roddick added, 'We have found no heroes, no modern-day heroes anyway, in the business world. Not one company that associates honest profit with

53

social awareness. We are, I dare say, the modern equivalent of the Quakers who made so much money by working hard themselves and treating people decently. The new word is values, and we're still looking for them . . .' A fierce glance, here, at the well-fed faces in her audience. '. . . Instead, we see tired executives of huge corporations, dying of boredom. The inertia of gigantism!' Another telling pause, then the *coup de grâce*: 'We believe they are doomed.'

She sat down to polite, if doubtful, applause. But Anita Roddick's philosophy does not include wanting to be liked, certainly not by the players at the biggest table of all, the heads of commerce and industry. In the United States the battle cry of this evangelical firebrand – who is changing not just the faces of the men and women who buy her goods but the whole nature of cosmetics – could well, I believe, start a second American Revolution.

'I believe we are the agents of change,' she frequently declares. It is a change that has been followed by many, but none with more zeal for the environment, more consideration for those who work for and with her, than Anita Roddick. 'Our aims are morale, a sense of purpose and achievement, and form,' she says. America and the giants of the conventional cosmetics industry will find, as others have found – some to their cost – that this can have an almost mesmeric effect.

There are, however, doubts about her ability to change the rules, to transform the industry built on puffery and sizzle. Leslie Kenton, an American writer and beauty editor renowned in Britain for her discreet judgements of the industry, shares them. 'Anita Roddick is sincere,' Kenton told me. 'She has tried to counteract the high cost of cosmetics – which in my view is the worst thing about them. But she is naïve, and the industry is full of sharks.'

A growing number of Body Shop customers would disagree. Roddick's naïvety – if it exists – is a refreshing change which they welcome. 'Even on an English winter's day, her stores smell like summer,' a customer commented recently. This is not only due to the natural fragrances she sells. It also radiates from her staff, who say they enjoy working under her guidance – and, no doubt, from the satisfying profits accruing to those scores of shopkeepers who operate one of her franchises.

Yet there is little doubt that the chain's main attraction for those who have to – or like to – count the pennies is Body Shop's downmarket prices. These, combined with Roddick's support for

Friends of the Earth and Greenpeace, her popular concern for saving whales, and her shops' emphasis on selling only natural, cruelty-free products, have created a highly persuasive commercial tool. Its effect on the giants of the industry has yet to be seen, but they would be foolish to underestimate its power.

Mrs Anita Roddick is, after all, no friend of theirs. Speaking in her usual racy, comic-book style, she told BBC-TV presenter Sue Lawley in February 1988: 'I am very embarrassed about being part of the cosmetics industry. It's run entirely by men. It reminds me of a sort of medallion-man uncle – you know, with lots of jewels. They [the big players] are not well known either for being relevant [i.e. caring], or for putting anything back into society. So I tend to zap in the opposite direction. Which is probably why I'm not your sort of doyenne.'

In her novel approach to the game – underselling products that women find pleasant to buy and are often as good to use, if less ritzily bottled and packaged, as the big companies' wildly expensive products – she is currently no threat. So the captains of the industry believe – or say they believe. But if her Body Shop spreads – and she has announced expansion plans that make even outer space seem a likely destination before too long – there is no doubt that it will affect the industry in its most vital and sensitive area: profit. Should this happen, should Body Shops proliferate, as she plainly intends, across the whole planet, should it take away even a particle of the billion dollar beauty business from the big cats, they will surely make every effort to eat her alive.

In 1987 Body Shop reported a turnover of £28.47 million, and the Roddicks were holding on to most of the reins. But in 1984 the company had sought and acquired a public quotation, so a take-over became a possibility if either or both of them ever had to sell. Meanwhile, the most likely way their embarrassing encroachment could be stopped was by merger.

With anyone else, that might be possible. With Roddick, it seems less likely than the election of a black woman president in the United States. She is not one of 'them', and says so. Whenever she appears in public, gabbling her daringly simplistic yet persuasive comments on life, business and cosmetics, she burns yet another boat with the cosmetics establishment. 'I've not met one cosmetics chemist who was fifty-five, or forty-five, or whatever they are, who looks twenty-five or thirty-five,' she complained to Sue Lawley. 'There is *no* application, no topical application, that will get rid of grief or stress or heavy lines.' She told another interviewer: 'There's nothing, but nothing, that's going to make you look younger. Nothing.'

So it is neither friends, nor business partners and allies, that she is after. Indeed, while working on the strategy for her global invasion she spares nobody. 'I have to challenge anybody, you know, that is daft enough, *daft* enough, to buy a cream that is more expensive than £5 a pot. Cream is basically oil and water. And it's brilliant – I mean a moisture cream is superb for the skin. But there's nothing magic about it at all. And, in the end, apart from packaging, it's no more . . .'

Her statement, as it often does, trails off before she can suggest that a good scrub with a face flannel would be as effective as some of her own products, as well as those of the highly priced competition. It is public comments like this that, to the delight or embarrassment of her PR people, make it indelibly clear to the business world that Anita Roddick is not afraid of shooting a hole in her own foot.

'You know what Revson said?' she asked glibly. 'He ran this company, Revlon. And what he basically said was, "What women want is hope and dreams." I simply don't believe that. I think they actually want a good cream, to stop their skin getting dry.'

Her own creams include such natural wonders as carrot, jojoba oil, hawthorn, and sage and comfrey. None costs more than £3.50 in Britain ($5.50), against ten or twenty times as much charged for the big-name products.

In late 1987, *Soap, Perfumery and Cosmetics* carried an announcement that Body Shop's autumn preview would include 'a Banana Conditioner for normal to dry hair'. According to the magazine, one thousand hand-peeled bananas would be mashed into a tonne of conditioner. In the projected new range there would also be a 'bodyscrub' containing olive-stone granules, and 'an aloe lip preserver in a roller ball pack'.

Sophisticated women, who had been spending small fortunes on the mysteries of night repair and similar well-hyped creams and potions, were all too ready to turn to these novel, unglamorously packaged items, forsaking the big names or doubling up on them. While the companies wrote Roddick off as a rival, believing her very low price structure would place the entire Body Shop operation exclusively among the lowest, mass-market cosmetics, there was one thing that they seemed to have overlooked.

Body Shop was classless. A British society woman, asked if she had tried these 'new-fangled preparations made of seaweed and so on', told a party of friends, 'My dear, every countess in Britain is using them.' Nobody seemed surprised by the exaggeration, and all confessed that they, too, 'had a pot or two of those nice creams that do your skin so much good'. In doing so, too, they did nobody and no living creature any harm, while actively helping to relieve poverty in the Third World, to assist rehabilitation for Britain's unemployed youth, and to ally the user with all humane and cruelty-free causes.

If the established major companies are underestimating the strength of this appeal, they are doing so at considerable commercial risk. Body Shop products not only save money (something that countesses and the wives of Wall Street tycoons and oil billionaires alike share a craving for whenever possible), but they also cleanse, moisturize, protect and nourish skin *without* any of the questionable, mildly frightening chemicals with long scientific names used in the major and more expensive brands. Furthermore, Anita Roddick's marketing strategy, for all its seemingly amateur and Greenpeace-tinged appearance, has proved hard-hitting and cost-effective enough to run any number of smaller – and some larger – traditional competitors out of town on a fast rail.

In the United States, there are those who believe that she will prove far less easy to get rid of than Dr Barnard's Glycel or the products of others who have tried in vain to climb aboard this bandwagon. Indeed, the wide social range of her popularity could devastate the vast, arbitrarily stratified US skin care and beauty market altogether, unless an early way is found to stop its invasion.

The question being asked by Roddick's many friends and admirers (but not as yet by her foes) is this: how long will it take the giants to wake up – how long will they let this novice get away with it? It seems she may have a clear run, at least in the early stages, for at present the big companies, comfortably dominating the super-profitable prestige end of the market, do not see her as a threat. She is beneath their notice. But all that could change very quickly. Amelia Bassin, who met and advised Anita Roddick when she made a preliminary, fact-finding trip to the United States and Canada before entering that market, knows this. When I spoke to her early in 1988 about Body Shop's chances on her territory, the acknowledged expert was hedging her bets.

Bassin told me: 'From everything I hear – I don't know. We

had a wonderful talk. She really wanted to come to the States –
this is where the market is. I told her the competition would be
pretty strong, but she's got a different story to tell. She's got some
aromatherapy products and stuff like that. But I don't know if her
prices are all that low – and "all-natural" products? To me, that is a
ridiculous claim! Many people are allergic to natural things – look
at poison ivy as an extreme example. And quite a few suffer from
rose fever.'

Bassin's realism is known, and respected, throughout the industry.
Her words are read and noted by everyone, and influence markets and marketeers alike. How Roddick will fare on this jealously
guarded battleground will largely depend on how people of Bassin's
kind in the trade regard the 'message' behind Body Shop. And
perhaps, also, behind a new wave of similarly 'natural', cruelty-free
cosmetics marketing outlets which are already gearing up to follow
any success Body Shop has in the USA.

At present, Bassin tells me she simply won't buy Roddick's belief
that 'synthetic' spells worse. 'There's nothing wrong with synthetics.
It's just a dirty word, like chemicals is a dirty word. In fact, very
often it's the synthetic ingredient that enhances the fragrance. It
makes it last longer and may help it to blend. For instance, all
musk is synthetic because of the government ban – rightly – on
killing musk deer. So "natural", in my opinion, is a phoney – but
a very successfully phoney – commercial term.

'In the seventies,' she continued, 'when all the big companies were
saying "It's a passing fad", I remember giving a talk on natural
products in the UK and showing one of my slides featuring crushed
bananas. They thought it was funny – well, it was. But then herbal
essence came out!'

This found a strong market foothold and acceptance. Though
Bassin and her peers warned that natural products had disadvantages, there was a marketing boom in them. 'They do have a greater
tendency to spoil,' she told me. 'And preservatives are chemicals.
They won't hurt a product at all – in fact they may help it, because
then you don't have to keep it refrigerated – but you can't use them
and still say the stuff in the bottle is all "natural". And you can't
preserve it without them. If you put a bottle of purely "natural"
product under the light for a while it will be rancid in no time at all.'

Roddick is aware of these problems. At the time when her company's shares were first quoted on Britain's unlisted securities stock

market, she told a woman friend in the trade that one natural product 'smelled like nurses' knickers'.

Would Amelia Bassin, I asked, buy shares in Roddick's US Body Shop invasion?

She thought about it. 'Well,' she said, 'she'd be very low down on my list. But I don't think it's something I would never buy. For instance, I would never buy stock in Revlon or Fabergé, because I don't think they're going in the right direction, and I hate all that. If Anita Roddick came out here and wanted to do another Obsession, or something like it, I wouldn't give her two weeks. But she's a very involved person who is right on top of things, and she knows what's going on. It's going to take a lot of money, but she does have something new to say and she's done very well up to now.'

In the early part of the year in which she was planning her American and Japanese ventures, the lady who has something new to say said some of it to British broadcaster Russell Harty, who sadly died less than six months later. 'Some critics say that you have achieved the perfect marriage between commercialism and do-gooding,' Harty told her. 'Is that so?' It was an ideal springboard for Britain's big business anarchist and she leaped on to it.

'I just don't know how *anyone* manages to run a company that is as successful as ours without having that attitude,' she said. 'I don't know how they inspire their staff, or sleep easy at night. So, I reverse the tables. I think there is an enormous responsibility for companies with high media profiles, like the Body Shop – and who are obviously fairly anarchic, fairly entrepreneurial – to talk about their images.'

'Anarchic, did you say?' Harty asked her.

'Yes. I think we are fairly anarchic. I mean, we tend to break the rules a lot, in terms of business. And the things we *don't* do are quite interesting. For instance we never talk about the profit. There are no big meetings where profits are discussed, and we don't have marketing departments.'

She believes, she went on, in inspiration rather than the rule book. 'We inspire, and I encourage, a whole culture of ideas, and I do think it is quite interesting, and often very different. We put an incredible emphasis on creating trade, but not just on selling a product and getting profit from it. Right now, we're creating trade in the Third

World, doing some extremely interesting projects within the inner cities, and in housing committees up in Scotland. This really *is* the creation of trade.

'It means,' Roddick told her interviewer, 'getting off your backside, walking around the streets, being a little bit streetwise, and having a bit more sense of humour about the whole damn business thing.'

It is a philosophy that has earned her the devoted allegiance of her staff, the admiration and often love of nearly everyone connected with her. However sourly it may have been received in conventional city circles, Body Shop has established itself in the hearts as well as the minds of almost everyone in any way connected with it.

Yet the captains of the industry refuse to see it as a threat. Stanley Kohlenberg's knowledge of the business is immense, yet the former head of Sanofi seemed only mildly interested when I talked to him in New York in late 1988. 'Some things travel, others don't,' he said enigmatically.

In London, Shiseido director 'Sam' Sugiyama was even less concerned. 'I don't see her as competition, no. We're not really in that end of the market. What we're looking for is the Harrods-type market, so we are not completely worried by Body Shop, though I know they are starting their operations here and in Japan very shortly, and the concept is good. It is carefully marketed, and I think it should be very successful, but it doesn't compete with us.'

Then who, in his experienced eyes, does Body Shop compete with?

'Look at any market survey,' Sugiyama advised. 'The top and the bottom are doing well. The middle? There is no middle. Here in Britain, you'll find Body Shop and Boots and the Marks & Spencers' house brand all increasing rapidly. And so are the prestige lines, the ones sold in Harrods. It doesn't matter where you look, it's the same story.'

But isn't the concept of Body Shop as a new, cruelty-free, natural and 'caring' operation capable of widening its attack to threaten all aspects of the market?

Sugiyama isn't so sure. 'Maybe. Nevertheless, the fact remains that the competition in this field is very tough. She'll need more than that to succeed.'

Rightly or wrongly, he and the other giants refuse to open their eyes to anything but this proven fact. They don't see Roddick's invasion as being aimed at their precious citadels of power. They know what it has cost them, individually, to gain the positions in the cosmetics marketplace they hold today, and take comfort from this fact. Theirs is not a game that anyone can play, or even take a hand in.

As Bassin said, it takes a huge lot of money even to take a seat at the big table. Anita Roddick's proud boast that she has 'never paid for an advertisement' suggests that she believes she can scoop the pot in the game without it. But if she aims to try and wrest a part of the vast US prestige market away from the billion dollar regular players simply by the appeal of her downmarket, caring philosophies – and without using high-priced hype and publicity – she is more than likely to find herself in a put-up or shut-up situation.

Without the thrust of an expensive promotional campaign to back her product, there isn't a single major American store that is likely to give Roddick an inch of floor space – 'real estate'. It is their domination of this, the prestige marketplace front-line, that is the greatest and most potent weapon in the armoury of the major league players. It is why, almost without exception, they are currently giving Roddick's Body Shop no more than a momentary chance of longevity in their market.

How strongly promotion has been used to influence trade is shown by the failure of many. The cosmetics industry has witnessed the demise of any number of punters who have tried to buy their way in, then found they had less than the resources needed to pay for all the puffery and hype of a major launch. The costs and commitments involved in one of these launches are a game in themselves. It is a game that sometimes makes the owners of the Western world's glossiest magazines, the makers of the cosmetics industry's videos and filmed product commercials, sweat blood as they consider what would happen to their businesses should it ever dry up.

7

PUFFERY AND HYPE

To see how insidiously advertising has become an addiction in the beauty business, consider the early days of scent selling. Delicate, discreet ads were tucked away in the society pages of 'ladies'' magazines. They appeared only where those wealthy enough to consider the use of such adornments might see them: in the pages of *Vogue* and the *Tatler*, the *New Yorker* and the *Illustrated London News*. No lady worthy of her coronet would admit to using such devices of allure, any more than she would tolerate excessive use of it by others.

'Women who wear too much scent can only be called fast,' wrote a society columnist. 'In the heat of India and the tropics, a little may perhaps be tolerated. One must never, never, wear musk, which belongs only in the lowest bazaars.'

Houbigant's popular Quelques Fleurs was unveiled in 1912 with the reticence of a shy bride. It followed such forgotten favourites as their Fougère Royale (1882) and Guerlain's Jicky (1889). There was no ballyhoo until World War I, when, in reaction to the stink of the trenches and the austerity of civilian life, a perfume craze began. Coty's daring Chypre appeared in 1917.

But not until the late twenties and early thirties did the power of perfume take off. In 1927 the French firm of Lanvin (also known for its couture) launched its magnificent Arpège. Here was a fragrance in the finest tradition of the top Paris houses, and Lanvin wanted to sell it in the huge new market of America, where flappers and their beaux were freshly awakening to sensual pleasures and possibilities. It could be achieved only by advertising. With considerable courage and ingenuity Lanvin allocated hundreds of thousands of francs to a campaign, using billboards and hoardings to attract the emergent automobilists on America's new highways. The slogan 'Promise her anything . . . but give her Arpège' became the most seductive, powerfully compelling advertisement anywhere.

To sell a perfume, a French fragrance, in this bold, sexy way was something altogether new – the birth of hype. The 'Promise her anything' slogan rang like a peal of bells. Almost for the first time, money was being lavished on a dream. It also led to a change in the marketing of cosmetics. If puff and hype could sell a mere scent, stuff in a bottle, to a nation, what would it do for the creams and compounds of Elizabeth Arden, Helena Rubinstein and others in the new cosmetics dreamland?

Today nobody knows the answer to that better than Estée Lauder. To the ladies of Palm Beach who play bridge with her, Estée's ability to sell roast beef to religious Hindus has never been in doubt. Even so, they are sometimes astonished by the sheer effrontery of the Lauder company's hype. Reportedly once in 1988 Estée put down her cards and pulled out a sheaf of photographs and proofs of advertisements. At first her companions were no more surprised than if she had touched their faces – as she often does with total strangers – to feel the texture of their skins. Indeed, they were happy to look at the pictures – they were resigned to being used as Estée's guinea pigs on these occasions. The pictures, it was explained, were to illustrate an exciting new fragrance – Knowing – that Estée was launching as part of a campaign to change the entire Lauder image. What did they think?

The company, she explained, was adjusting its sights. In future Lauder would aim to attract a more sophisticated woman, a woman 'who had lived'. Thus the girl in the pictures was expressing this more mature and sexy, role-model female. The ladies could hardly have missed the point. Czech model and film star Paulina Poriskova's half-opened mouth and yearning expression gave an altogether different impression from the fresh innocence of her predecessor – virginal, seemingly untouchable Willow Bay. This was a U-turn, and the bridge party expressed mild surprise. Gone was the 'purity' image Estée had been so consistently, and expensively, emphasizing for a decade. Nobody had expected *sex* from the Lauder house. Could it be Estée's doing?

Rather more tartly, Mrs Lauder explained that she was not showing them the pictures simply to introduce Willow's successor. She wanted her lady friends to see and applaud the perfume she was about to launch in a $6 million campaign. Estée, personally, had named the fragrance Knowing because she felt it gave exactly the right hint of women's deepest intuitive sense, their secret intelligence of a male-dominated world. As to the new, sexier image that her son Leonard and his wife Evelyn were giving to the company, these had been agreed by her only reluctantly.

In Estée Lauder's shrewd old eyes (Josephine Esther Mentzner was born on 1 July 1908, according to biographer Lee Israel) the switch was a gamble. But she also knew, and was being soberly warned by her business executives, that something in the way of a booster was needed to keep ahead of the growing competition. Leonard was insisting that the company needed a fresh and different image. It was he and Evelyn who had picked Paulina, while Estée was putting all her strength into the launch of the new fragrance. It was Leonard who was to announce that, 'If today's woman wants sex, Estée will give them sex.'

She had said no such thing herself. In her view, the new fragrance was all that was needed to remedy the decline. She had wanted her friends, who represented the wealthy circle Estée depended on for her company's billion-dollar-a-year turnover, to share her confidence in it. Instead, they seemed interested only in the model. As she later explained, 'They couldn't have cared less about the perfume! Oh, they said it was fine. But what they were interested in was the girl. "Just look at that girl!" they kept saying. "Isn't she great?"' But Estée's disappointment ('I'd designed the bottle and everything!') was quickly eclipsed. In Paulina, the company had found a winner who would spin a web of fantasy and myth around each of their expensive product lines.

If launching her has cost the Lauder family business more than enough to ransom half the hostages of the Middle East war, that is the price of staying on top. Cosmetics monarchs depend more and more on hype and image. That launch also symbolizes the terrible, driving need of today's fragrance merchants to lay out fortunes in the hope of staying at the head of the game.

Paulina, billed and plugged by the newspaper-sized Lauder publicity department as 'a woman who has lived', and given the title of 'the most famous "name" in a bathing suit' by *Vogue*, was the latest in a line of only three previous Lauder models, Shaun Casey, Karen Graham and Willow Bay. Through her daringly adult appeal – and the expenditure of those six million promotion dollars – she was destined to 'sex-up' the Lauder image and put dramatic and revolutionary pep into the vast Lauder sales force. In the business this is no more than 'selling the sizzle'. One of the ad men summed it up during photo sessions with the new model: 'God, look at that. That's *today*.'

Unquestionably, the girl who was to give Lauder a dramatic face-lift was, as one story headlined her, 'the six-million dollar woman' – and, to the company, worth every cent. But if anybody was going to have to pay for this hype-rocket, fired into international orbit at such enormous expense, it was the consumer. Nobody in the company, or among its dealers, questioned such extravagance. The wealthy women sweeping into smart stores around the world to purchase their Estée Lauder make-up and skin care preparations took it as a matter of course. No voice complained about the price of the product, in which every penny of the hype, of the changed image and style, was meticulously costed in.

For more than half a century, women in the top bracket of the prestige market have been accepting such extravagant seduction without a flicker of complaint. The flood of necessary artwork for such campaigns, the purchase of acres of space in glossy magazines, costs large fortunes. It adds enormously to the cost of what we put on our faces and bodies. But does that matter, so long as it keeps the dream alive?

In only one issue of one glossy magazine in Britain in 1988 – the April *Harpers & Queen* – the big cosmetics companies (with a minute intrusion by lesser lights) spent close to £100,000 on full-page colour advertisements that rivalled one another in alluring promises. In eighteen full-colour pages with guaranteed positions at the front of the magazine, emphasis was so subtly diffused, so seductively displayed, that it would have been hard for a visitor from another planet to fathom its purpose. The main aim, as one of the magazine's advertising executives explained to me, was reassurance. 'The readers will see their favourites, the well-designed bottles and pots of their precious creams and lotions, shining up at them from the pages of a magazine as unmistakably 'classy' as a Rolls-Royce radiator,' I was told. More emphatically, 'Not only the customers, but the staffs of the cosmetics companies are affected by it. Their sales people need this back-up.'

At any price? Doesn't it matter that it will have cost their company a secretary's salary for a whole year for a double-page spread in that particular magazine? Or that production of the artwork alone has exhausted a further small fortune? The really awkward question seems to be that, if advertising and publicity did not (as even the players admit they do) massively increase the market prices of these outrageously over-priced embellishments, would their purchasers be as pleased to put them on their dressing-tables? And if the cost was sharply reduced by cutting this out, would they feel as satisfied in buying the stuff?

It is this aspect of the business that confuses socialists and psychologists alike. If, instead of unwrapping a minute quantity of basically inexpensive fragrance or cream from a costly cocoon of glamorous packaging, the consumer simply opened an ordinary pot or bottle – something she had bought at the chemist or drugstore without any alluring advertising to direct her – would she feel the same rapture of possession? Would it, in fact, do her as much good?

Anita Roddick of Britain's Body Shop, of course, believes, and seems to be proving, that it would. She does not depend, she says, on promotion in the accepted sense. She uses not one inch of space in the glossies. Her UK promotional machinery is contained in one relatively small PR office in London. If her New York offshoot on Broadway, headed by the experienced Michael Waldock, adopts a more conventional marketing approach it is unlikely to be with her unstinting approval.

Roddick has shown that it is possible to market cosmetics, skin care and make-up, without hype. In doing so she is cutting right across all the old market definitions. It is now an established fact that her products belong as much to the prestige, high-class end of the business as they do to the down-market mass end. Both countesses *and* the modern equivalent of chorus girls buy at the Body Shop.

And at least one of the very biggest players, Lindsay Owen-Jones of L'Oréal, rejects the idea of hype as the most important and influential card in the game. 'There is a fundamental misunderstanding about cosmetics, both in the financial community and by some in the industry,' the new chairman of this French company (according to UK trade magazine *SPC*, 'No. 1 in the world league, with £4.1 billion sales') told Fiona Walsh of the London *Sunday Telegraph* in June 1988. 'The most stupid man in the world was the one who once said, we sell "hope in a jar". Our products have to be based on serious research. This is not a frivolous business.'

If Owen-Jones' philosophy was universally applied, not only would prices drop but several famous magazines would be forced out of business. According to the UK's Media Expenditure Analysis, a total of £161½ million, including £44 million on press advertising, was spent on hype in 1988 by the cosmetics and toiletry companies. L'Oréal, which takes in Lancôme, Cacharel, Ralph Lauren, Paloma Picasso, Guy Laroche, Biotherm, Vichy and many others, was one of the main contributors. As the chairman explains, 'Marketing is extremely important, but success cannot be based solely on that. Those are the companies who sell hope in a jar. It is not us.'

On the other hand, as Owen-Jones would agree, myth can be infinitely potent. So much so that the Lauders and the other big names are justified in relying on it, as their sales show. It is a quality that has stood politicians and statesmen in good stead throughout history.

An astonishing example of its strength occurred in 1988 in Uganda. Alice Lakwena, described as a 'white witch', led her fanatical Holy Spirit followers into suicidal attacks on the army with only her own brand of cream to protect them. She had told them that, by rubbing shea-nut oil – which she had specially prepared – over their bodies, they would be protected against bullets. It took the slaughter of scores to destroy the myth, but even so others were waiting to take the place of the dead, still convinced that they were invulnerable.

There is no doubt that there will always be those who accept myths, however outrageous and even dangerous. Nothing the sceptics and doubters say will alter that. The editor of the British *Sunday Telegraph*, Peregrine Worsthorne, told his readers last summer that 'people die and kill for myths, which they don't willingly do for facts and figures'. He added that 'myths are just as much part of reality as facts and figures and the small print of treaties; more real in many ways'. Estée Lauder's voice would be among a chorus echoing that.

Yet the facts and figures present a fantasy all of their own. According to Goldman Sachs' July 1987 Data Base report on the Personal Care Industry, 'In response to materially slowing volume growth in 1980, manufacturers boosted prices significantly and failed to increase advertising efforts. *This introduced price sensitivity in mass and product lines, which ultimately impacted earnings*' (my italics). Without hype, in other words, product sales based on myth lose their momentum.

And Britain's sharp-eyed Media Expenditure Analysis watchdog has noted a considerable increase in money spent on advertising by toiletry and cosmetics companies during 1988. This was in all branches of the media – most significantly in television – at a time when sales of cosmetics in the UK were barely more than static. As my advertising executive informant confessed, 'I really don't know how cosmetics companies cost their products. But in my personal opinion a large part of it – the cost of the product – has to be in hype and packaging. Because, without these, they simply could not compete.'

So, whatever the myth machine costs, it has to be worth it to those playing for the highest stakes in the game. Without it the main players – Estée Lauder and Revlon, L'Oréal, Avon and so on – would lose their socks. The perpetuation of myth is as crucial to their sales as fertilizer is to the farmer – which may or may not be a good analogy.

Thus, perhaps understandably, they go to stupendous lengths to protect and screen the purity of the image which all this expensive puffery and hype concocts. This reticence applies, in my experience, as much to the cosmetics kings' and queens' personal lives as to their products and marketing techniques. Lee Israel told me how Estée Lauder had reacted to *Estée Lauder, Beyond the Magic*, her well-researched and revealing biography written without the subject's approval and published in America in 1985. It seemed to suggest an extraordinary reluctance to face the truth other than through the devious channels of puffery and hype.

Persuasion amounting to bribery, and bullying attempts to prevent adverse publicity, are by no means unknown. They have been noted in several cases where the big American companies and their luminaries have been threatened with exposure. And Lauder, as I mentioned in Chapter 2, had rushed into print with her own book – rumoured to have been dictated in Barbara Cartland style at her Palm Beach poolside. 'And as soon as my publishers, Macmillan [in Britain, Arlington Books published it the following year], announced the book,' Lee Israel told me, 'they [the Estée Lauder company] tried to buy me off.

'They first threatened to injunct against the book, saying that I had misrepresented myself as having written it with her authoriza-tion – which of course I had never done. Then they claimed to have a tape recording to prove this. Of course, when I challenged them to produce it it never materialized. But after the threats came the bribes.'

A close friend of hers was approached by a lawyer and told: 'She can have $2 million if she doesn't do the book.' Whoever made this outrageous offer, and whether it was genuine or not, Lee Israel rejected it out of hand. Her book was published and well reviewed in both countries.

A leading columnist on one of Britain's biggest-circulation daily newspapers has since been offered a large sum to withdraw an unfavourable account of another leader of the industry. The disease is spreading, and not all reporters and writers have the moral strength of Lee Israel. I know of journalists who have had stories critical of cosmetics or the people who make them rejected or cut by editors for no accountable reason.

The vast financial weight of the hype machine, spending millions annually with the media, seems effectively to ensure that nothing damning or detrimental to the industry ever reaches the buying public. Estée Lauder herself may have known nothing of the efforts made to suppress Lee Israel's candid, unauthorized work. It is good to know that, whoever instigated them, they failed completely. But the need for those protecting such a fabulously wealthy and powerful woman to have gone to such lengths as they apparently did says much for the value such people place on absolute discretion.

What did they fear, on her behalf? Was it the fact, established by Israel, that Estée Lauder was not born in Europe, as she had previously claimed, but in Corona, a near-slum district of New York? In the book, the author pays due tribute to Lauder's extraordinary success, and to her talent for promoting her products. It is certainly not a malicious work.

Presumably the high cost of hype – and the vulnerability of a business which (despite Lindsay Owen-Jones' feelings in the matter) universally claims to be selling no more (and no less) than dreams and hopes – makes for extreme sensitivity among many of the top names. Before any major interview with them can be authorized or given, a would-be interviewer will be screened more thoroughly than Palestinians entering the United Nations building. At Avon's Manhattan headquarters, Jim Preston's PR office informed me primly: 'We make it a rule not to be associated with any work of a personal nature.' Estée Lauder's front office echoed this: 'It has never been the policy of the Lauder family to contribute to a work of this sort.' Almost without exception I was asked to define the 'thrust' of the proposed work before I had even decided what possible views my researches would lead to. Without this precondition, I was told, no interview could be set up or help given. With notable exceptions

– chiefly Shiseido in Tokyo and London, Clarins in London and Paris, Revlon in New York and New Jersey, and Sanofi Products in Manhattan – I found them suspiciously unwilling to open their doors to any reporter or writer who would not commit himself or herself in advance.

In his profile of Ronald Perelman – 'the new Mr Revlon' – in *New York* magazine in 1985, David Blum wrote that

> [he] would seem to prefer that no one ever utter his name. He would rather that no one know the details of his personal life . . . his financial status . . . how he lives. His corporate headquarters, which doubles as his home, is off-limits to the press. He would prefer to be a businessman no one talks about, a face no one recognizes, with a past no one remembers.

The attractive thirty-five-year-old woman who presides over Calvin Klein Cosmetics in New York's Trump Tower, Robin Burns, is almost equally *recherché*, though she did allow writer Marguerite Smith to penetrate her eyrie last year. This rising star, whose erotic advertising style for Obsession has featured entwined nudes, says she 'strives for balance' in her personal life. This means getting well out of reach, salmon fishing in Iceland or at her Long Island home where she buries herself away during spring and summer weekends.

In 1984, when Lindsay Owen-Jones was promoted from running L'Oréal's American company, Cosmair, and whipped over to Paris to be groomed for the chairmanship, there was – according to *Forbes* magazine's 12 March issue that year – only one black mark against him. 'He'd wowed US cosmetic folks with his marketing success – not to mention his charm and good looks,' the magazine reported, 'but L'Oréal's Paris executives dislike his visibility and willingness to talk to the press.' Things obviously were going to have to change. It added, 'And [he] refused to be interviewed for this story.' Despite repeated requests, he did the same to me.

Unlike Sam Goldwyn, who didn't mind what anybody said about him, 'just so long as they spelled the name right', the chiefs of the cosmetics business prefer life in the shadows. If their reticence gives rise to suspicion in the media and elsewhere that they have skeletons in the closet, that is a price they seem willing to pay. In the crisis now facing them over the definition and claims made for some of their products, it could prove highly expensive. And if it does, nobody will pay for it but the people who continue, like well-fed sheep, to buy their products. 'The actual ingredients cost 10 per cent or less of what they pay for them,' a woman who had worked for Helena Rubinstein and *Vogue* confirmed to me. 'The hideously huge mark-up is to cover the cost of advertising and all the technical research they put into the products these days.'

In Paris Pierre Dinant, the great perfume bottle designer, made this point even more forcefully. 'Let's say an ounce of a fragrance like Opium is going to be sold for $150. I would think the bottle costs no more than one dollar. The carton could not be much more than another 50 cents. Perhaps 1 per cent of the retail price in all!'

So what can possibly account for the other 99 per cent? It is true that essential oils, from which all top fragrances are blended, can be expensive. As Stephen Mannheimer, supplier of them to the leading perfume houses in New York, had already told me, 'Jasmine sells, wholesale, at $1000 a pound. Rose can cost three times as much.' But this is for the basic raw essence, in its natural form. Only a minute quantity of that would be found in any pure perfume today because, as Mannheimer points out, few natural essences are used.

'Giorgio and Poison do not rely on naturals,' Mannheimer assured me. 'They do contain them, but only in very small measure. Seventy to eighty per cent of them, I'd say, are synthetics.'

On that basis, it seems unlikely that an ounce of Opium, or any of its three-figures-an-ounce rivals, would cost the maker more than a few cents, or pence, at most. 'Yes, but you are also paying for the research, which gives you safety, stability and efficacy,' 'Sam' Sugiyama reminded me. 'With the cheaper brands you don't get that. It is a matter of choice, left to the good judgement of the consumer.' Shiseido can say this with pride, laying out, as it claims to do, $50 million a year on its huge research plant in Yokohama. Comparatively they spend, as Sugiyama says, 'only peanuts' on advertising. But dreams don't sell themselves.

Like many skin care companies, Shiseido has a 'magic ingredient'. It is a rare and valued substance called hyaluronic acid. Whether or not it is as effective as the company claims, women all over the world are rubbing it on their faces and bodies in increasing numbers. The most elegant Parisian I know wears it. The marketing success of this clinical-sounding substance is already fully established, and there are many others.

Maybe they work, maybe they don't. But the mystique created by

71

them, and the vague promise of miracles, carries its own ring of confidence. Every woman knows, when tempted to buy an outrageously expensive new skin cream, that she is paying far too much for it. And, of course, she has more sense than to believe that it will permanently take away her forty-five-year-old furrows and lines. But, ah, look – it has 'X' in it! So all is well.

8

MAGICAL MYSTERIES

Opening a beauty salon in London in the early eighties, when the secrets of the business were not as familiar as they have since become, seemed an attractive proposition. Judy Black certainly thought so. She invested £30,000 in a course of the latest treatment techniques, found a partner, and opened up in the West End.

How women like Judy Black are lured into the beauty business depends largely on their gullibility. Black had read an article by a leading beauty editor supporting the notion that 'cold laser' treatment – applying an electrically vibrating needle to the skin for stimulation and 'toning' – would help lose fat. She told me, 'Some French lady was doing the laser treatment, and the article said how successful it was. I called the magazine and they gave me the name. The next thing I knew I was over there, on a long-weekend course costing about £500!'

What she learned on the course convinced Black that, if nothing else, laser-toning was a wonderfully persuasive tool for extracting money. 'I really didn't get to know an awful lot about the therapy side of it, but I could see that it was a money-spinner. There I was, on the outskirts of Paris, asking myself "What the hell am I doing? For God's sake, get me out of here!" But all the time I couldn't help wanting to make a fortune.'

'I tend to be an empire builder,' she explained to me. 'I can't mess around with bits and pieces. So, having invested money, I went into everything I could get to make the company larger.'

'Collagen,' she was told by the representatives who called at her new salon, 'is a magical substance. In its natural form, in our bodies, it provides elasticity and shape. Adding it, in creams and lotions, or by injection, is the greatest aid to beauty since the discovery of the hair comb.' If that was so, Black reasoned, she plainly must offer it, too, to her clientele. 'I never really knew what it was,' she admits now. 'I advised it, without really understanding anything about it at all.'

But to the fourteen British, eleven continental and two Japanese chemical companies offering it to her in its different grades for as much as £75 a kilo, the tough, rubbery substance was a money-spinner. Advertised as an animal product similar to the protein in our bodies, the spongy layer which firms up the flesh between the inner and outer layers of our skin, it came originally from the carcasses of dead cattle in slaughterhouses. Abattoir owners were only too glad to get rid of the stuff.

All Judy Black knew, from the encouraging persuasions of the reps who sold it to her in quantity, was that it was the one ingredient women craved. Collagen would make their wrinkles fade and disappear. Collagen was the new wonder skin care ingredient of the age. They had to have it, even if they paid as much as £45 for barely more than an ounce, which the most expensive salons were charging.

'I didn't charge anything like that, but even at £10 or so, depending on the range, it made a profitable and popular addition to the wide range of cellular preparations they advised me to offer to the customers,' she told me.

Finding a scientific basis for its popularity as a 'magical' wrinkle and age-line remover was, she found, very much harder. In the opinion of Buddy Wedderburn, a retired senior biochemist with Unilever, the effect of rubbing collagen on to the skin is negligible. Even when injected, she told me, there is no scientific evidence that it will do more than temporary – literally 'cosmetic' – good in banishing wrinkles and lines.

This experienced chemist dismisses any suggestion of 'magical' properties in collagen. 'I don't think it does a damn thing,' she told me. 'It is perfectly true that collagen fibres are in our bodies, in the collective tissues. But they exist below the dermis. As we get older, their natural elasticity goes. Eventually, the fibres are absorbed and we lose that sort of cushiony, spongy mass underneath.'

Can they be replaced? 'No, you can't do anything about that,' Wedderburn told me. 'Except by good diet, exercise and ensuring that your circulation is working really well. There's really nothing anyone can do, permanently, to stop the process of collagen loss. I don't know of anything that gets into these areas – certainly nothing that will stop wrinkles. *Nothing* in science is magic!'

But Judy Black had been given a very different view. She was told, as were many of the three thousand members of the British Association of Beauty Therapy and Cosmetology, that the substance had powers of rejuvenation which did indeed seem supernaturally wonderful. So Black filled her salon shelves with it. 'We had collagen creams and collagen lotions. They were supposed to give you "that youthful glow". I always thought it was something like yeast, which bucks you up. Then I went to see a man who injected it into wrinkles, filling them up, and everything he told me seemed to me to be a lot of rubbish.'

But in the meantime she had become 'totally immersed' in the whole business, and taken courses to learn every aspect. 'Some of the situations were quite amazing – like a Soho sex shop! They used to really embarrass me. They'd say, "Oh, there's a terrible drama, dear. Could you go down and sort out what's going on in the sauna room?" I'd go down and see all these naked women, and go totally blood red! I was a disaster – I was so shy about the whole thing.'

There were even times when she found it funny. 'I had to take one woman off her slender-toning, being done with our laser machine. Poor woman, I think I was electrocuting her I was laughing so much! I almost had hysterics. I thought, what am I doing? There was this fat woman covered in suction pads and I was trying to pull them off. A nightmare! But then the whole business is,' she can now say with hindsight.

Though she had an experienced beauty therapist partner, at the outset Judy Black had financed the entire venture herself. She was then faced with having to try and get her £30,000 back. 'I'm a good businesswoman, and I wasn't going to lose £30,000 just like that. In the end I just about got all my money back – but, my God, I had to work for it! I did special parties – virtually Tupperware parties. I thought, oh, if only I can get my money back, I'll forgive myself.'

It was hard and distasteful work, but she had to do it or lose everything. In the end she managed to recover most of her capital. 'People were literally queuing up to be given this miraculous new laser treatment. They were begging me. "Please, please, make me younger!" They were crying down the phone! "Yes, I'll take the whole course of treatments. How much? A thousand pounds?" I'd say, "No, no." But the money was absolutely hysterical!'

Gradually she found herself growing disenchanted with many aspects of the business. 'What's really terrible is these sad women all wanting desperately to be slim,' she told me. 'I say women –

but I'm sure there are equally sad men – women who were trying to hold on to their lovers, or trying to get their husbands back. I've got letters – poetry – begging me for appointments. Mostly from middle-class women, or women whose husbands were highly successful, running big companies and so on. They'd come in with handfuls of cash, imploring me to give them a treatment.'

In 1984 she sold the salon. It was across the road from a major studio, and had become fashionable enough to attract television and movie stars. 'We were doing people like Joan Collins, though only odds and ends on her. She never came to us for any important treatment and I think she was very wise not to.'

By this time, the salon business disgusted Judy Black. She became convinced – and she admits it now – that: 'It was a load of rubbish. I suppose I'd known that from the start really, but it took a long time to sink in.' She acknowledges that she had little or no idea, for instance, of what the laser treatment really did, though she was charging £23 for a five-minute session. 'I can see now that it was a total waste of time. On the course in France I hadn't known what the hell they were talking about, and nobody else who was on the course with me knew either. But we were all passed out as fully trained laser therapists!'

She described an imposing 'graduation ceremony' at the Selfridge Hotel in London, where she and her whole class were issued with a 'wonderful scrolly thing' by the people selling her the laser machine. 'They told me it was my certificate of competence to operate a laser toning machine, costing several thousand pounds – which, of course, I was expected to buy. Now, they said, I would be able to recoup the cost of it in a matter of months.'

Yet there were times when she believed she was doing some good. 'I did get a nice feeling sometimes. And my partner was amazing – she's got these magic hands. Clients would say, "I'll pay anything, I don't care what she does to me. Just let me book an hour with her." She'd go to their feet, feel the points we'd learned about in reflexology, and tell them, "My God, you're constipated, aren't you?"

'I'd think, "How does she know that?" But you can tell these things from those points – I really do believe in that. Certain things are not rubbish. And, even when they are, if the person you're doing it to *believes*, then it can do a lot of good.'

In the same way, she came to respect some of the mystery ingredients of skin creams. 'Don't knock all that they do,' she advised.

76

'Maybe it's just an ordinary cream base, but if the right few drops are added, it will do good. We had a certain cream which we didn't actually invent – we had it made for us in a pharmacy and it was amazingly cheap. It was most probably cow dung or whatever, but it was so pure and it contained lanolin – that famous word which *has* to be all right!'

Black's cream was made entirely from natural ingredients. 'Honey and all the rest of it. I thought, "Well, at least this is pure, it can't do any harm" – even if they were paying £15 to £20 a pot for it. You have to realize that the whole cosmetics world is built on the fantasy that the more you pay the better the stuff is. We could never sell anything we put too cheap a price on.

'Why do you think the top companies spend X-millions a year on advertising? And do all that wonderful packaging? It has to *look* amazing. That's what counts. If women get one that isn't packaged and puffed, they don't get the same pleasure from it.'

Judy Black looks back on her salon years with something approaching self-revulsion. 'I hated myself for doing it, and I couldn't believe there were so many crooks,' she told me. 'This is the very first, and I hope the very last, time I'll fall for anything like that. Somebody sits down and talks to you, you ask questions and they come up with the right answers – and, bingo, you give them £30,000! I didn't have £30,000 – I had to borrow a lot of it. And, you know, there were people on the course not just buying those lasers, but taking options to buy more!'

Laser-toning was the flavour of the age. 'Women everywhere were demanding it. They only had to hear about laser-toning to believe that, at last, something approaching the fountain of eternal youth was in sight and attainable. It could – it did – work miracles on ageing skin! They'd heard that it did. Somebody, so-and-so, had told them it was simply marvellous. The very word "laser" held magical, indefinable possibilities. If nothing else, it was brand, spanking new.'

This was as important as anything else. 'Ageing, beauty-conscious women,' Black reflects, 'know in their hearts that nothing really works for long. It's only when something new comes along that their spirits soar and their hopes – dashed so many times – rise. It is why, in the beauty salon business, there always has to be something new, something even more wonderful, coming along. Women will pay anything to get their hands on it.'

It is this incessant pressure for novelty – for something that might,

77

just might, do the trick at last – that drives the companies to bring out ever more magical products. It makes them claim in their costly advertisements that 'Now – at last – comes the breakthrough every woman has waited for . . .' Or dreamed or longed or prayed for.

It is only people like Judy Black (whose real name has not been used in order to protect her from those who resent any outspoken revelation of their secrets) who learn to their cost that these claims are not always to be trusted. But there are many thousands of honest beauty salon owners, and dedicated women who work in them, who would argue that her feelings are unrepresentative.

Myra Sims, for instance, is constantly adding new and improved techniques and cosmetics to the range of beauty treatments offered in her London salon, and believes in all of them. With obvious pride she showed me one of the latest. It is called, I was told, the Tsunami electro-toning facial machine, and differs from Judy Black's laser in ways too subtle for me to comprehend but which I accept.

'Is this another laser?' I asked Sims.

'No, not at all,' I was told. 'It's a Japanese technique which I found and imported from the States.' She walked over to a table on which a machine like a small tape recorder was standing, and switched it on. A pleasantly melodious hum, alternating in tone as she moved switches, came from it. 'It stimulates the acupuncture points of the face,' she told me.

Sims had picked up twin metal probes attached to thin wires leading from the machine and was fitting small cotton-wool pads to the tips. 'Perhaps you'd like to try it?' She moved the soft pads in a light circular movement over my forehead, then round my eyes and closed lids. The effect was a mild tingling of the skin, more gentle than that of my electric razor. By itself wholly innocuous, I thought. But the humming was persuasive.

After a few moments my eyes began to feel heavy. Sleep became an attractive prospect. 'Is it supposed to be hypnotic?' I asked.

Myra Sims laughed. 'If you're lying down, it can make you very drowsy. Unfortunately it does affect the operator, too. So I have to turn it down a little when my girls use it.'

It can also, I gathered, make a sharp difference to your bank balance. 'We do a course of twelve – you can't do it in less – for £200. That's less than £20 a session, and it includes an initial full consultation, which means a treatment with it. If you consider the cost of the machine and our trained staff, plus the overheads, that really isn't expensive.'

Her soft, pleasing voice became mildly critical. 'But we can't charge top prices here – the women won't pay to improve their bodies. Not like the French! British women prefer to let them go, and then cover them up with expensive clothes.'

Fifteen years ago, four beauty salons were opened around London by a friend of Myra Sims, an energetic businesswoman called Maureen Barry. In her Chelsea home where she and her husband now operate a business 'putting together kindred interests' (including health farms), then launching them on the stock market in well-promoted public flotations, Barry told me, 'All these things go in cycles. I started with a South African slimming machine, the Faradic, which Professor Hawkins – a friend of Dr Christiaan Barnard – was franchising. You lay there and it exercised you by sending a little electric charge into your muscles. After forty minutes, you'd be pouring with sweat – it had actually done the work of about eight hours' exercise. Of course, it couldn't do anything about weight loss, but it could help people who got saggy.'

Barry shares her friend's belief in the new Japanese machine, but from a business viewpoint. 'The Japanese are making tremendous inroads. And according to Myra, who has all these actresses coming to her salon, it gives a very convincing demonstration. The way she does it, she only treats one half of their faces. Then they look in the mirror and say "My God! It's amazing!" '

Barry had let Sims give her a treatment of the humming Tsunami. 'I must say, I did feel very, very fresh afterwards. It's supposed – you have to laugh – to be the equivalent of a face-lift! The idea is that the electric current is going into your cells and – you really *do* have to laugh – regenerating them!'

At £20 a throw I shouldn't have thought that laughter came into it. But Maureen Barry is first and foremost a businesswoman. 'Cosmetics,' she says, 'are endlessly fascinating. It's the psychology of how you look, and how you want to look. Looking good is so very important.'

So why did she give up the salons?

'Well, after five years, I saw the desperation of women. Not really their faces, more their personalities. I began to find it wearing, maddening! I'd reached the stage where I wanted to scream out at them, "You're a selfish, heartless bitch! Why don't you think of somebody other than yourself?" It wasn't their faces that wouldn't attract a man, it was *them!*'

Yet she has, she says, 'a lot of time for women. They work hard, they're terribly courageous, they're loyal, selfless. And the women who just came in to better themselves, or because they'd got a bit of money to spare, were practical about it. That was fine. But certain ones were absolutely deadly!'

The buzz-word in Barry's day was 'liposomes', which Morris Herstein had told me about. They were then being marketed with considerable hype by Dior, and were said to contain mysterious powers of skin rejuvenation and moisturizing. Their mystique has since been taken on by Lancôme, part of Owen-Jones' L'Oréal group. 'Basically,' Barry says, 'I was told that a liposome was a molecule – discovered during research in Britain for a cancer cure – that was supposed to carry other substances deep down into your skin. But then I read that Professor Kligman, who is the world's leading dermatologist, said he didn't think anything could go right through the skin, simply because the skin is made to be a natural barrier. I tried it myself, and I didn't notice any difference at all.'

As Herstein had pointed out, the claim for liposomes was that they ferried other materials – such as the all-important collagen – into areas of the skin where wrinkles were. 'So it was said to be the great breakthrough in cosmetics. If you could take this stuff into your skin you could almost have the promise of eternal youth.' As we now know, she said, that promise remains a long way from being fulfilled.

But there are many who believe that both liposomes and collagen work miracles.

Collagen, of course, can be implanted under the dermis by injection. But there seems to be no evidence that it will *permanently* replace shrinking body tissue. Dev Basra, a soft-voiced, gentle-mannered Sikh who runs a Harley Street practice as an aesthetic plastic surgeon, uses it. He injects animal protein collagen ('a solution of cowhide and pepsin') in a process he calls zyderm. Dr Basra admits that it has very little, if any, lasting effect. 'For about two months,' he explained to me, 'it stays there and adds bulk. But that's before the body naturally removes it. And, in the process of removing it, the body does lay down a certain amount of tissue.' Ultimately, as Basra candidly confirms, 'the whole lot is removed. So you come back to square one.' At which point the magical, mysterious properties offered by such products must surely be seen, at best, as an expensive disappointment.

Yet there is always one more trick up the sleeves of the skin game players. Where collagen has failed, the salon operators can tell their anxious customers that there is every chance laser-toning will succeed. Does the candid Dr Basra, who has written a book on ageing skin which carries an enthusiastic foreword by Dr Christiaan Barnard, approve the use of a 'cold' laser in such circumstances?

'No, I do not,' Basra told me. 'All it does is increase the amount of blood flowing in that area, so you get a swelling around the lymph for about fifteen days. That's how it works. But all that stuff about getting collagen laid down isn't true.' There are, however, people who will benefit, he insisted. 'Whether objectively or subjectively, we don't know, but some do seem to find an improvement from laser-toning treatment. Mind you, it's only a very small minority. And I think it's because the name "laser" spells magic for them. That is the appeal. That and the fact that the treatment is so easy. People think: there's no penetration of the skin, so let's try it. And if they're having a course of it, they probably don't notice that the effect only lasts for fifteen days. So they go away happy.'

Hearing this professional denunciation of one of the industry's most profitable 'miracles' recalled to mind the words of John Ledes in New York. 'Respectfully,' Ledes (who never wastes respect lightly) had told me, 'when it gets down to injections, for me that's not cosmetics. That's medical, and I disapprove of it. It's the anomaly of what I call the drug culture. You'll see that I write articles asking, "What do I have to do to be a drug addict?" That's my way of showing how wrong it is that these things pose as part of our industry.'

At the marketing end, however, it is extremely doubtful if women care what distinction has to be made, for legal and commercial reasons, between one product and another, one technique and another. What matters is the net effect – does the thing work?

A trained physiotherapist, Felicity Hone is in an unusual, perhaps unique, position to know this. She runs a busy London suburban beauty salon as well as lecturing in cosmetics at the London School of Fashion Design. 'If they ever find a miracle ingredient I'm sure to be one of the first to hear about it,' she told me. 'And maybe they will. But one of the most potent arguments against them doing so seems to be the impenetrability of the skin. When clients ask me, "But it doesn't go into the skin, does it?" I tell them, "No, and you should be extremely glad it doesn't!" Most of those things I certainly don't want swishing about in my body.'

It was left to Morris Herstein, the pharmaceutical scientist who had discussed liposomes with me in New York, and who sees the cosmetics industry playing an increasingly important role in our future lives, to offer positive hope of a major advance. 'Collagen,' he told me, 'is useless by itself. It does not penetrate the skin. But what I have seen is that if you use proper collagen – very pure, very expensive, what's called "native collagen" – some of the amino-acids, a small chain, do get into the skin and stimulate the collagen already in there.' As a result, he says, fresh vigour *can* be added to ageing cells by the amino-acids passing directly through the dermis. 'Yes, this has been proven. You can put a radio-labelled tracer on one of those acids in very good, high-quality collagen before you apply it. What you find is that it's the new collagen which has been produced, that is now carrying this radio-labelled marker – not the other.'

This, surely, would focus unwelcome FDA attention on the substance, discouraging those of us with lines and furrows corrugating our faces from using it? If high-grade collagen contains acid, which can penetrate our bloodstreams, then surely the classification of such an ingredient has to be 'drug'. And, as Ledes rightly points out, the industry prefers to regard all such ambiguous substances as against the rules, pending a change in the arbitrary boundary between drugs and cosmetics.

Herstein, primarily a chemist, argues against this. 'No, it depends what you want collagen to do,' he says. 'Collagen by itself does not penetrate the skin. It is only compounds of it, which cause stimulation of other actions, that can do that. And those take place *inside* the skin. You have to remember that collagen is a universal word, and there are many kinds of it. Some comes from bone, some from skin. They all do different things.'

He firmly believes that the cosmetics industry cannot remain narrowly concerned only with the skin's surface – not if a genuine antidote to the signs of ageing is to be found. 'They'll have to look outside,' he says, 'to study the level of research being done in three major groups. And one of these is the very serious work being done on anti-ageing by the major pharmaceutical marketing companies in Asia, the USA and Europe. Then there are the universities, functioning in an academic environment but heading the same way. And thirdly we've got – mainly in France – independent laboratories doing serious research into new and active ingredients.'

It is these last, the independents (of which his own company is one), that Morris Herstein sees as the fore-runners. 'Their highly scientific approach equates with the universities, but is applied on a commercial basis. I believe that a company that establishes collaboration among these three – a triangle, if you like, taking in the internal research of the commercial firms, the external research being done by the independents, and the academic contact – is the company that will have the optimum resources for this problem.'

A trumpet blast for his own company, Laboratoires Séro-biologiques?

He admits it. 'Yes, we are No. 1 in the field, a French-originated company that has been doing this for forty-three years, and we sell our products to all the leading cosmetics companies. We do very serious research for them. But again I am proposing a partnership, a collaboration, because I don't think anyone has an exclusive licence on brains. And in my opinion it is the company that forms such a partnership that will have the greatest chance of being successful. It will win the race.'

Furthermore, Morris Herstein assured me, the goal is in sight. 'It's real. It's happening from all points. You've only got to look at the progress made in the last five or six years. What will the next five years bring? I believe an even more rapid advance. But I do think that much of the research will have to be carried on in the medical field.' This, he believes, may be closely linked with the work currently going on in virology, in the search for a cancer cure and an antidote to AIDS. What Herstein and others seem to be saying is that, if we want a final answer to our ageing problems, new and ethical challenges will have to be faced. And the question, as these gather pace, will be this: how far are we prepared to accept even more 'miracles' and 'magical mysteries' in the name of beauty?

9

SELLING CELLS

The most highly controversial raw material of all rejuvenating cosmetics – injected living cells taken from an aborted human foetus – is seldom mentioned. Yet cases on record tell of pregnant women in poor countries being persuaded by professional dealers to sell the child in their womb for this trade. The aborted foetus then becomes part of a highly organized supply line. The 'living cells' are sold for a high price to cosmetics producers in Europe and the United States. Sums of money which vary according to the term of the pregnancy, but which seldom exceed £200–300, are offered to these women. They and their families are thereby freed of the burden of another mouth to feed.

Speaking on a BBC television programme last year, Dr Ian Kennedy of London University raised the possibility of a spread in this ugly trade in what is clinically called 'foetal tissue'. 'Would it be lawful,' he asked, 'for a man to give his wife, suffering from Parkinson's, a child simply in order that the foetus thus created could be aborted and used to treat her?' Dr Kennedy was echoing the shocked sentiments of many viewers when he concluded that, 'This is fundamentally unethical. I would say it is also quite intolerable that a living being should be used in this way.'

His concern is shared by many in the medical world. Human foetal tissue is reported to have been implanted in the brains of sufferers from Alzheimer's and Parkinson's diseases. The likelihood that cosmetics users may also be involved raises a far more fundamental question. How far is the ageless, beauty-seeking world prepared to push its physical frontiers in an attempt to find – should it exist – the fountain of youth?

To the world's more persistent observers it has been evident for some time that a lucrative undercover trade in human foetal tissue exists, centred in particular in Third World countries. The

French writer Dominique Lapierre graphically exposed the Calcutta problem in his recent book *City of Joy*. His description of the true case of a woman who died during an abortion for the sale of her unborn child detailed the risk to human life involved in the trade.

Lapierre's story is about a woman he calls Selima. Living in the teeming slums and already the mother of three children, when she became pregnant again Selima was haunted by the difficulty of feeding yet another child. Her husband was out of work and there was hardly enough food to keep the existing family alive. Selima was seven months pregnant when she was approached by a neighbour who, due to her large girth and comfortable lifestyle, was suspected of having an illicit source of income. The neighbour told Selima that there was no need for her to bear such a heavy burden. 'Let me offer you an interesting proposition,' the woman told her. 'Instead of having the child, we will pay you to lose it.'

At first Selima was horrified by the proposal. Then, when she thought about it, there seemed little alternative. She could have her child aborted and, instead of adding to the financial difficulties of her household, would receive in exchange 2000 rupees (£120) – a small fortune to this destitute woman.

Lapierre's researches revealed that Selima accepted the offer out of sheer necessity. She had wanted the child, but the bribe offered was irresistible. 'You needn't have any fears about yourself,' her procuress neighbour told her. 'The operation is always carried out under the very best conditions. It takes only a few minutes. You'll be away from home for three hours at most.' In fact, on the makeshift operating table of the 'clinic' to which she was taken, a massive haemorrhage ended Selima's life. Her premature child died with her, but not before its body could be refrigerated and packaged for transportation abroad.

Lapierre, who has donated half the proceeds of his book to helping Calcutta slum children, told me: 'I can vouch for the truth of the story. The details were given to me by a leading Calcutta journalist. He also supplied me with the name of the ex-pharmacist whom I name in my book. He it was who was putting up the money Selima was to get for the foetus of her unborn child.'

This journalist told me: 'The mainsprings of the industry are a network of foreign buyers.' Lapierre confirmed this. 'They scour the Third World on behalf of international laboratories and institutes doing genetic research. The majority of these buyers are Swiss or

American. They use the embryos and foetuses for scientific work, or in the manufacture of rejuvenating products and cosmetics.'

There is no doubt in my mind that the money for this illicit trade in human misery comes from the pockets of the rich and privileged people who trade with them. Some are the suppliers of expensive, reputable health farms and rejuvenation clinics in Europe and America. 'Just £120 was paid for the double murder of Selima and her unborn baby, but thousands would have been realized from the sale of the child's living cell tissue,' Lapierre told me. 'The man who ran the operation in Calcutta could ship consignments out via Moscow, on the regular Aeroflot flight, labelled as urgent medical supplies.'

Selima's fee was higher than most because her pregnancy was well advanced. There are clinics, I was told, specializing in abortions which pay as little as 200 rupees (£12) for foetuses aborted after only two months. But the market is forced to depend on criminal sources for its supplies only when they are not obtainable from a respectable hospital or clinic.

When Bobbie Long, a Canadian married to a history professor, gave birth in an Ontario hospital, she saw evidence of the 'legal' trade in 'living cells' for cosmetics use. Mrs Long told me she was surprised to see the nurse who had attended the delivery 'scoop up the placenta and put it aside, as if preserving it for future use'. When she asked why this was being done she was told, 'Oh, yes, we don't let these go to waste. There's a big trade in placentas going to the cosmetics industry.'

In some countries, the use of human placental liquid in face creams and lotions is already banned. In the United States there have been a number of actions and counter-actions about its use in cosmetics over the years. As the cosmetics giants now know to their cost, using these so-called 'living cells', such as exist in placental liquid, has created an explosive controversy.

Pundits and doctors have long contested and argued against the inclusion of human cells in cosmetics, on both ethical and scientific grounds. Nevertheless, the trade goes on. Morris Herstein, executive vice-president of Laboratoires Sérobiologiques in America, was speaking for many of his colleagues in cosmetics research when he told me, 'I don't think we should be using *any* human products in cosmetics. Not at this juncture. But, provided they are totally safe, I think it is surely acceptable to use cells from placental liquid obtained from animal sources.'

During the winter of 1985, questions had been raised in the House of Commons about the use of human foetal tissue. They were provoked by an investigative BBC television programme, *Tomorrow's World*, which had described 'revelations which suggest that the sale and use of human foetuses for cosmetic and other commercial purposes does go on here in the UK'. The programme quoted a government spokesman, junior health minister Ray Whitney, as saying that 'the government has no plans for legislation covering the trade in human foetal tissue'. It went on to detail 'unsubstantiated stories, particularly in Europe, that human foetuses from abortions are being sold'. The programme further claimed:

For example, French customs intercepted a consignment of foetuses from Eastern Europe apparently intended for a French producer of beauty products. And other reports have come in from Austria, Germany, Italy and the United States. One French cosmetics firm even went so far as to advertise the fact that they were using fresh, foetal cells. In the result of the furore that followed these allegations, it has now been made illegal in France to use such extracts in cosmetics.

In Britain, no such protection existed.

Alarmingly, there is no legislation . . . foetal material is being offered for sale. In fact we found two companies in the UK who were prepared to supply foetal tissue and organs. In reply to an enquiry, one of these said: 'Before we supply you with any of our products, we would like to know if you are a cosmetics manufacturer . . . we shall then supply you with human foetal, spleen, liver or other foetal organs.'

In Philadelphia I showed Professor Albert Kligman a transcript of the programme, and his reaction was a blend of disgust and astonishment. 'Well, of course, that's fantasy! Some of it is ridiculous. The rest is religious bias, one way or another. I mean, killing, murdering foetuses is . . . well, it's outside my game – and I'm not a religious man.'

When I told Kligman about the Calcutta case recorded by

Dominique Lapierre he was characteristically blunt. 'They're selling their foetuses for embryonic tissue?' He shook his head. 'Sick! And they're no doubt claiming that living cells, put in the skin along with prayer and God knows what, can work miracles. I've gone into some of these salons where they have chick embryos flown in from Sweden – though why they have to fly them in from Sweden is beyond me – and they don't do a darn thing. In the skin, you see, most of these things are just downright incapable of doing anything.'

But aren't the surgeons in Mexico and elsewhere, who are implanting human foetal cells into the brains of sufferers from Alzheimer's and Parkinson's diseases, claiming exciting and positive results? And doesn't that at least excuse their use, even if it seems to give encouragement to the terrible trade in Calcutta?

'No, not *human* tissue. At least that's not my understanding,' Kligman told me. 'Anyway, let's say it's animal foetal tissue, and implanted early enough to overcome incompatibility before it's rejected. There may be a logical explanation for that. If it can be verified that the disease can be reversed in these cases, then that is a fact and would have to be recognized.'

It is the distinction between the use of animal and human foetal tissue for cosmetics, as opposed to the treatment of serious diseases, that raises the thorniest ethical barricades. On ex-presidential speech-writer Pat Buchanan's *Crossfire* cable TV programme broadcast from Washington in 1987, the professor of neurology at New York University, Dr Abraham Lieberman, was asked if he could defend the use of human material in cosmetics. His reply was, 'No, I cannot.' I asked Dr Lieberman to amplify this, and he told me, 'I think it's terrible. Basically, we're using a living human being for vanity's sake.'

Lieberman is genuinely concerned that foetal tissue has to be used at all. He told me, 'I do have patients who are desperately ill with Alzheimer's – people with serious, debilitating, life-threatening illnesses, who will die if nothing is done to help them – which is one thing. But to use human tissue for people who have wrinkles – however psychologically upsetting – is monstrous! It comes down to how you feel about abortion. If you believe that the foetus is a living being, then we are using murder to help old people.'

In a related BBC television programme, *Horizon*, shown in Britain in January 1988, Dr Lieberman repeated his cautionary views. These were challenged by another American specialist, Dr Arthur Kaplan. 'The tissue is there,' Kaplan told viewers. 'It has to be disposed of. Unless one has a kind of indifference to sufferers, why not use it to help them?'

It was left to Britain's Dr Jonathan Miller to clarify the controversy. 'Moral judgements,' Miller said, 'are negotiable issues.' But not so negotiable, apparently, that consciences are untroubled by it. In some bodies of scientific opinion, I learned, the use of human cells in anti-ageing cosmetics is seen as completely unnecessary.

'There are other ways,' my self-confessed 'pseudo-scientist' informant, Morris Herstein, told me. 'In biological ageing, every cell is programmed to have so many revolutions and then it ceases to exist. So what do you do? You can either implant younger cells that have a longer lifespan, as we are doing now in certain of our products. Or there are materials – oh, yes, there *are* materials – whereby you can affect the life-cycle of that cell.'

If that is so, then why does the terrible trade in human misery go on in Calcutta?

'We have demonstrated in the laboratory,' Herstein continued, 'that we can slow down that life-cycle. We can alter it so that it does not go through so many revolutions so rapidly. And we can depress those cycles still more, which means that there will be more cycles spread over a longer period of time.'

This means, presumably, that Morris Herstein and his colleagues believe they can rejuvenate the cell structure of our ageing bodies as effectively as any implant or injection of living cells from foetuses, placentas or any other biological by-product. So where is this magic to be obtained? Why have we not heard of its anti-ageing properties on the market?

'It has not yet been put into practice on human beings,' Herstein explained. 'So far, we have only demonstrated it in the laboratory. And I am not saying it is the only way. I just want you to be aware that there are *two* avenues of approach, not just one. Either we can put younger cells into the body, or we can alter the life-cycle of existing cells. And in a perfectly safe way.'

This, as Aldous Huxley's fiction of a generation of cellular-adjusted hominids approaches realization, will be welcome news to the squeamish. What, I wondered, were the feelings of today's youth? Christopher Collins, a twenty-one-year-old trainee surveyor, had no particular feelings about the matter until I told him that human cells were being used in this way. Did he care?

'I wouldn't mind it being done to help cure disease,' he told me. 'But not just for cosmetics. That verges on the obscene!'

Yet cosmetics can cure, as post-operative surgical ward nurses know. A touch of blusher and lipstick, a hairdo and some face cream, often provide a better impetus to recovery than drugs. An argument can therefore be made for believing that the refusal of the British government to introduce legislation banning cell-tissue imports was ultimately in the public interest.

The media certainly would not have supported any such argument. On the morning of 31 October 1985, hours before the BBC showed their alarming *Tomorrow's World* programme, the London *Daily Mail* broke the story of 'A sickening trade connected with abortions'. Frank Dobson, the Labour opposition health spokesman, was predictably reported to be 'horrified'. He it was who raised the issue in the House of Commons that same afternoon. The point was that, though carefully controlled use of foetal tissue was not illegal, the report of the Peel Committee of 1972 had strongly recommended that no commercial trade or 'any monetary exchange' should be allowed to take place in its supply. Now the *Daily Mail* bluntly claimed not only that foetal tissue was being offered for sale, but so too were other cellular products – of liver, spleen and pancreas. The two British companies alleged in the story to be 'willing to enter into commercial transactions over the sale of human foetuses and foetus material' were made to sound like abattoirs.

Dobson's question forced the government to reveal that no legislation covering the trade in human foetus material had been enacted following the Peel Report, and that none was planned. But as a spokesman for one of the two firms named subsequently told Mrs Virginia Bottomley MP, there had been no mention of 'human' in what had been admitted to.

Nevertheless, in the following days a flood of questions was raised in the House. A harassed government claimed that 'inquiries have been made and no cases of foetal material used in cosmetics in the United Kingdom' brought to light. No mention was made of products and ingredients imported from abroad. The matter, therefore, did not in any way breach the British Cosmetics Products Regulations of 1984, which 'are concerned with safety in use only'.

Pressed still further, a week later the government was asked by an Ulster Unionist MP, the Rev. Martin Smyth, if an investigation into 'alleged breaches of the code of conduct on the use of foetal material' would be ordered. Also, whether it was 'still satisfied that there is no evidence available to substantiate allegations of a trade in human foetal material'. And, thirdly, what action had been taken against the two named firms said to 'supply foetal material for cosmetics'?

In reply, the Secretary of State for the Social Services, Mr Hayhoe, could only repeat that investigations into the allegations made on the BBC television programme were still going on, but that 'no other evidence' had been received relating to a trade in human foetal tissue. The code of practice, he said, was non-statutory, and the Human Tissue Act 'does not apply to the use of foetuses or foetal tissue where the foetus was delivered dead before twenty-eight weeks' gestation' – which, in the tragic case of Selima of Calcutta, had been exceeded.

In Britain, therefore, the law alone need not deter importers of human foetal tissue, or human foetuses, aborted prior to this term. Michael Trend, writing in the *Spectator* on 16 January 1988, said that 'researchers are waiting, as is everyone else, for one central decision to be made on the question of experimentation on human embryos; and it is a question that could have been settled some years ago.'

Trend agreed that

If you take Dr Jonathan Miller's view [that 'moral judgements are not absolute, they are negotiable'] then the past decade will have been a very exciting time . . . but if you prefer a rather more traditional view of the 'non-negotiable' value of human life, then the past decade would have been one of ever-increasing anxiety, most specifically on the question of whether a human embryo should be created for the purposes of scientific experimentation, or for any other purpose except that of enabling a woman to bear a child.

He concluded, 'The question is one that most people feel is entirely separate from all others and should be settled separately in law.' Until it is, both in Britain and in the United States, the possibility that human cell tissue taken from aborted and discarded human foetuses may find its way into ingredients used in cosmetics, whether or not the companies marketing them know they are there, cannot be ruled out and should not be ignored.

Marion Kelly, director-general of Britain's Cosmetics, Toiletries and Perfumery Association, takes a more encouraging view. 'Somebody once asked me if it was true that there were human embryos in Oil of Ulay. Well, frankly, at the price, it is quite evident that there are not. Nor do Oil of Ulay make any such claims. But the question has come up.'

I can confirm this. When I talked in Liverpool to Unilever's chief cosmetics research chemist, David Thom, I asked if his company – which had failed in a take-over bid for Richardson Vick, the company marketing Oil of Ulay, but had become one of the world's cosmetics giants with the purchase of Chesebrough Ponds, makers of Vaseline and Ponds Cold Cream – was using placental liquid? He assured me that 'to the best of my knowledge' neither he nor Proctor & Gamble, who now own Oil of Ulay, was doing so.

'If we're honest,' Thom told me, 'placenta extracts tend to be used, if at all, only at extremely small levels. And really only so that the companies can make a claim that their product contains material from living tissue. We're not in that game at all. I wouldn't even know where to get human placenta if I wanted it.'

As he said, 'There is no doubt that there are products – hormones and so on – which nourish the body and which are there to be used. The question is, what would they do on skins?'

So what did he think of Lapierre's tale of Selima in Calcutta, and the trade in human embryos for cosmetic and scientific research?

'Horrifying!'

Though Marion Kelly's office is in London, she is not concerned only with what goes into cosmetics in Britain. She represents her members in the Council of Europe, which recently debated the issue. 'The conclusion was, basically, that there was no question of human foetal tissue being used in the UK,' she told me. 'France was then put under the microscope, because the French do have a slightly different view from the UK. But the French minister of health made a categoric statement that they were not using it in their cosmetic products.' This statement was believed.

But Switzerland, where rumours of cellular treatments to prevent ageing abound, was more suspect, perhaps?

'Well, the Swiss have always had these clinics where they use rejuvenation techniques. Actually, somebody on a television programme recently made an assertion that human embryos were being

sold there, for use in cosmetic products. I believe it started in Italy
– somebody said they had seen a consignment of human embryos
bound for cosmetics companies. Then, in the USA somebody else
said yes, his abortion clinic supplied cosmetics houses. But when they
traced him, he told them he had only said it to make an impression
on TV. The clinic existed, but he didn't have any connection with
it. It all became very nebulous.'

Not, though, to experienced old hands like Stanley Kohlenberg
in New York. To him and his peers, the probability must always
be there. 'Oh, sure, the clinics are still doing it,' he told me. 'There
must be something to it. Also, in the same area, there's this cell
therapy. Obviously it's going to have to be controlled by the medical
profession, because we do know that people will keep on going to
these clinics, whether they are controlled or not.'

He believes this is a potential threat to the entire industry. 'The
danger is that there have been no controlled studies,' he complained.
'And the cell is a biological time-bomb. Who knows what effect it
has? Unless you can synthesize it, and break it down, you're taking
an awful chance.'

And nobody is 100 per cent clear what it is that cells, whether
from 'living tissue' or in collagen and the other 'magical mysteries',
are able to do once they penetrate the bloodstream. Marion Kelly is
an untiring champion of her British member companies, but even
she cannot be totally sure that all is and forever will be well. 'Our
statement on the use of human embryos,' she told me, 'is that our
members do not, have not, and will not use them in their products.'

But Miss Kelly also told me that before she issued that forthright denial she personally had telephoned every single one of the
managing directors and chief executives among her members. She
had requested them to 'double-check their own companies, and to
let [her] have their absolutely categoric assurances that they were
not using them in any of their products'. As she, and everyone
with a lively interest in the cosmetics industry's surprisingly little-
blemished safety record knows, there can be no such thing as too
much caution. The beauty jungle grows more impenetrable by the
day. And more deadly.

10

SAFETY MEASURES

Some years ago a British woman journalist, with tongue in cheek, wrote a gushing commendation in the London *Evening News* of one of the biggest – some say the most audaciously high-priced – characters in the business, Erno Laszlo. 'The Erno Laszlo Institute,' she exclaimed, '. . . combines mystery, exclusivity and promise with a deep-rooted knowledge of feminine psychology . . . I can think of nothing except a new love affair more guaranteed to entice, intrigue, and – well – *hook* the average woman.'

Sadly, the Laszlo hook does not always offer such tasty and enticing results as these tributes suggested. One of those who later swallowed its bait was a top New York model. In November 1987 the US Supreme Court awarded Teresa Rae Norris damages of $1.3 million against the Laszlo skin care company, of which the Institute is a part. She had endured, the evidence disclosed, a 'nightmare experience' after using one of the face creams made and sold by the company as part of its 'specialized skin-care system'.

Teresa Rae Norris, whose hitherto flawless face was well known to readers of *Vogue* and other glossy magazines, had allegedly spent the dollar equivalent of £250 on Laszlo skin cleansers and associated products. 'As I was using them,' she told the court tearfully, 'I started to break out [in spots and weals]. It got worse and worse.'

Soon it became impossible for her to work in her highly-paid profession. In deep distress, the model rushed back to the Laszlo clinic. According to reports of the trial, she was there assured that the pock-marked acne which had suddenly flawed her face was 'just a passing phase'. Yet eight months later dermatologists told the court that they were prepared to testify that the model's skin would remain 'beyond repair'. At this point her lawyers produced analysis reports which, they claimed, showed that the Laszlo creams 'contained ingredients that could be harmful'.

Despite all arguments and protestations of innocence by the company, its case was lost. The model whose face was her fortune was awarded damages based on the income she had lost by using their treatment.

It is perfectly true – and supported by a large and unarguable body of documentation on the files of all the major companies – that the amount of distress, injury and permanent suffering caused by any of the skin care or make-up products on the legitimate market of the wealthier countries of the West has always been minimal. The Teresa Rae Norris case attracted world attention partly because of the huge amount of the damages, partly due to the beautiful young girl who was its victim, and partly because such actions and settlements are extremely rare.

It is also a fact that any number of 'ingredients' in cosmetics – most especially in those at the expensive end of the market which frequently contain fragrances and natural essences – are injurious to some. Fortunately, such allergic people form only a tiny fraction of the populace (according to Marion Kelly 'no more than one in ten thousand').

But they can never be ignored by the cosmetics manufacturers. Nor can precautions (such as those being demanded by the FDA in America) fail to be rigidly enforced on all the major companies. As Teresa Rae Norris told well-wishers outside the courtroom who had come to congratulate her on winning her case, 'Yes, but I'd happily return the $1.3 million if I could have my complexion back.'

It is unlikely that anything less than long, costly and medically supervised treatment will provide her with that – if indeed it will ever be possible. Where an allergic reaction has been set up in the skin's outer layers, the epidermis and underlying tissue, the chances of returning it to normal are not very great. 'Once the cell programme has been altered, the skin will continue to malfunction – rather like a computer with a bug,' a dermatologist explained.

This proneness of the skin to reject certain ingredients is a persistent, critical problem that the cosmetics companies have to face. It has been growing markedly in recent years as the use of exotic and stringent ingredients, aimed at reducing wrinkles and lines, has been forced on them by competition.

Pharmaceutical companies have, of course, been aware of the need for safeguards for decades. They are constantly in the firing line from media snipers and over-zealous members of the public, and reaction to new drugs, to poisons and acids which can enter the bloodstream, is carefully monitored. But recently a controversial series of cortico-steroid creams and ointments for the treatment of excessively dry skin have led to complaints which touch closely on the beauty business.

In the seventies the medical correspondent of the London *Sunday Times*, Oliver Gillie, reported that 'some twenty thousand people a year in Britain' were suffering problems from the steroid drug. 'Yet only two out of the eleven firms that manufacture cortico-steroid creams and ointments issue any warning to the public about the product's possible side effects.'

Bearing in mind the toll of late twentieth-century tragedies involving other dangerous drugs, notably Thalidomide and Opren, it is not surprising that safety and security are unremittingly on the minds of the big players. These are haunting reminders of what could result if the use of questionable substances was allowed in their products. The irony is that, in the race to find the most potent cosmetics against the ravages of age, tempting incentives to take risks increasingly arise.

It is also a fact that the present public inclination to buy only 'natural' ingredients, such as those used in homeopathic and herbalist medicines, is forcing cosmetics chemists to include more and more natural and organic essences and ingredients. These both tend to deteriorate more quickly and are more likely to set up allergic reactions.

Some, if improperly used or administered, can actually be dangerous. As Carole Baldwin, a London-based PhD student pharmacist, explained, 'Too many people think that if something is herbal, it's OK. They don't realize the damage herbs can cause.'

However, properly used, derivatives from herbs and other plant materials can provide great benefit: digitalis from foxgloves, for the treatment of heart disease is just one example. The important thing to realize is that herbs and indeed all chemicals can be toxic if too much is given but are safe when used in appropriate doses or forms.

Last summer British newspaper reporter, Celia Hall, asked David Phillipson, who holds the Chair of Pharmacognosy at London University, what he thought of the herb, comfrey, which is contained in popular tablets and herbal teas. The professor plainly did not favour it at all. Hall quoted him in an article signed by her in the *Independent* on 12 July 1988 declaring, 'I would never take comfrey.'

I asked Professor Phillipson if this meant that he regarded it as dangerous. He told me, 'Yes, comfrey is potentially poisonous if swallowed or absorbed into the bloodstream through cracked or broken skin. But the herbalists won't thank you if you say so. They maintain that there is no proof of its toxic effects.' He also told me that 'comfrey has been identified by pharmacognosists (herbal chemists) as a potential cause of severe liver damage and even cancer.'

Comfrey is also an ingredient in certain herbal cosmetics used by thousands of women. Dr A. J. Jouhar, consultant pharmaceutical physician, argued that 'there is no published evidence that damage has occurred as a result of comfrey's absorption through the skin.' He pointed out that comfrey and many other herbs contain substances known as pyrrolizidine alkaloids – a fact confirmed by Mrs Warren Davies, a senior Member of the National Institute of Medical Herbalists, who told me that these alkaloids have been found in the spike of comfrey's young leaves. As Jouhar pointed out to me, any toxic effect from comfrey taken by mouth is due to these alkaloids.

Though traditionally known as 'knitbone' and used as a remedy to promote the healing of wounds, internal ulcers, bone fractures, and bronchitis, Phillipson told Hall that 'root and leaf' he regards the herb as 'potentially poisonous to the liver'. The writer listed it in her article under 'herbs which need careful handling – with possible toxic or unwanted effects.' Comfrey, as well as all other herbal medicines, is under review for efficacy and safety by the British DHSS as part of their licencing procedures.

According to Hugh Mitchell, Secretary of the British Herbal Medicine Association, 'It is true that comfrey has been on the doubtful list for some time, following published evidence in Australia that it caused liver damage in rats, to which it had been force-fed. The British Health Authorities are refusing to renew product licences for medicines containing it without justification of the toxicity in each case. So comfrey can be sold, and can be taken internally, but not in medicine.'

Dr Jouhar emphasised 'The published evidence is that, among a number of plants including some of the common vegetables, the substances which may cause these problems are pyrrolizidine alkaloids. The comfrey extract which skin-care products use contain infinitessimal quantities of such substances, hence the products themselves contain virtually none.' He also pointed out that any body exposure from use of such a skin-care product would give a safety margin some 100-fold greater than that accepted by the Health Authorities for food additives.'

The laws of countries differ, but in the United States cosmetic marketing companies are legally bound to list all ingredients in their products. Furthermore a watchdog media keeps up constant pressure on the companies in the beauty jungle to guard against production or marketing of any substance that could possibly provoke an adverse, harmful reaction.

In spite of this, over the years there have been several cases of allergic reaction and injury to skin caused by make-up and skin care products, and many of these have proved costly both to the profits and reputations of the companies concerned.

This, perhaps, is no more than a risk the big players have to take in return for the vast sums they make from their products. It is certainly the reason why so many of the larger companies in the beauty jungle invest millions in research facilities, such as Dr Brauer of Revlon's well-equipped complex of laboratories, libraries, archives and high-tech instrumentation.

'I'll stand in front of the commissioners of the FDA and defend this product,' Brauer volunteered as we watched some of his immaculately clean, white-coated lab assistants mix ingredients for the production of Revlon's famous Ultima II sun-screen and skin care cream (advertised as a help to 'prevent premature ageing'). 'I want you to know,' Brauer insisted, 'that the claims we make for this I can defend to anyone. It really works! We say it helps counteract premature wrinkling, skin discoloration, age spots and leathery texture. Well, that's exactly what it does. I say that, not just as a dermatologist – though as a dermatologist I will get up in front of my peers and they will agree with me – but also as the man who makes it! Ultima II not only works, it is one of the best products we've ever put out.'

Nevertheless, nobody knows better than Earle Brauer what risks are involved in marketing creams and potions – even those that 'work' and are believed to be 100 per cent safe to the user. The present controversy over Professor Kligman's Retin A is fuelled by dark suggestions that it causes peeling and damage to some skins.

When products are marketed in all corners of the world, under every sort of condition of temperature, pressure and hygiene, it is virtually impossible to ensure total safety.

Dr Brauer stands under the same daily threat as the people he works for. Like them he knows that danger can come from areas outside his control. Increasingly, top-selling lines put out by the major cosmetics companies are being pirated, and copies imported through illicit tax and excise-evading channels, into the United States and other countries. This fraudulent trade, labelled the 'grey area', is a constant threat and worry to all major cosmetics companies.

In the summer of 1988 John Ledes reported in *Cosmetic World* that 'grey area' invasion had spread to include the worldwide demand for Retin A, even while it was still undergoing tests by the FDA for use as a skin care product. To exploit the enormous demand for the drug – American women were bombarding their doctors for prescriptions, if only under its present licence as a cure for acne – unscrupulous foreign firms were shipping in products which, so they claimed, contained the magic ingredient, retinoic acid. Traders, located by FDA investigators, were allegedly providing doctors and cosmetics houses in the United States with products containing ingredients used in Retin A. According to the FDA commissioners, 'watered down', unauthorized versions of it were in danger of swamping the market. Too many doctors were anxious to obtain the drug in any form, so as to satisfy their clamouring patients.

Johnson & Johnson, manufacturing the genuine article at its subsidiary, Ortho Pharmaceutical corporation of Raritan, New Jersey, had come across products with such passing-off names as Retinyl A and Retinol A. These, the company said, were being prescribed and sold as if they were the real thing. 'The bogus look-alikes are out there,' Ledes warned the industry in his newsletter.

Genuine firms were thus forced into making determined, concerted efforts to have these practices outlawed. So far they have been unsuccessful, and the undercover merchants have outwitted them. Cosmetics branded with the top names in the business are increasingly entering the United States from Mexico and the Far East. Customs and other agencies are apparently unable to halt the flow. When these goods find their way into mass-market outlets such as drugstores, they can do irreparable damage to the expensively hyped images of the major companies.

Not only are these their *actual* products – they are being sold at cheaper prices. And the fact that shopgirls and typists can then buy and wear exactly the same fragrances and skin care items as the richest and smartest in the land destroys their 'exclusive' hallmark.

On the corner of Union Square in New York, a street vendor with a tray full of bottles offered to sell me three quarter-ounce 'copies' of famous fragrances. The price was $5 for the lot. One was labelled Joy – once the world's most expensive scent. Others I chose were Giorgio and Poison – both selling in top stores at over $100 an ounce. I could have had any of the most expensive brand names.

Some weeks later, in a village market in the south of France, I came across a young woman selling similar 'copies' of famous scents. When asked if they were genuine, she assured me that they were not 'copies' at all. They were, in fact, the real thing. As she explained, they could not be advertised as such, 'for obvious reasons'. The way they were obtained, she hinted, was by back-door black-marketing of the essences. This illicit trade was conducted, she said, either by employees from the factories producing them, or – which seemed more likely, in view of the wide range she was offering – by the suppliers who blended fragrances at source for the manufacturers. Once a formula is known, any quantity of the most expensive scent can be made up for only a few francs.

Thus 'knock-offs', as these copies are known, are – like the 'grey area' imports – serious threats which continuously harass the major companies and threaten their markets. 'Knock-offs' make the major manufacturers' carefully fostered reputation for safety and exclusivity harder and harder to maintain. They also imperil the industry's best defence against the popular belief that it is charging prices way over the top.

Consequently, the need for scrupulous care in maintaining safety and purity in all products has become a top priority. The risk of being faced with an action for heavy damages, of being branded as the cause of physical and mental injury, is always with the big companies. Shiseido's £50 million budget for research and development by its four hundred scientists is an illustration of the price these companies are paying to keep out of trouble. Avoidance of contamination in any of their creams and lotions is worth no less.

Robin Vincent, managing Clarins' British offshoot from his Mayfair office, is frank about this. His company has an impressive array of safeguards for their famous, if expensive, range of skin care creams and lotions. 'Firstly we make it clear that we only treat the epidermis, and nothing below that,' Vincent told me. 'Then we retain a leading dermatologist, Dr Ian White, to deal with any problems.' Besides acting as consultant for Clarins, Dr White is in charge of the contact dermatitis clinic at St Thomas's Hospital in London.

Robin Vincent is rightly proud of this. 'If any problem crops up that we can't deal with – an allergy or a reaction – we simply say, "Go and talk to Dr White." Or if we need a formulation of one of our products, all of which are listed and registered, then Ian White will give it to us. Everything we make is pure and harmless, as he knows.'

What I saw, when I was shown over Clarins' immaculate factory at Pontoise, outside Paris, confirmed it. Robin Vincent had made it clear that his chairman and founder, Jacques Courtin Clarins, was a stickler for purity, possessed of an almost neurotic determination to keep his company and its products whiter than white. Here, it was obviously so in all its gleaming, eat-off-the-floor splendour. 'I have to tell you,' Vincent had said, 'that Courtin Clarins is *manic* about quality and the consumer. Every complaint has to be minutely examined and explained. He's never afraid to tell us that it is *his* name and *his* reputation on every bottle, every jar.'

When I met this paragon in his Paris office, Courtin Clarins' precision showed in the neatness of his desk. It was not hard to believe that his prime aim is to ensure that nothing leaves his factory without his personal guarantee that it will be harmless and in perfect condition. Behind the desk were electronic screens reflecting the most recent complaints – and plaudits – from Clarins' consumers. In due course these would be sent to join many thousands of others kept on record by the chairman. Most of them, I was assured, testified to the effectiveness and purity of the Clarins range. First, though, the conscientious chairman would vet every one of them personally. 'I like to control every aspect of what happens,' Courtin Clarins told me. 'That is why we make everything we have under one roof.' As Robin Vincent had said, 'Clarins is a real "hands-on" business.' So it seemed.

I was reminded that, as Erno Laszlo has found, nothing is more important than consumer safety. When Clarins ship out their lines to the 106 countries where their products are sold, a little leaflet is included in each carton. It invites the consumer: 'Please, do tell us how you found it? And how you were treated?' That, as Vincent had proudly explained to me, was 'because most of our business is with salons and treatment centres'.

Yet in spite of this impressive show of care not all salon owners, I found, would agree that Clarins is the acme of perfection. In her beauty clinic in Bromley, Kent, Felicity Hone sells a great many skin care products, but those of Clarins are not among them. In her other role as cosmetics lecturer Hone has to know what is good not only for her customers but also, in academic terms, for her budding beautician students. So I wondered what had made her reject the Parisian creams which, according to the enthusiastic proprietor, are among the purest and finest in the world?

She told me frankly, 'First of all, Mr Courtin Clarins is always sold as the most wonderful cosmetic chemist, with a deep care for women, which I'm sure he has. But first and foremost, in fact, he's a marketing man. And a lot of his money goes into marketing, as well as into research and development.

'Obviously,' Felicity Hone told me, 'anyone can react to anything at all. But when I have to get on to a company and say "This lady has been using your product X and has developed this or that reaction", I'd expect them to take it seriously. To investigate, and do a patch test – this is where a product is applied under a protective patch and results observed over a period of time. Or, at least, to support me in doing so.'

But surely this is exactly what the Clarins company does? Jacques Courtin Clarins and his staff had assured me, vehemently, that they would rush to take care of each and every complaint or problem.

A keen businesswoman as well as an expert skin care cosmetician, Hone told me she had further reasons why she prefers not to sell Clarins products. 'They are extremely expensive. Some things will justify high cost, but Clarins' mark-up [the discount to retailers, on which her profit depends] is also poor.' In only one respect do Clarins preparations earn high regard from her. 'They are beautifully marketed,' she told me. Hone also admits that it is the low profit margin that mainly shapes her view on Clarins' product range. It is decidedly not one shared by Robin Vincent.

He proudly told me, 'In five years we have risen from among

the smallest – thirteenth out of fourteen roughly – to our present position as No. 2 in the UK. In Margaret Thatcher's words, we must be doing something right.'

Yet the risk remains. Dr Kligman in Philadelphia sees the worst results of it every day. The photographs of deformities caused by skin diseases and allergic reactions which hang on his office walls offer dramatic proof. Any temptation to overstep the safety mark could lead to similar horrors. Only when cosmetics are treated with the same amount of care that is given to them by the most responsible manufacturers will they be truly safe. Professor Kligman knows better than anyone what can result if they are not.

He is critical of what some of the companies are doing to prevent damage occurring. 'Some of these things are actually injurious,' he told me. 'In some wrinkle creams and anti-ageing preparations, we see this being done deliberately . . . My study of the materials indicates that what is really happening is that they are producing low-grade vascular damage in order to puff out the skin and remove the wrinkle. This leads to an injurious inflammation and consequent leakage of pituitary into the tissue.'

Two years ago the professor first began to doubt claims being made for wrinkle creams. 'I don't want to single out anyone – it's embarrassing,' he said. 'But when I first heard the claim being made for some of these things – that they would reduce wrinkles – I thought it probably wasn't true. Then I made a further study, and it *is* true. These things actually *will* reduce wrinkles. It's clear, by photography and image analysis, that they can do it – and Dior can certainly produce people to demonstrate that this has actually happened.

'So then you have to ask whether it's good or bad. The consumer, of course, will say it's good – fewer wrinkles. But it's really only like taking a prune and injecting water into it, inflating it. I think there's a low-grade inflammatory reaction taking place in the skin which is the explanation. Looked at that way, wouldn't you want to make sure your wife didn't use it?'

Professor Kligman's doubts about wrinkle preparations stem from the fear that many manufacturers will use these harmful methods to get quick results. 'I have complex relations with the industry,' he admitted. 'They come out every week with some new, incredible thing. Beautifully advertised, packaging superb –

103

they deserve applause for it! But we see the consequences. Women are becoming more sceptical of this bunkum, and they know that some of these things are actually injurious.'

In Europe the body governing safety in cosmetics is the Scientific Committee on Cosmetology which, as Marion Kelly of Britain's CTPA points out, 'require certain tests, or the product will not be listed and approved.' Though animal testing is not legally enforceable, in many areas it is the only safe guarantee of satisfying the Committee. And though the tests must be done in accordance with their stated requirements, animal testing is never likely to be dispensed with altogether while these regulations remain in force.

'Legally, in the UK and also in the EEC, certain ingredients are prohibited in cosmetics,' Kelly explains. 'Others are limited, by warning notices, levels, etc. But then there are three positive listings: preservatives, sun screens and colours. If you market a product containing a preservative, say, that is not on the list [i.e. tested for safety] then it is against the law.'

Most cosmetics, with the exception of largely alcohol products or those composed almost entirely of essential oils, have a preservative in them. As Kelly says, 'You could not market a cream without one. It would be unsafe, and therefore not allowed by the Committee's directive. Even if the product was sterile when it came from the factory, once somebody had put their finger in it it would be contaminated.'

Many commonly used preservatives have, as Kelly says, 'been around for so long that human use is considered to be sufficient. One can't undo the past. But I think if you did a tox[icity]-line search on any of these ingredients, you'd find that there had been animal work done on them, back in the sixties and seventies. Once they've been positively listed and approved as safe, nobody needs to do any further testing.'

This allows firms boasting 'cruelty free' products to claim 'No animal testing', when in fact they may be unaware of whether any of the 'listed safe' ingredients in their products have been originally tested on animals or not. 'Only if they have an entirely new set of ingredients, as well as a newly discovered preservative, can they be completely sure,' Kelly explains. 'And then they would have to have each one animal tested, or they simply would not get them listed. As things stand, the only way all tests can be avoided when formulating a new product is by using only those preservatives that have already been positively listed, and are therefore considered safe.'

Another difficulty for cruelty-free firms like the Body Shop, which genuinely seek to avoid using ingredients that have been tested on animals at any time in their history, is, as Kelly says, 'that they may very well be using ingredients which have come to them from abroad, and they can't really know what has gone on in the country of origin. In Austria, for instance, there is an ingredient for "pearlizing" lipstick, nail polish and face powder. As Austria is not in the Common Market, there is no way this ingredient can be controlled by us, though it is in wide use everywhere in the industry.'

These are facts the consumer must not be told. No hint of any lack of safety, or unwelcome animal-testing experience, must be allowed to filter into the alluring copy of the glossy advertisements. Certainly it cannot enter the near-holy atmosphere of the 'real estate' counters in the big stores. The cosmetics industry's reputation for safety and purity, and for having suffered as little contact with cruelty and distress as possible, is too valuable an asset to be risked by exposure.

As the manufacturers of the highest-priced cosmetics fight an insidious invasion by cheaper 'knock-offs' and the illicit practices of the 'grey area', so the safety reputation of their products becomes increasingly important. Even after a lifetime in the business, Amelia Bassin speaks for nearly every woman alive when she says, 'I still today believe that if it costs more, it's got to be better. And I *know* it's not true. But it still gives me a kick to buy that stuff!' It is pointless to argue, as research chemist David Thom did during our talk in Liverpool after his British company, Unilever, became world leader in the mass-market field with its acquisition of American Chesebrough-Ponds, that 'Whatever it costs, putting a cream that is not a drug with a big, expensive molecule ingredient on top of the skin doesn't do a thing. It's not technically possible for it to get through. Whereas our products contain small molecules, which hold water and actually do penetrate.'

When asked by salesmen of expensive ingredients – say hyaluronic acid, at £7000 a kilo – to add them to his popular brands such as Ponds creams, Thom's answer is brief and to the point: 'Go away.' But cold common sense will never quench a woman's innate desire for an occasional pot of the best-packaged, highest-priced cream for her dressing-table. No more so, as America's doyenne of cosmetics, Hazel Bishop, says, than man's belief that a more expensive motor car will bring him greater status among his peers.

One of the oldest laws of the business is that whatever a woman lavishes on skin care and make-up will be more than worth it to her if she *thinks* it is. There is always that faint murmur of hope telling her that perhaps, just perhaps, it may be as good as it looks and feels. Hope without reason, maybe, but well worth the money. After all, what is the alternative?

11

SNIP AND TUCK

There is only one way to turn the beauty clock back permanently, and it is a path that is always risky and often painful; cosmetic surgery. In New York, a young cosmetic surgeon told me with a contented smile: 'We can't make a woman of sixty-five look twenty-five, but we sure can make her *seem* forty-five.' How many of his patients, I wondered, lived to regret the reassurance of that 'seem'? This man's speciality can correct nature's worst defects with only a gentle snip or two in those superficial areas of a woman's body where half a centimetre makes all the difference. But one slip of his scalpel could turn fading beauty into lifelong beastliness.

Cosmetic – or, as some people like to call it, aesthetic – surgery is a newcomer to the beauty business, despite the fact that it has been in use in India and China for the past two thousand years. In Europe, women hesitate to think of it as more than a last resort in the struggle against ageing, but in the United States more and more people – of both sexes – are turning to it for fat reduction (mainly by suction), for reshaping breasts, for face-lifts, hair transplants, nose jobs and tummy-tucks.

Women in top executive jobs, and those who support high-profile public figures, are known to have accepted the need for surgery as fearlessly as their mothers and grandmothers faced operations for appendicitis and the trauma of unassisted childbirth. Men, too, are discreetly surrendering to its skills, though not always for appearance's sake. The cosmetic guru can restore potency, and every ageing lothario is as much afraid of failure in that department as he is of being declared redundant.

Since nearly everybody wants to be young, for whatever reason, it was no surprise to find the young Manhattan specialist pleased with life. His net salary is over a million dollars – though insurance against legal actions for disfigurement cuts into that savagely. He

107

is an essential part of today's social and economic fabric because, for the average career woman, as for her husband or lover, it is no longer a question of how they want to look.

What *has* become vital for them is not to look their age, other than in a distinguished way popularized in soap operas. The older they get, the tougher the battle becomes – as competition from rising, younger generations hits harder. There is only one sure way to trick nature out of its tell-tale ravages, and the plastic surgeons have got it sharpened and ready.

Businessmen are increasingly finding themselves in desperate need of them. Beyond a certain age (apparently getting lower all the time) they can feel nakedly vulnerable. Many are haunted by the fear of being replaced by one of the rising tide of yuppies they see climbing the ladder behind them. If unlucky enough to be bounced out of their job, there is, as they quickly discover, an urgent need to make a major readjustment to their appearance. No prospective employer will want to take on a man with sagging cheeks, thinning hair and brown age-spots on the back of his already shaking hands. Whatever it costs to get rid of some of these disqualifying factors must be well worth it. One visit to a waiting room filled with other, younger candidates for the same job will convince him of that. As a result, a vastly increased public awareness and interest in age-transforming surgery is mushrooming all over America, and making tentative inroads in Europe.

'I'd undergo it, yes,' middle-aged Berthe told me in Paris. A week before we met she had split up with a long-time living-in lover. 'But only if skin care, diet and exercise fail me.' A month later she was asking friends for the address of 'a reputable surgeon'.

You meet people like her everywhere. But not all of them will admit to it. 'You had eye surgery?' I asked Stephanie in London. She had been introduced as 'someone who has had it done – and went through a simply terrible time'.

'Yes,' she said, 'and I had a very good man, not a shark. He told me straight out: "Look, this is not a miracle, but it'll make a magical difference to you. You'll look a lot better." '

Had it made a significant difference to her?

'I had this dreadful overhang and bags. He said the operation would be "nothing" – he did say that. So I had both done.'

And did she ask how much it was going to cost?

'Oh, sure. Because I didn't have much money. He was most reassuring – made it sound so simple. Just a little local anaesthetic, he said. I'd be able to walk in and walk out in half an hour!'

Is that how it was?

'No, it certainly wasn't. The first surprise came because I had no idea what it would really be like. When he started cutting, I was in a state of shock. I told him, "Look, I'm going to faint." He'd given me no sedation. And what made it such a terrible experience was that I knew I had to keep still at all costs, because of what he was doing. Ugh! It was disgusting, awful, I hated every minute of it!'

Hadn't she expected it to be unpleasant?

'Yes, but not like that. Because, even though he'd given me a local, I was aware of everything. He was scraping underneath – here, and here. Scraping away the fat. It took forever! All I thought about was "How am I going to stay still, and put up with it?" '

How long had it taken?

'I suppose about ten minutes. Then, afterwards, I felt I couldn't walk, I was so faint. Fortunately I'd brought someone with me. They took me home.'

And then?

'The next day – don't forget, I'd had both the tops and bottoms done at the same time – my eyes were not only swollen, as I'd expected them to be, but they were completely stuck together. Nobody had told me that that would happen. Or that I would suffer such acute discomfort, with no medical supervision whatsoever. I was torn between ringing up the surgeon and asking "Is this right? Should I be having this? What's happening to me?", and waiting to see if it would clear up on its own. I decided to stick it out, but it was holy hell!'

How long for?

'It lasted about two weeks, during which I was totally unable to cope – you simply can't do anything when you're in that condition. I tried dark glasses, but they were no help. It was much, much more than I'd bargained for.'

And how much had it cost her?

'It wasn't all that expensive. Only £150. But that was six years ago. And although the surgeon had consulting rooms in London I actually had it done in Brighton, in a clinic, which was cheaper. But I also had to pay for my time in the operating theatre – about another £30.'

Not exactly a rip-off, then?

'No, not at all. But I could have done with a little more after-care. I've heard since that there are surgeons who won't let you out for days. Of course, you pay for that. It's when people like me, who haven't got the money, try to cut corners that the trouble starts.'

What sort of trouble?

'Oh . . . I've seen what can happen. A friend of mine, a woman in her fifties, had a face-lift quite recently and had the most terrible experience. She'd had no idea what it would entail. Like me, they gave her just a local anaesthetic – for a full face-lift! – and apparently she was a bleeder. She became unconscious. All she remembers is hearing the assistant say, "Oh, my God! Oh, my God!" Of course, it totally devastated her. Then, on her first day, she got up to go to the loo, fell on her face and had a heart attack – I think from the traumas.'

Did she recover?

'Yes, but she told me she felt violated, and deeply disappointed. I nursed her, and it was frightful. She kept blaming herself for even having entertained the idea of having it done.'

So why did she?

'I think it was mainly for herself. She'd kept telling people she knew, "Look at me – look at my neck! What's happening to me?" That sort of thing. I think she felt disgusted with how she looked.'

Did the face-lift improve her?

'No. It certainly wasn't worth it. It didn't make any fundamental difference to her that I could see. There's much more to one's appearance than just tight skin. You are who you are. I could see what it had done, but she was still herself. To those who knew and loved her, she was still the same person.'

Was she married?

'She was divorced a long time ago, but she didn't do it for that reason – because she was losing her man – nothing like that. She's a tremendously popular person with a wonderful personality, who has worked in the film industry and has no end of friends. No, I think she just felt fed up with the way she thought she looked.'

Wasn't it a high price to pay for vanity?

'I don't think it's vanity – not entirely. I think it's embarrassment. Having to face the world, looking as you believe you look and with your confidence destroyed. Maybe it's a stage women go through, when they are physically changing and find it very hard to accept.'

Losing their attraction?

'Well, yes. But I don't think they do it for men. I certainly didn't. My only reason for doing it was because I felt embarrassed to look at people with my eyes, knowing the bags were there.'

Would she go through it again?

She laughed. 'Absolutely not! At the time, I just didn't stop to think. Me, my sister and my sister's friend all did it together. My sister only had the bottom done and she was fine. The other girl wasn't satisfied – one eye was different from the other, and she was left with a scar. She went back and he did it again for nothing.'

Why in her opinion were more and more women having it done?

'It must be something to do with the age we're living in, I think. Television, marketing – everything today is to do with how you look, the image you create. Or the image you feel you ought to create – whether you fit in or not. I suppose it comes down to the stupidity of women, but a lot of men do it, too.'

In New York two weeks later a reassuringly professional male voice crackled out of my bedside radio. 'Why face life with unwanted lines?' it asked. 'Why live with wrinkles and bulges? Why look older than you need to look?'

I dialled the telephone number the voice gave, and the same voice greeted me with cordial and engaging frankness. 'Hi, this is Dr James Reardon speaking. . . . Yes, I am a plastic surgeon, one of three hundred certified by the American Board of Plastic Surgery . . . Yes, we are permitted to advertise. Does that seem strange to you?'

I postponed the answer until I had put a face to the voice. At 737 Park Avenue, the door of a high-rent ground-floor apartment was energetically swung open by a fresh-faced man in his forties. Dr Reardon led me into his 'office' – the professional name for his neat, well-equipped surgery and operating room complex. He settled comfortably behind his desk with the cheerful self-confidence of a salesman who has more than made his target.

'There are more than a million cosmetic surgical operations being done each year in the USA,' he said. 'Since 1979, when a bunch of Arizona attorneys fought the case all the way up to the Supreme Court and won it, we doctors and lawyers have been allowed to advertise on radio and TV here in the States, though some of the doctors who jumped on the bandwagon are still frowned on by their colleagues, and several have got into trouble.'

111

Reardon himself, he explained, had led a blameless professional life. The damaging effect of the law enabling his colleagues to use publicity had been over-rated, he believed. 'Yes, there hasn't been the tremendous onslaught of advertising that was expected. It's mostly board-certified doctors and surgeons who do it. I do it, constantly, on radio and TV.'

The refusal of Britain to follow this trend (while permitting a doctor, or group of doctors, to form a company and advertise itself and its treatments) surprises him. 'They're very slow over there. In France they're almost on a par with us here in the United States.'

Earning an estimated million dollars a year each, he and his fellow cosmetic, plastic or aesthetic surgeons neither complain nor apologize for the work they do. 'I started private practice in 1972,' Reardon told me, 'after an initial period doing reconstructive surgery on people who had had fingers mutilated in industrial accidents, and similar work. Since then I have averaged between five and seven hundred operations a year. By now I must have accumulated seventeen thousand or so friends or enemies out there – hopefully, all friends! I certainly get a lot of patients recommended to me by those I have worked on.'

Shortly before I arrived, Reardon told me, a woman patient who had had breast implants provided by him in 1981 had telephoned. 'Now she wants her eyes done. In fact there are so many areas of the human body related to cosmetic surgery that, if you do a good job on one of them, you can pretty well rely on the patient coming back for more in some other part.'

Doesn't that make the practice sound a little like the garage business?

'Not quite – no, it's not. But if you go to somebody, and you're happy with what's been done, why not go back a second time? I have had many patients on whom we've done face-lifts, who came back seven to ten years later to have it done again. Only because they liked it the first time.'

In company with the growing wave of American operators in this lucrative field – the majority of them certified by no one at all, but each likely to be earning far more than his or her (there are some, but not many, women cosmetic surgeons) congressman and senator combined – James Reardon possesses the confidence of a man proud of having given happiness to many. 'Everyone gets older,' he said happily. 'A lady just left. She hates this turkey wattle-wattle under her chin. I told her it can be tightened up in a several-hour procedure, and this gives her a certain amount of satisfaction. She's sixty-four years old and a physical fitness expert, and she needs to look good and feel good. She tells me she's looked in the mirror and seen how old she looks. Her face has gone, though her body is still in pretty good shape. She tells me, "I look like my mother! I love my mother, but I don't want to look like her now." Well, I can help her.'

In return he, like most successful US plastic surgeons, can charge fees which may seem considerably inflated for what, on his own admission, can involve less than an hour's work. How fair are the prices he and his colleagues charge? I asked. How much would the woman with the wattles have to pay him for his undoubted skills?

'It's pretty reasonably priced, I think, as far as surgery goes. A face-lift can run from three to four thousand dollars, up. Whatever the market will bear. Some people charge ten thousand for an operation, others four or five. In her case, face and neck are going to cost her about five thousand.'

Does that cover a stay in hospital – surely necessary after surgery lasting, in this case, 'several hours'?

Reardon seemed pleased by the question. 'We do *outpatient* cosmetic surgery – and that's a good selling point. The work can be done in hospital if they like, but the bulk of our patients like to go home. That way they don't have to put up with the impersonality of a hospital, plus the risk of infection.

'My private office' – he waved an arm in the direction of the small suite of rooms he had led me through – 'is maintained the way I like to live. The patients come in the morning, they have the surgery and go home later the same day, with a dressing on. If necessary, one of our nurses goes with them. Either we arrange for a relative or friend to stay with them overnight, or we provide a nurse. Then they're seen the next day, and treated as outpatients.'

Fine, but what if things don't go smoothly thereafter? What if the patient reacts as disastrously as British housewife Doreen Sweetman did after an operation just to remove wrinkles? Her case, exposed on the front page of a tabloid newspaper and on television in February 1988, seemed unbelievably shocking to those who saw the pictures of her swollen, scarred face.

Mrs Sweetman's husband told viewers that, when he saw his wife in the hospital she had been rushed into in a semi-conscious state two

113

days after the operation, 'It was like looking at her body, but with a monster's head.' She was oozing blood from her nose, ears and mouth, he said. 'A big pipe was sticking out of her neck, and she'd got white towels all over her covered in blood. It was horrendous . . . I can't put it into words. I just completely fainted.'

According to the programme:

> Some three to four thousand people, mostly women, wake up in Britain after cosmetic surgery to find that, instead of their looks being enhanced, they've been severely disfigured. Many cosmetic operations are successful, but where they go wrong the results can be humiliating, even catastrophic. Worse still, our investigations indicate that many of the failures are due to inadequate medical care, yet there is no way for the patient to know in advance who is a reputable surgeon and who isn't.

Surprisingly, other than the National Health approach through one's GP – in which case the patient is likely to be referred only if suffering from a seriously disfiguring deformity, or injury caused by an accident or illness – there is no available list of qualified specialists in Britain or the United States. Peter Davis, long-time consultant at a major London hospital and secretary of the British Association of Aesthetic Plastic Surgeons (the body representing active and past plastic surgeons operating in the National Health Service), firmly believes that there should be. Is James Reardon's optimism justified? I asked him.

Davis was emphatic. 'No, it is not,' he said. 'One of the problems in America, of course, is that it is commercially based. If they were to admit to a 10 per cent failure rate, which is normal in our experience out of every thousand face-lifts, they'd lose their practice. Take the breast prosthesis we've been inserting for years here – I'm being very honest when I tell you that it has a 70 per cent complication rate. Yet there are people in America quoting 1 per cent. *One* of us has to be telling the truth.'

One common problem with the prosthesis – which is a silicone implant deftly inserted through a small slit, sometimes made under the woman's arm and almost invisible – is that it can harden unbearably for the woman who is trying to pass it off as a natural breast. Davis explained what he does then.

'The body's natural reaction is to get rid of foreign matter. So what

114

it has done is to compress round the implant and form a membrane, like a capsule. When that gets to a certain strength it becomes tight, hard and very unnatural. There's only one thing to do.'

He flexed muscular hands. 'I just get my hands on it and nutcrack it! It makes a noise like a small balloon bursting, and they go "Aah, that's better!" And that's that. The membrane is only like a thin polythene bag, which makes it easier. But sometimes it won't crack open. Then I have to operate again.'

As a National Health consultant, Mr Davis will only see patients who have persuaded their own doctors that their condition is serious enough to be referred to him. If men seek a cure for impotence, it is more likely that they will be sent to a specialist in urology. 'But we do have ways of doing it – several, in fact. I sometimes use a long stick of silicon, which I put up the penis. It has a little, soft base which sits on the pubis and puts the man into a permanent state of erection.' He laughed. 'Difficult if you drive a bus!'

But no joke to the elderly man 'assisted' by it – or, one would think, to his lover. Davis has other, more modern techniques to use in such difficult cases. 'The new types are inflatable, and there's a small valve in the scrotum, a little reservoir somewhere up in there, and then two inflatable balloons down at the bottom of the penis. You pump up the valve in one direction and it inflates, and you pump it in another and it deflates. That costs about £1000, and the erection will stay up for as long as you want – forever if you like. The only grievance I've heard about that one has been from the wives, who say, "He won't stop using the damn thing!" No, the wife satisfaction is not very great on those.'

Giving 'satisfaction' has to be the highest aim of cosmetic surgery, since it can hardly be said either to cure or to heal. 'You can't put a new framework there,' Dr Davis agreed. 'You can only alter whatever you had to start with, and people are often disappointed by that. They say, "But Michael Jackson has been transformed!" I have to tell them that the pop singer has had three or four operations. From the look of him he's got a very distorted, over-corrected nose – dreadful, I think. He's a real example of what plastic surgery should not do.'

In Davis' opinion there are several other things plastic surgeons should never attempt to do, certainly not unless they have had long and wide-ranging experience. He would like to see the introduction of a specialists' register, listing each surgeon's qualifications, which would be available in every public library in the country. 'They say they can't permit it because it would be tantamount to advertising,' he explained. 'Actually, I believe the reason is that it might affect some people on the fringe – surgeons and doctors who could usefully advance frontiers by their wider experience and approach. I can understand why they are reticent about doing it, but it wouldn't have to be exclusive.'

It would also, in his opinion, save people from falling for the beguiling cosmetic surgery advertisements of British 'companies', formed by financially interested businessmen and in some cases employing dubiously qualified surgeons to operate in their clinics. 'There are only about 127 mainstream practising plastic surgeons in this country,' he told me. 'Of these, the people doing regular plastic surgery and organizing themselves into groups would not, I should say, amount to more than twenty. Whereas in California alone there are about five hundred board-accredited plastic surgeons and about five thousand non board-accredited.'

Such a figure might suggest that British, and perhaps European, women and men – according to Dr Davis, in the UK only one-twentieth the number of men as women seek such help – are lagging behind Americans in using this radical, often effective, means of coping with physical shortcomings and the ravages of age. At present this may indeed be so. But, statistically, the number of operations being carried out on women in Europe is rising at the same rate as in the States.

It is only European men who are holding back. 'I'd expect one out of every five of my patients to be male in the States, from what I've heard,' Davis said. 'But then, I don't think I could practise my job over there with my eye-bags. Nobody would come near me! I'd have to have them done.'

He doubts, too, that Britain will ever accept the same standards as those which apply in America. 'I'm told that people there can go to a plastic surgeon and say, "I'm up for a job, and I'll never get it with these ears," or whatever. And the surgeon has to do it. I just can't see that happening here. Not in my generation.' He doesn't deny, though, that things are changing all over the world. 'In America, of course, there are considerable pressures on men to have things done, both in a business and a social sense, and it isn't like that here yet. But having said that, I do get young men coming in with big noses who are just devastated with their appearance.'

116

One young man, brought to Davis by his mother, had been living almost as a prisoner in his room for the previous two years, refusing to leave the house except for essential purposes. Mr Davis told me, 'He was a big, powerful chap who'd had his nose altered, and he simply couldn't stand the result. It was true it hadn't been done very well, but it wasn't all that bad. It certainly wasn't something to get desperate about. But he felt he just couldn't be seen in public.'

He and his colleagues see quite a few men who feel morally outraged by some feature of their appearance. 'Yet there are plenty of Cyranos walking about who are perfectly happy with their noses. The sort of men we see most on the Health Service have usually broken their noses four or five times playing sport, or fighting, and some of them are proud of how they look. It depends what they've done, but we can usually make something of those.'

He deplores the 'counsellors' who represent a number of high-pressure companies offering cosmetic surgery through advertisements in magazines and newspapers. 'They tell everyone it's going to be no problem at all, but they have no idea how difficult some of the work is. A first-time nose is a very difficult operation to do. If it has to be done again, it's harder still. And the third and fourth time you can get into real trouble. All the time you're sliding down the slope a bit more. The people who work as counsellors don't know about that – all they're interested in is selling the service.'

When an applicant who has read an advertisement for the company telephones or writes, one of these counsellors will discuss their needs with them. Some, I learned, are qualified cosmeticians and beauty specialists running or working in clinics. But others are simply employed for their ability to persuade callers to sign up for treatment, and are paid commission on the business they bring in.

In Dr Davis' view these lay counsellors are quite unqualified to offer advice, and certainly should not be persuading people to commit themselves to operations which may prove difficult and dangerous. As he says, 'We don't mind cutting people about, and we all want to earn enough to send our children to school. But if you are only doing it for gain, and taking more and more chances, it is easy to start getting into catastrophes.'

The fees he charges his National Health patients are vastly less than James Reardon's 'reasonable' fees in New York, but that is only to be expected. For £3000 (approximately $5000) Dr Davis will carry out a four-and-a-half-hour operation on both top and bottom of a patient's eyelids, and do a face-lift at the same time. 'I keep them in hospital three nights for that, whereas a private room outside would cost, say, £300 a night. And our anaesthetic fee is only £150.'

At a tenth of the cost of a private anaesthetist, this is a bargain – provided you can get your GP to recommend you.

But what does the cost matter, if it is going to make an unbearable life worth living? To those who can afford it, maybe very little. So Dr James Reardon has every right to look pleased with life. After all, he believes he is selling happiness. 'The people who come in for surgery in their late seventies and eighties don't necessarily think life's all over for them,' he explains. 'They say, "Well, doctor, I've got a few more years and I want to enjoy them." I have to realize that, to them, those few years are a long way off, in the distant future. Sometimes it amazes me, but I know how they feel.'

But not everyone with experience of what prompts some people to risk more than they should, and of the little-qualified practitioners who enrich themselves at their expense, see it that way. Dr Leslie Gardner, reinstated after being struck off Britain's medical register for publishing a book on his pioneering cosmetic surgical work which was construed as advertising, told me, 'The whole of cosmetic surgery is full of gimmicks. In my opinion the only thing that really matters, and is professionally correct, is the nose. An ugly nose can be a great disadvantage. After that, the eyes, the breasts and the face-lift to remove nasty lines can be good operations. And everything depends on the surgeon.'

Everything, that is, within his power. But accidents happen. Taunted by schoolfellows for his 'sticking out ears', in August 1988 a Yorkshire schoolboy was given a cosmetic operation in a London hospital to make his life more bearable. Simon Boot died under the anaesthetic. Nothing so fine as beauty had been his quest, but the price he paid was a risk run by everyone who seeks surgery as a cure for his or her problems.

If there is a moral in Simon's tragic fate, it is surely that cosmetic surgery is no different from any other surgery in that both can be fatal.

12

SLURP AND SLICE

The expensively produced full-colour brochure for the National Hospital of Aesthetic Plastic Surgery, discreetly hidden amid the green fields and twisting lanes of the rural Midlands, radiates the comfort, ease and health of a first-class country hotel. It looks enviably calm and attractive on the cover – cows graze in the meadow beyond the swimming pool – and utterly at one with the reassurance of the words printed across the opening page: 'All you need to do is relax . . . we'll take *great* care of you'. It was disturbing, therefore, to know that this was not a holiday spa, but a booming beauty clinic, and that such things as suction pumps were at work inside the white walls, slurping fat out of people's thighs and bellies.

As its businessman proprietor John Terry assured me, the clinic had grown in the mere eighteen months since its opening in autumn 1986 to become one of Britain's leading private centres for many of the more advanced ways of staying young, including such aesthetic bodily improvements and refinements as 'liposuction'. Having seen this done elsewhere, I would describe it as being about as relaxing and reassuring as crossing the English Channel in a gale. From the moment the surgeon stuck a syringe full of local anaesthetic into the flesh of the patient, the whole operation that I was allowed to witness took on the aspect of a horror film.

Using a scalpel, he cut a small slit over a bag of lumpy fat. That was the end of the surgery. Next, a pipe, known as a cannula (named after, and as far as I know identical to, the instrument used in French abortions) was inserted into the slit. Then the machine – like a powerful vacuum cleaner – was switched on. As it sucked out what I was told was largely 'subcutaneous matter' (fat), a tube at the far end conveyed this greasy substance into a bucket on the floor beneath the patient. The sound of this product of self-indulgence over willpower slurping and gurgling into the enamel receptacle was nauseating.

Peter Davis at St Thomas's Hospital had previously warned me that the operation was not one that he, or his fellow surgeons, enjoy performing. My discomfort, apparently, was nothing to that which, according to the doctor, would almost certainly face the patient in the days and weeks that were to follow. 'Don't let anyone tell you that there is no pain,' Davis had advised. 'Liposuction is surprisingly effective, and on the whole people are very pleased with the result – after all, for a woman who's never been able to wear jeans due to bulgy thighs, it is a marvellous thing. She'll most probably be thrilled. But patients feel as if they've been kicked by a horse after it, and the bruising can be dreadful, to a really frightening degree. It sometimes even upsets the surgeon!'

Complications were also remotely possible, Davis explained. 'Mortality, I believe, is reported to be up by 10 per cent in America. We've had one or two cases of thrombosis in the veins, and I know of one case of infection. But irregular contour and flaps of loose skin are the most common complications. If it's not evenly done, liposuction can produce a very lumpy result.'

Fat reduction by suction is nevertheless probably the most popular cosmetic operation in America at the moment. According to Mr Davis, it 'leads to a lot of abuse, because it doesn't require much skill. You can put someone to sleep, charge an awful lot of money for it, and do what appears to be a clever thing in reducing a bulge. It's really a bit of a brutish procedure compared to, say, a face-lift, which will take three and a half to four hours and calls for a tremendous amount of experience. Liposuction is donkey work. You end up sweating a lot, trembling with fatigue and a bit disgusted.'

But John Terry is resolutely proud of his hospital's expert use of the technique. He boasted to me of having been responsible for putting right many other surgeons' mistakes – apparently he was unbothered that this cast a poor light over aesthetic cosmetic surgery as a whole. The sad fact is that a large number of mis-shapen catastrophes have indeed occurred, though none at this hospital. Terry explained to me that his surgeons dealt with the victims 'at far less cost than the fees charged by the fashionable operators who botched them'. The suggestion that a patient may benefit more from paying more – to obtain greater experience and skill – was not an argument he was prepared to accept.

'We've just sent a woman back to the isle of Jersey,' he informed me. 'She'd been charged £4000 for liposuction by a London clinic.

120

The man who had done it was an ordinary doctor in general practice, not a surgeon as she believed. Her legs were a mass of dents, bumps and lumps. They'd taken fat out of her all over the place, but not at all evenly. It was so bad that she'd gone back to them and they'd tried to do it again. It was still terrible.' Terry's surgeon, a consultant at a Birmingham hospital, had been able to smooth these out, he said, 'but only after a long and arduous procedure. The whole area where she'd been worked on had been damaged with the cannula, and it was a struggle to make the skin stick back in smooth clumps. Anyway, we did it. And I think we only charged her about £2000 for the whole job.'

The operation, he explained, is not simply to remove fat. 'People talk a lot of rubbish about it. Bullshit! I'll tell you what it does. The edge of the cannula tears up the skin, causing all these lesions. When we stick it back down it is a lot firmer. I'm not saying it doesn't remove a lot of fat as well, but a litre of fat doesn't make so much difference, to be quite honest. The real secret is the tightening up of the skin.'

Until less than ten years ago, liposuction was almost unheard of. James Reardon in New York told me he had been reluctant to use it at first. 'I didn't think it would really work. But then a senior associate of mine persuaded me to take the course with him, and now I do two to three cases a week.' Since then, he said, the sound of fat slurping into enamel buckets has been on the increase all over the United States. 'Yes, it's a growing procedure,' Reardon explained. 'They usually come in worried about their thighs, buttocks or knees. I've had many women – including two tennis players – with very heavy pads of fat on their knees. I removed the fat, and for once in their life they could knock their knees together and really hear them!'

He regards the actual operation as simple: 'All you do is just go in with a little suction catheter and break up the fat.' But he accepts that it can lead to problems. 'There can be relatively minor complications. The trouble is that, at the beginning, there were cases of unlicensed people doing it and pulling out tremendous masses of fat. Then the body fluids poured into the area and the patients went into shock. There were a couple of cases of infection and death in those early days. But today, in the hands of a competent surgeon, the risks are fairly low.'

Only fairly?

Reardon went on to stress further possibilities which not everyone would enjoy hearing before submitting to liposuction. 'It *is* an operation. You're sticking a tube in the body, removing fat. There has to be a potential for infection, blood clots, breakdown of the skin and haematomas – everything is there.'

Nevertheless, he and an impressive list of his colleagues in the field now regard the technique as a useful procedure. He emphasized that liposuction has come a long way since the early days. 'Nowadays it is only considered dangerous to remove more than a limited amount at any one time.'

In Britain, John Terry confirmed this. He assured me that, in vacuuming out fat, the risk of causing bleeding, scarring and infection is no higher than in most cosmetic operations. But that is only so if the work is done by a skilled and experienced surgeon. More serious complications, such as pulmonary embolisms (obstruction of blood vessels in the lung), subcutaneous fluid collection and even death were recorded in the past when little was known about the amount of fat that could be safely removed at one time.

How much was too much? I asked James Reardon.

'About a thousand to two thousand cc is the maximum,' Reardon advised. 'It might be nice to get it all out sometimes, but Steady Eddy wins the race. The shock to the system does lead to trauma, however well it works. And there has to be a limit to how much fat you take out if only on account of the need to contract the skin successfully afterwards. We used to cut away all that excess skin. But that left big, wide, ugly scars. Now we only make a tiny slit and pull the stuff out. But there are still problems of appearance, and unfortunately you can't make everyone's body beautiful at one go, just like that. There has to be a limit.'

In London, not every surgeon will perform liposuction. Out of consideration for his patients, Dev Basra told me he has given up the process altogether. 'I used to do it,' he said. 'But it is pretty revolting, especially with a really obese patient. It's so very hard to meet their demands, you see. You can only take out a bulge, not the whole lot. And then, if it doesn't seem to have made enough difference you're left with an unhappy patient.'

That is something which he, and others operating in this lucrative field where a happy patient may encourage others to come in for treatment, understandably dread. Basra's decision to exclude the technique from his repertoire (there is no mention of it in his

informative book, *The Ageing Skin*), was made as part of a larger
policy change in which he has moved completely away from body
surgery. As he explained, 'I think body surgery has a lot of sexual
connotations, because it isn't as straightforward as facial surgery.
It is very hard to meet a woman's demands if she thinks she knows
what would make her body more attractive, whereas with the face
you can draw a line and stick to it.'

For removing what is called cellulite – lumpy collections of fatty
tissue under the surface of a woman's skin – liposuction can nevertheless be useful. Basra explained that cellulite is 'fat under tension'.
With liposuction, he says, it is possible to remove it completely.
'Because it is only like an overstuffed pocket, impeding the lymphatic
flow. Once you've taken away the excessive fat, you've cured the
cellulite.'

For how long?

Peter Davis had expressed heartening views when we spoke on
the technique's lasting benefits, once the patient has recovered from
the traumas and bruising. 'It's the question of the suitcase and its
contents. If you tip the suitcase out, it won't fill itself again. No, I'd
say that the effects can be lasting, but of course the operation doesn't
take away the reason why the fat was there in the first place.'

From the doctor who had declared publicly that 'three to four
hundred cosmetic operations go wrong every year', this sounded
like a solid commendation for the treatment. But Davis has no
more regard for liposuction than for anything else in the cosmetic
surgical lexicon. In the British television broadcast which exposed
Doreen Sweetman's tragedy he startled viewers by complaining, 'I
have seen a young man with his eyelids pulled down from his eyes
so that there was no contact with the lower lid at all on both sides. It
needed a skin grafting operation.' And Davis told me, 'I've seen scars
on breasts which have reached almost to the armpits. Normally, in a
breast-reducing operation, they should all be around the nipple or
below it. They should *never* be above it. And I've also seen people
who've had tummy-tucks, as you call them, with a criss-cross of
scars on their abdomen as if somebody really didn't know what
they were doing.'

His argument – one that every candidate for any sort of cosmetic
surgery, including liposuction, would do well to pay heed to – is that
there is nothing wrong with the science behind liposuction, but there
is an ugly question mark over some of the unqualified people who

practise it. Desperately unhappy fatties, Davis told me, are prone to rush into operations which promise 'seeming miracles'. They, he said, should be warned that what has been called 'the kiss of the cannula' can, when wrongly or inexpertly used, blight their lives far more than the predicament by which they currently feel afflicted.

In the early eighties British journalist Peter Brock underlined this caveat with startling clarity. 'The procedure is said to pull away the fat cells without doing much damage to surrounding blood vessels and nervous tissue,' he wrote, 'but above the surface there can be a rippling effect – a sort of subsidence.' Of a particular case, reported by the American Society of Plastic and Reconstructive Surgery, Brock commented, 'The before and after pictures are gruesome . . . suction lipectomy [the name then given to the operation] is not a cure for obesity and should be used only to remove localized fat deposits resistant to diet and exercise.'

Furthermore, he declared, the American Society did not accept that deposits of cellulite would succumb to the suction treatment in the same way as ordinary fat. 'Used against the surface dimpling in women known as cellulite, it does *not* work,' the journalist reported. He went on to question any optimism about the lasting 'suitcase' effect of the treatment. 'The long-term effects have yet to be assessed. The procedure removes fat but does not inject the will to control eating.'

At the same time, Brock plainly shared the specialist's concern over the danger of the technique being used by inexperienced hands, in what was already then becoming a boom item in beauty salons and cosmetic surgery clinics. 'The slurp technique offers considerable scope for abuse,' he cautioned, 'and there are already reports of at least fifty surgeons, who have not undergone the special training required, asking where they can buy the suction equipment.' This, he concluded, 'serves as its own warning'. It still stands today, perhaps even more urgently as the 'slurp and slice' treatment becomes universally accepted.

There are, of course, conscientious beauty salon owners who would hesitate to recommend anything as extreme until every other form of fat-reducing treatment, including diet and exercise, had been rigorously tried. A leading London salon owner told me she neither uses liposuction, nor does she advise her clients to undergo it. 'I don't know anything about it really,' she told me, 'but I do have a client who comes to me at the moment who has had it done. When she described it to me, it sounded horrific. The pain she suffered afterwards was awful. It certainly isn't something I would want to have done to me.'

But another beautician running a busy West End clinic, Sally Wilson, described the treatment gratefully to me as 'God's gift to women'. Wilson does no lipo-surgery herself, but she will recommend to her clients a practitioner she respects if they seriously want it, and if they are prepared to go through their own doctor first. 'In Britain,' she complained, 'if a woman goes to her GP with a double chin he pats her on the behind and tells her to live with it. In France, it's quite different. There, the women insist on getting the treatment they want.'

To John Terry, the problem women face – whether or not they can convince orthodox medical channels of their needs – is that so many sharks lie in wait for them. In his view, liposuction may be 'God's gift to women who gain satisfaction from it, but for those who are led into dangerous operations by largely unqualified practitioners it can be and often is a disaster'.

He told me, 'I'd say that an honest cosmetic surgeon – one who'll say "No, you can't be helped" – may be quite hard to find. The reputation we have built here over the years is due to only one thing – we don't take on "aggro" [aggravation]. If the problem is beyond us, we say so. We never undertake what we cannot do satisfactorily.'

Just as it is 'the patient's right to come to this hospital and spend money', Terry declares, so it is *his* right to refuse to take on what he cannot do. 'There are hospitals operating on women who don't need it – persuading them to undertake the risks, the injuries, the tragedies for no good reason except profit. Until these are controlled – which they seem unlikely to be, because there are too many fingers in the pie – it won't be stopped.' He is confident that the resources offered at his own National Hospital avoid these pitfalls. 'Here, the first person who'll tell you what's wrong, and what can be done to you, is the surgeon. Nobody else. Not somebody with a lot of meaningless letters after his name and no real qualifications.'

His partner, Mel Green, was even more specific in warning against 'cowboy surgeons' who offer to reduce any amount of fat in one go. 'Cosmetic surgery in this country is a market based on greed,' he told me. 'Our frustration is that we have to be lumped with all the unqualified people who are allowed to practise it, and who give plastic surgery a bad name.' Their hospital, Terry explained, 'has never been sued, and we carry malpractice insurance purely as a precaution'. His estimate of the cost of similar insurance in the United States, due to the colossal awards which have been made there against some surgeons, is in the region of half to three-quarters of a million dollars a year. 'So quite a few carry no insurance at all,' he said. 'They put the business in the wife's name so that, if damages are claimed against them, they can announce: "I have nothing, and if you want to sue you'll get nothing." '

As an even stronger disincentive to claiming against them for bad work, American surgeons are now threatening to counter-sue. Lawyers who offer to represent dissatisfied and damaged patients on a 'no fee unless successful' basis can find themselves facing a suit from the surgeon for 'vexatious litigation'. As always in those areas in the States where a lot of money is involved, the plastic surgery marketplace has become a legal battleground. 'And unfortunately we're heading the same way,' John Terry complained.

Even a hospital as well run as his claims to be is vulnerable, according to him. 'This is a minefield. It needs a lot of pruning. We know that about one in thirty-five noses will have to be done again, and about one in twenty eyes. We've had patients on the table three times. What can you do? We've got a very competent man doing the job, but if the symmetry – which is the enemy of plastic surgery – has gone, there are bound to be problems.'

According to Mary Stein, writing in *McCalls* magazine in June 1987, one San Francisco plastic surgeon, Samuel J. Stegman (who was also president of the American Society of Dermatological Surgery at the time), cautioned that liposuction, when used to remove eye-bags, had been known to cause blindness. On record in Britain is the case of a young woman who was unable to close her eyes in sleep after a cosmetic operation.

Stegman told Stein that inner thighs, breasts, mid and upper abdomen and the centre of the face are high-risk areas for liposuction treatment. Its most effective use was in reducing pouches of unwanted fat – 'saddlebags' – from outer thighs, the underside of the chin, the inner side of the knees, the abdomen below the navel, the buttocks and the ankles. Yet what *People* magazine has called 'the mirror's daily disappointment' is leading to more and more people, and not only in the United States, trying it.

American men and women lead the field. In 1986 liposuction operations there had increased by an astonishing 78 per cent during the previous twelve months. In the same year overweight Americans were reported to have spent more than half a billion dollars on cosmetic surgery. Remoulding the body had come out of the closet and become highly fashionable. Celebrities openly paraded their improved shapes and appearances.

The need to retain the contours of youth, to be as beautiful and lissom as in adolescence, was pouring gold into the coffers of the industry. In the words of Michael Elam, the man described in *People* magazine as 'Phyllis Diller's faceman' and the surgeon responsible for the American star's unique ability to conquer the ravages of age: 'You can be as healthy as a horse. But if you look like one, that's another story.'

13

LIVING DREAMS

At the time when the magic of Rubinstein's paints, Arden's creams and Revlon's lipsticks had begun to fade with advancing years, something even more compelling came to take their place. A middle-aged Swiss doctor heard the universal cry of the rich and famous – to free them from wrinkles, banish the terrors of approaching senility and death and help them to look, and feel, years younger. His name was Paul Niehans, and he set up a clinic to do just that.

Niehans understood that ageing was an irrevocable cellular process. He knew that every cell in the human body was programmed to replicate no more than fifty or so times before reaching its death. If he was to tap the waters of the fountain of youth, it could only be by restoring vitality to the human body itself. How better than by replacing worn-out and dying cells with new, living, vibrantly active cells?

By injecting fresh animal foetal cells into the buttocks of his patients, could he not restore and reactivate the whole process? Science, perhaps, offered no conclusive evidence that this would effectively lengthen their lifespan, or that the cells already there would accept the invaders. Science, indeed, took rather the opposite view, clinging to the conviction that the protective immune system of the human being rejected all invasions by 'foreign bodies'.

But Niehans reasoned that, if he could prove science wrong, a goldmine would lie within his grasp. It was all a question of which cells were to be used, from which animal they were to be taken, and, above all, how fresh they would be when injected. He began by studying the effect of cells taken from a number of different species – even, according to reports and rumours current at the time, experimenting with the emulsified spinal cords of squirrels. Finally, he settled on the cells of a breed of specially reared black sheep.

128

The results surprised him. He set about treating patients with his discovery, and within a few years had established himself universally as a protector of the old against their most feared enemy – approaching impotence and death. World-renowned figures followed discreet inquiries with carefully concealed visits to Niehans' Swiss clinic. Among them were such luminaries as Somerset Maugham, Noël Coward and Gloria Swanson. Many others, too shy to reveal their famous names, submitted to the course of injections. It was even rumoured that among the distinguished visitors were Winston Churchill and the Duke and Duchess of Windsor. When a newspaper printed a story that Charles Chaplin had undergone the Niehans 'cellular therapy' it so angered him that he sued. The suggestion that this prolific family man was lacking the full potency of youth was apparently unbearable to him. Others, with less reason to hide their craving for more years to live, and added potency while living them, came to Niehans with open minds and ready cheque-books.

The doctor was always obligingly ready to greet them, and his magical elixir was available to anyone who could pay for it. Niehans knew how desperately many of his patients had tried, and failed, to keep young by more orthodox means – by exercise, diet, cosmetics and surgery. His course of injections required little from them other than the time he insisted that they stay with him at their expense while the newly implanted cells did their work.

His answer to the body of orthodox science which refused to accept his claim that the cells were doing all that he claimed for them was: 'Prove it otherwise.' In this, he never varied. In 1953 he was magnificently, if unscientifically, rewarded by a call to the sickbed of the ailing Pope Pius XII. Arriving in Rome with a pair of pregnant ewes, Niehans was given facilities in the Vatican to remove the foetuses a few days before birth, prepare a serum of tissue from them and inject it into His Holiness's infallible posterior. Fortunately, the Pope recovered. Niehans was given the chair of medicine in the Pontifical College which had once been occupied by the British discoverer of penicillin, Sir Alexander Fleming.

It was no surprise, therefore, that, although Niehans died in 1971, his famous treatment centre, the Clinique La Prairie, has survived him. It stands on the grassy banks of Lake Geneva just outside Montreux, and is still doing capacity business among the rich and famous. Some of these were leaving as I arrived there one morning in the spring of 1988. Frail, elderly men and women, warmly wrapped up against the mild lakeside breeze, were being helped into chauffeur-driven limousines. One had to assume, as they did, that the cells freshly implanted in their bodies were already doing the work of rejuvenation.

The essence, after all, of Niehans' dream is faith in an impracticable illusion. In the opinion of many to whom I talked in the scientific world, it has no basis in fact. Could an injection of fresh cells, taken from the still-living foetus of an unborn lamb, restore the inevitable chemistry of deterioration in our ageing bodies? I asked.

It was about as likely to do so, I was told, as it was for a complete cancer cure to be found before the end of this century. Nevertheless, the Clinique La Prairie continues to fill its twenty-eight beds. The discreet staff are seldom bothered by vacancies. And the list of those waiting to occupy its comfortable rooms, with views of lake or mountains, continues to read like a society gossip column.

Since Paul Niehans himself did not manage to live forever (the founder succumbed, according to those who follow in his footsteps, at the age of 'about ninety', but more accurately eighty-eight – and not until he had injected his patients over half a million times), it falls to his disciples to perpetuate the dream. They are professionally guided by one of the most loyal and devoted of the acolytes, Dr Ellie Eddé.

Dr Eddé, now senior doctor in charge of the clinic, told me how well Niehans' dream has survived as a profitable reality in his care. 'We are the only clinic in Switzerland giving the patients fresh and live cells,' he said. 'We inject the same day as they are taken from the lamb embryo.' Sitting behind a large desk, he was impressively sure of the value of his unique treatment. 'Where all other injected substances, such as collagen, can be rejected by the human body,' he assured me, 'we have none of these problems with ours.'

La Prairie's brochure promises that the fresh cellular therapy, 're-stores energy . . . reduces menopause troubles and works favourably on sexual problems'. A herd of six hundred specially selected black sheep, their resistance to cancer assured, are reared under conditions as sterile as possible and impregnated to supply the foetuses from which the cells are taken. They are, I was told, chosen with great care for this honour, and tended daily under the strict and expert control of veterinary experts.

According to Dr Eddé, many of the patients who have received their cells feel fully rejuvenated. Only one whom I encountered was less discreet, and less well pleased. A South African restaurateur who had had the full treatment told me that he has since felt no beneficial effect whatever that he could attribute to it. 'Nothing that I can honestly say is due to anything going on in the cells of my body,' he told me. 'I went to the Clinic with an old friend, who wanted company. As far as he was concerned it can't have done too much good, because he died soon afterwards – and he was almost ga-ga for what remained of his life.'

With the memory of Lapierre's chilling story in mind – the Calcutta slum mother who sold the unborn child in her womb for foetal tissue – I asked Eddé whether he or Niehans had ever used human cells.

'Never,' the doctor assured me.

Was their objection mainly ethical?

'There are many reasons. Number one, because it is not convenient to take them from the human embryo. And also, yes, from the ethical point of view that material is very hard to obtain.' Dr Eddé did, however, admit that he had heard reports of human foetuses being imported into Switzerland.

Were they being used for experimental work in laboratories such as his?

He had no idea.

Would he have any objection if they were?

'I don't like it,' he told me. 'Maybe in Calcutta they need the money. . . .'

In La Prairie, clearly they do not. Since 1980, when he joined the clinic as medical officer in charge, responsible to the owner – who, he told me, is a Zurich banker, Ermin Mattli – Dr Eddé has been largely responsible for setting the scale of fees for the treatments. 'We charge around 9000 Swiss francs, or some $5000, but that is for everything including the patient's stay here for three days after the injection, which is the time it takes to allow the body to accept the new cells.'

The fee, he says, is justified by the costs. 'What is expensive is the material, taking the cells only from lambs which have been found, after extensive tests, to be free of any problems. We take the foetus two or three weeks before it is to be delivered, while it is still dormant in water. We cannot wait until it is born because then it would be alive and the cells would be animated. There is a big difference.'

131

It is one that may have surprised Dr Christiaan Barnard, who was appointed an honorary consultant of the Niehans clinic. Barnard took the La Prairie treatment twice from Dr Eddé, in 1981 and 1982, in the hope of curing his arthritic hands. 'He told me he could not understand why the cells were not rejected,' Dr Eddé remembered. 'He said that whenever he transplanted a heart there was always the problem of rejection. I explained that the cells we use have not yet been brought into use. They are living, but unborn.'

In Dr Eddé's view, Dr Barnard's treatment was completely successful. 'Now, he doesn't have any pain in his hands. I am told that it is only because he has no time that he no longer performs his operations. I gave him the shots myself, and as far as I know he certainly has no complaints about the treatment he had here.'

Barnard himself has never denied that the injected sheep cells may have increased the life of his own ageing cells.

At La Prairie five assistant doctors, beside specialists and nursing staff, tend the often delicate and sometimes extremely old patients. Those whom I saw leaving were settling their bills at a reception desk resembling that of a luxury hotel. On either side of a brightly lit corridor leading from the reception area were laboratories and offices with white-coated men and women preparing for another of the clinic's injection days.

'We only inject on Thursdays,' Dr Eddé explained. 'Then they leave here on the Tuesday, having spent five days here in all. Niehans used to make his patients rest for three months, but I have taken tests on patients and found that after two weeks they can comfortably return to normal life. Except that they must keep out of the sun.'

In the nine years he has headed the clinic's medical team, Dr Eddé insisted that he has had no problems or lawsuits. He is now hoping to receive official scientific recognition of the clinic's claims. 'At present, we have no proof that the treatment works. But we have a team of six specialists operating in Europe and America who are monitoring and studying its results. For the past six or seven years they have been reporting to us, and we will soon be in the position to publish their findings. The difficulty is that in Switzerland there are no medical reviews, so it will have to be done abroad.'

And Dr Eddé is confident that the reviews will justify much of his work and establish the Niehans dream in the realm of scientific reality. At a time when a controversial battle is being waged in the United Kingdom over the use of animal organs in human transplants, and when American neuro-surgeons are excited by the curative possibilities of foetal cells implanted into the human brain, this could ensure another form of immortality for La Prairie's lucrative popularity. Even today, the Niehans dream world that Mr Mattli of Zurich ('too busy to take the treatment himself, but hoping to do so') has inherited, can hardly be less than highly profitable.

'The benefits of the treatment last from two to five years,' Dr Eddé told me. 'And, of course, it can be redone as often as necessary – one man, an American who began with Niehans in 1950, is about to have his thirteenth go! I had the shots myself five years ago – the usual four to six injections on each side. How old do you think I am?'

I studied the grey-haired man in front of me. 'About sixty-five?' His face fell.

'Not yet sixty,' Dr Eddé said stiffly.

There was an awkward pause. 'Well, thank you for being so frank,' I said.

He smiled. 'I have nothing to hide!'

Could the same be said for the makers of La Prairie Premiere Collection of seven Serious Skin Essentials from the World-famous Clinic? It seems less than plausible. The magic properties of immature cells, depending as they do – and as Dr Eddé insists that they must do – on being drawn and implanted within hours of leaving the womb, cannot be retained in them. Even if the ingredients are from the same source – the unborn lamb foetus – putting the creams on the skin's surface could not have anything like the effect of injecting them.

Yet these luxury skin care products are being sold on prestige cosmetics counters, and through La Prairie Skincare Centers set up to market the mystique of Montreux in fashionable stores such as Bloomingdales of New York. The actual extent of their connection with Paul Niehans' Clinique La Prairie is a well-guarded trade secret, but it is reasonable to ask how these creams can contain the same quality of 'elixir of youth' cells which Dr Eddé claims for his clinic's injections – and which, in a subtle way, is implied as being fully available in them?

The answer, of course, is that no such claim is scientifically possible. Nor do the manufacturers make it. Whatever cells are contained in the creams, they are certainly no longer the fresh tissues taken from an unborn lamb foetus, such as are injected at the clinic. They can no longer be vibrant with the crucial properties of immaturity which, as Dr Eddé is convinced, prevent rejection by the body's normal immune system.

Indeed, by the time these skin care products – five pots of different applications and two tubes – go on sale, the principles which Dr Niehans made famous cannot conceivably be involved to any significant degree. Yet the great name of the clinic, and the promise of anti-ageing it contains, is undoubtedly what sells them. Advertisements put out by the stores offering the creams stress that these so-called 'serious' skin care products are all 'based on the pioneering research into cellular rejuvenation at Clinic La Prairie'.

This, naturally, is more than enough to guarantee interest, and the resulting lure of the cellular-based creams has made fortunes for the American owners. Indeed, since the La Prairie line was launched in the early eighties it has changed hands several times, due to its profitability. Stanley Kohlenberg, whose former company, Sanofi Products, was its owner until recently, is fascinated by the La Prairie line's astonishing success.

'It's a fantastic story,' he told me in New York. 'When it was started here by a fellow in Kansas City, a lawyer (I guess in some sort of association with the Swiss clinic), they didn't really know what they had. It was an instant success. They had a very small distribution, only about seventy-five doors. Just in Saks, Neiman Marcus and I. Magnin, but in no time at all sales shot up to about six or seven million dollars.'

At this point, as customarily happens, one of the bigger players in the game, Jacqueline Cochran, moved in and snapped the line up. 'Then we bought Jacqueline Cochran out, in June 1987,' Kohlenberg continued. 'But as we already had a treatment line, Stendhal, we soon sold it on again.'

Last year, the La Prairie Collection passed into the hands of a New York society lady by the name of Georgette Mosbacher who, as Kohlenberg says, 'had no connection with cosmetics, but she'd been married at some time to George Barry, from Fabergé. So I guess that gives her a cosmetics background. Anyway, she's always loved the industry, though she's now married to Bob Mosbacher, who is oil and gas. And she wanted La Prairie, because it was at the high end of the scale, a real prestige product.'

What will be its fortune now? Knowing the business as he does,

Kohlenberg forecasts that La Prairie will continue on much the same profitable course. 'My guess is she'll go the way of the individual entrepreneur again, and hope to build it on that basis. Which is really quite big.'

Whether it is also good business to market a skin care treatment that promises, as La Prairie does, that with its use 'fine lines seem to disappear as smoother, softer skin emerges' is the only question disturbing Stanley Kohlenberg. The tie-up of a product with a famous name and reputation is only now beginning to be fully exploited.

After all, the La Prairie success, linking a commercial operation with a world-famous clinic, is little different from what Irvin Alfin attempted, though unsuccessfully, with Dr Christiaan Barnard and Glycel. L'Oréal are continuing it with Picasso's daughter's scent, Paloma. And the apparently ageless charms of Elizabeth Taylor, marketing Passion as the fragrance bearing her name, will soon be followed by others.

Another seemingly miraculous anti-ageing treatment that lends itself to commercial use is Gerovital. Until her death in 1988 this balm was offered in Romania by Ana Aslan, a woman who claimed to be ninety years old and still actively working. Aslan, who styled herself 'professor', apparently gained experience of the well-known nerve-deadening drug procaine during World War II. Working as an assistant to a Romanian physics professor, she observed that procaine, when injected as a local anaesthetic, sometimes led patients to claim that it had made them feel rejuvenated. In certain cases, there were even reports of hair colour being restored.

Convinced that procaine, suitably stabilized, could stimulate vitality and delay ageing, Ana Aslan set up a clinic behind the Iron Curtain. It provided hope and dreams to many ageing and even infirm people who heard about her 'miraculous' results with the famous. Names such as George Hamilton, Presidents Nixon and Kennedy, Mao Tse-tung, John Wayne, Marlene Dietrich and many others among the royal families and nobilities of Europe and America – including Elizabeth Taylor herself – have been advertised as having undergone her treatments.

In Britain, Sally Gilbert-Wilson continues to represent the Aslan treatment from her clinic in the West End of London. She told me she is a confirmed believer in the anti-ageing powers of Gerovital (the name reportedly given to 'procaine, stabilized by benzoic acid and metabisulfite' – a sterilizing agent used in amateur wine-making). She recommends patients to go to Aslan's clinic in Eastern Europe and try it out, as she herself has done.

Yet, so far, scientific tests have discounted the assertions that Ana Aslan and her disciples have made for it. Unmoved by her claims that Gerovital has increased the maximum lifespan of rats, authorities in Britain advise against taking it. The professor, they say, has been unable to provide any solid proof that it delays ageing in human beings. Thus Orthodox professional bodies are steadfastly refusing to accept her treatment.

The *British Medical Journal* has reported that tests in which Gerovital was given to demented old people made no effect whatsoever on their lifespan. Procaine, the journal said, was merely an acceptable anaesthetic and anti-depressant drug. The ageing process was, or appeared to be, wholly unaffected by it.

In her book *Growing Older, Living Longer*, published in Britain by the Bodley Head in 1988, BBC science department producer Teresa Hunt added a damning conclusion. 'It is not easy to disprove all the claims that are made for it, but it is equally difficult to find scientific evidence to support those claims. So it seems the advice on Gerovital has to be *don't* keep taking the tablets.'

None of this has prevented the late professor's publicity-minded helpers from circulating a brochure dramatically headed 'World Exclusive'. In this, an anonymous woman 'journalist' describes a visit to an Aslan clinic in Romania. There, she reports, 'visitors from over a hundred countries fly in to receive the "Cure".' According to the un-named reporter, they received 'a secret Youth Injection . . . used by Kings and Princes – the famous and notorious – even an American president'.

There are also excited reports of a 'secret corridor', allowing the superstar patients discreet access from their hotels. And a curt warning that 'the foreign press' will not be welcome, should they attempt 'to expose this heavily guarded secret side of Ana's fight against age'. These warnings follow a piece more notable for spelling errors and breathless adulation than objectivity. Since it also includes the late professor's belief that 'treatment should begin at the age of forty', costing £600 a go, and that 'it is recommended that you repeat it every two years for excellent health and youthful appearance', there seems more likelihood that the 'dispatch' has been written by a member of Ana Aslan's staff than by any impartial journalist.

As with so many anti-ageing 'cures', Gerovital is believed to encourage renewed and increased sex-drive. This elusive attribute is as earnestly sought by men as anti-ageing treatment is by women. While hormones may help the latter to enjoy sex past middle age, largely by increasing vaginal fluidity, there is little to help the impotent male whose member remains obstinately flaccid at vital moments, except the awkward devices and supports offered by plastic surgeons.

Thus the mystical yet unshakeable belief in the added sexual potency of ancient herbs, in particular of the Chinese root ginseng, has given it immense popularity among ageing males. Whether those ginseng products available in Europe and the United States are the real thing is questionable, since the original plant was so rare that it was once classified as a protected species in China. Anyone caught tampering with it was executed. But demand for the root, which the Chinese say increases the male 'yang', or strength, continues to rise.

Today, it is probably the most expensive root in the world. According to market sources ginseng sells in the raw state for around $50,000 a ton. Scientifically, it has been given grudging approval as an energy provider. Though how this translates into the reproductive organs is as hard to discover as is the truth that the former American secretary of state Henry Kissinger's use of it on his honeymoon with a much younger bride rekindled his sexual appetite and strength.

It is only when considered among the proposed remedies for ageing that ginseng, and regrettably every other known substance of its type including the whole range of homeopathic products (in France given almost the status of miracle drugs), has to be relegated to the level of wishful thinking. A controlled study on mice carried out in London provided no evidence at all that the root alters, or extends, lifespan in the slightest degree.

Clinics and health farms which supply ginseng can nevertheless claim impressive Chinese statistics in support of the root's powers. A London-based doctor carried out what he claimed were highly convincing experiments with nurses, showing that the root has the capacity for reducing stress and fatigue in humans.

Other experiments, too, have indicated that increased stamina can result from its absorption into the body. For this reason, and

137

since it is not listed as a drug, ginseng has become extremely popular with athletes, especially those undergoing lengthy tests of endurance.

It is equally possible that other forms of treatment, such as dieting and exercise, will have the same effect. Health clubs are increasingly being used by those who prefer to try and stave off the natural ageing processes of the body without the assistance of cosmetics or drugs. Sauna, steam and impulse showers are taken to stimulate the skin and tone the muscles. Whirlpool spas allow for complete relaxation after work-outs. Using exercises which combine aerobics, callisthenics and yoga, with optional additions of tanning, massage and electrotherapy, many of these clubs provide a viable alternative to the expensive products of the cosmetics industry. The big operators recognize this fact and have already invested heavily in the area, taking over some of the clinics and sponsoring others. The health kick has become a major money-spinner.

In the United States, scores of spas and health resorts are available to tired, stressed city workers. They can use them in their spare time for punishing, or pampering, work-outs according to choice. Ninety listed in *Travel Weekly*'s 1987–8 Reference Guide range from the Fontainebleau Hilton Resort in Miami Beach (where, for little more than $100 a day, the visitor can enjoy, or endure, 'unlimited fitness classes, body/beauty care, mineral baths and dermatology consultation') to New Age Health Farm (cable address 'Neverskink') in New York State, which mixes astrology consultations, hypnotherapy (at extra cost) and daily yoga and weigh-in classes in its 'holistic approach to weight and stress reduction'.

The independent proprietors of these health farms thrive on the new urge to put the clock back, to stay vital and attractive for as long as the life-blood flows. But to the manufacturers they also provide a welcome addition to the cosmetics marketplace, for unlimited amounts of cosmetics are sold by the spas and resorts to their captive clients.

Normally, health clinics will carry one cosmetics company's lines exclusively. Only these creams, toning and soothing lotions, sun block and other fitness aids will be pushed, which has led to intense competition in the trade.

The health farm outlets are seen as solid gold real estate by the major companies, especially since they get to the customer while sales resistance is at its lowest, thus adding healthy new dimensions to the profits of the game. But if exercise can build the body beautiful, it may also be relied on to magnify body odour. Thus the need for fragrances and fragrance-layered creams, lotions and deodorants rises with every work-out, and the value of scent – subtle or blatant – also rises in direct proportion.

For as long as it remains a duty to keep young and beautiful by pumping iron and other strenuous exertions, it will also be necessary to smell sweet while doing so. And fragrances have become the beauty jungle's sweetest blooms.

14

SWEET AND SOUR

In the Persian Gulf, where women walk veiled, a curious tradition marks the social life of the sheikhas. When these wives of the fabulously wealthy ruling families visit each other's palaces – usually for tea and gossip – they wear the finest and latest gowns, the most expensive *haute couture*, hidden under their veils. Each veil carries an individual hallmark which only their delicate nostrils can detect – the personal fragrance of the wearer.

As they enter, they discard the veils in a heap at the door, forming a mound of delicately perfumed gossamer. When they leave, each picks out her own veil by its scent. Unerringly, she knows it from the others because of the fragrance on it that is uniquely hers.

It is accepted in the Gulf States that every high-class lady has her scent blended to her taste. She has it made up for her in her teens, by one of the skilled perfume mixers of the souk. And since she wears no other scent all her life it becomes as familiar to her, its fragrance as easily recognizable, as the colour of her eyes. Indeed, I was told that it would take a bigger revolution than Women's Lib to persuade a high-born Arab lady to wear anything else.

Fortunately for the fragrance makers of the West, perfume is the easiest, subtlest and most seductive of all cosmetics. And this loyalty to one scent is not as religiously followed elsewhere. There are discerning women in the West who stay faithful to their own brands (largely because they have learned the secret of all well-blended scents – that it is the skin and body warmth of the wearer that create the final fragrance), but they are a diminishing band. And those who experiment are growing every year.

Even so, one wonders what it is, aside from the competitive urge to meet like with like, that has so afflicted the great perfume houses of Paris and the cosmetics creators of New York? Universally, they seem touched by a mania for gambling millions of dollars on the introduction of ever more new and costly fragrances. Yet the cascade of fresh brands gushing out of the great houses – superbly packaged and hyped to the skies by huge promotional budgets – is such that the entire industry could well be close to super-saturation. In this case it will either drown out the less affluent, or lead to a revolution in the traditional use of prestige fragrance as a luxury, to be worn only on special occasions.

It is true that the weightiest golden chips in the skin game come from successful fragrances, eaux de toilette, perfumed soaps, lipsticks, bath gels and related perfumed cosmetics. But fragrance is also the riskiest and costliest gamble in the game. In continuing to back each new delivery with millions of dollars of advertising and packaging money, the players are taking an increasingly slender chance. For consumers are thereby being encouraged to be fickle – to keep switching from one new fragrance to another. Thus the odds against the establishment of an enduring market for any one of the new brands lengthen with each launch. Indeed, in the opinion of experienced players, the risk today of launching a fresh fragrance into the game with any real hope of rivalling the sales of scores of existing perfumes and perfumed products looks about as secure as break-dancing on the parapet of the Eiffel Tower.

And the cost for those who fail is monumental.

In Paris, Pierre Dinant discussed the down-side of the fragrance game with me as he sees it from his side-table position. Having designed and supplied some 250 or more bottles and packages over the past 30 years for the new brands of the great houses – each taking him about a year to complete – there can be few who see the hazards more clearly.

What makes failure so frequent, I asked? Dinant explained, 'There are, of course, some that don't work simply because the stuff inside is absolutely terrible. Flop! And sometimes the design, I have to admit, isn't so good.

'But you have to realize what is involved – the amount of money it takes is phenomenal! Do you know, it can absorb as much as $20 million to make a success like "Opium" or "Poison"? Of course, you make a lot if you succeed. But if you don't . . . !'

Among those that have failed, one stands out in Dinant's mind above all others. 'Because it was one of the biggest. It was designed for the Prince Pierre Henri d'Orleans who, if there was a king in

France, would be "le Comte de Paris". This distinguished gentleman had decided to launch a fragrance under his own great family name, and as the d'Orleans crest bears the emblem of the fleurs-de-lys the fragrance was to be called "Lys Bleu".

'On the bottle, which was shaped like a jewel,' Dinant added sarcastically, 'were the words "désigné par le Prince Pierre Henri d'Orleans." Almost a royal warrant!'

The Prince, however, apparently believed that the scent would be successful on snob value alone. 'I thought the whole idea was cuckoo,' Dinant remembers. 'The fragrance was launched in the year that Mitterrand and the socialist Left came to power – so the King of France image was not a very good idea! The timing couldn't have been worse, and the whole concept was completely wrong – we cut off the neck of the king two hundred years ago, and to bring him back now was completely crazy! It was like calling a fragrance Charles I in England.'

According to Dinant, the company marketing the fragrance had to accept defeat. 'They sold "Lys Bleu" off to another company. It was a catastrophe,' he told me.

Such expensive mistakes in the marketing of fragrances are common, he says, to all. 'L'Oréal, which now claims to be No. 1 in the world, launched "Sagamore", a men's line, which has not been particularly successful. It happens to many of the biggest fragrance houses.'

A famous failure for which he designed the bottle – but which he describes as only technical – was the ill-fated Glycel, part of the Dr Barnard-backed range withdrawn by Irwin Alfin. Many more, he said, have failed for less tangible reasons – but all of them have wasted millions.

Dinant showed me the list of failed scents he keeps in his office. 'A really beautiful fragrance, to my mind, was Amalda. It was designed for the grand-daughter of the King of Saudi Arabia, Princess Amalda Ben Saud. And it is very popular in the Middle East. But, sadly, even her exotic charms could not make it a success in Europe and America. Then there was Balenciaga's Michelle, launched in 1980. The idea was to tie the perfume to the Beatles song, but the Beatles refused permission.'

We were only at the start of the list. The evidence of all these money mountains at risk, and of how much their write-offs must have added to the overhead costs of the big companies and the exorbitant price of their wares, was dramatic. Many have become collectors' items. Yet Pierre Dinant had more to reveal.

'We did one for Yves St Laurent, to follow his popular Rive Gauche. I'd designed the bottle for that one nearly twenty years before. Very successful. St Laurent thought he'd do another and market it under the name of Eau Verte. But it didn't catch on.

'Then there was Balmain's Ebène, which they brought out to follow their success with Ivoire. Unfortunately, they hadn't checked that it was the same name in English – Ebony – as a popular magazine for blacks in Chicago. They had a lawsuit over that, and lost.'

In Pierre Dinant's opinion, these failures and the financial losses involved are sometimes influenced by the opinion of one of the big players' wives. 'If the wife of the president of a big perfume company likes it, I've more than once known a new fragrance to be launched,' he told me. 'We designed a perfect bottle for Bloomingdales in New York when they wanted to market their own fragrance line, Bloomies. The bottle top was the head of a pierrot, or clown, and it should have been promoted as a young, fun fragrance. But they put an old-fashioned symbol on it, and it flopped. I was shocked. When I heard what they'd done.

'Shéhérezade by Desprez was another disappointment in 1983, but that was because they'd insisted on an old fashioned bottle in the style of 1860, which was going too far.'

There have been so many losers that, in Dinant's view, the number of new fragrances being forced onto an already saturated market today can only lead to more and more multi-million dollar disasters. As he says, 'It takes five to ten years for a previously unknown perfume to get its money back. The average is about seven years. If the money runs out before it takes on, that's it.' Everyone believed that Folies Bergere launched in 1981, was doing well. And so it was – for two years. But it didn't last; it lost money.

So a fragrance like Obsession, which has been going for only four or five years (and is known to be grossing $150 million a year) could yet force Calvin Klein to cut his losses and cease production. Only the insiders, and the big players' accountants, know this sobering fact.

The question is, how many more fragrances can the market be expected to absorb? Conformity, such as the sheikhas practise –

or the old-hat notion that a tasteful woman ought always to be identified by her personal scent, and by that scent only – cuts clean across the promotional aims of the big perfume houses. They believe that scent can be sold in much the same way as fashion; that the way in which the great couturiers offer completely new and different styles with each new season's collection will become an accepted part of fragrance buying.

Fashionable women, they say, will learn to replace their fragrances as often as they change their wardrobes. The new will take the place of the old for those who want to be 'in'. No limit exists to the number of beautiful bottles containing scents costing well over $100 a fluid ounce (to buy, that is – to produce, only a minute fraction of that).

The ladies of American and European 'nouvelle society' and those aspiring to it, they believe, will want to have a variety of prestige bottles decorating their dressing-tables. The age of 'designer fragrance', with all the snob appeal of the latest Christian Lacroix gown, is well on the way if not already with us.

And what can possibly be wrong with this? Annette Green, executive director of America's Fragrance Foundation, fired the question at me when we talked in New York. What, she asked, is so terribly shocking about the idea of women becoming accustomed to wearing a different fragrance on each separate occasion of their daily lives?

Green's vision is of a different scent for each mood and period of the day. It might mean wearing a floral fragrance in the morning, then changing into something more astringent at lunchtime. In the evening – and particularly on evenings when rendezvous and romance are on the menu – there are the deep, seductive pulls of musk, oriental and chypre to enhance the occasion. Or even, perhaps, to encourage a little 'après-TV'.

She also dreams of an age when office and factory workers will be psyched up by fragrance sprayed through the air conditioning. 'I know that medical science is experimenting with aromas,' she explained to me, 'and I personally believe that fragrances could play a much bigger part in our lives than they do now, and with very good results all round.'

Mostly, the cynics might say, they will be good for the perfume houses, who, as Dinant's casualty lists show, can lose their shirts as well as the market share they are seeking unless they get it right.

But Annette Green is convinced that her billion dollar industry will be able to take the consumers with them into a new, increasingly fragrant age.

The fact that, of the whole range of materials used in cosmetics, fragrance is known to be the most likely to cause allergy does nothing to quench her belief. And, to justify such outlays as the $20 million she believes Calvin Klein risked last year on the launch of their new scent, Gem, she showed me an expensive looking bottle in the shape of a clock. It had been given to her as a sample by the company. 'Look at what they have to do, how aggressive they can be! That's how Elizabeth Taylor launched her Passion, and already it's doing very well. She'll get the market, and will be a major competitor in the coming year. As Paloma Picasso did, too – she has done a marvellous job.'

Yet it is a fact, confirmed in the UK trade magazine SPC by their report of a market conference held in Britain last year, that another of the big fragrance players, Fendi, only achieved sales of around £120,000 in its exclusive four weeks at Harrods at a cost of more than twice that sum. The makers 'probably had to spend a quarter of a million to get it', the magazine reported.

And the fragrance marketplace faces other hazards, quite apart from consumer rejection. 'Knock-offs' – more politely termed 'replica fragrances' – are causing deep worry lines which even Retin A is unlikely to dissipate on the brows of the major manufacturers. Already toppling over backwards from a cost structure that depends on spending five times as much on advertising and promotion as on the product itself, today's fragrance industry is being neatly robbed by these priates to the extent of an estimated 10 per cent of the US market overall and not much less elsewhere.

Annette Green takes comfort from the fact that more and more big name perfume houses are being run on what she calls 'the old entrepreneurial lines'. And that some, like Yves St Laurent, are indeed showing confidence in the rich rewards of those who succeed, buying back their top-selling fragrance businesses from the big pharmaceuticals which took them over in the mid-eighties. As she points out: 'Until recently the trend was all the other way. Squibb, Ely Lilly and so on bought up the best fragrance lines. But now it's going back on itself. Fabergé have bought back Elizabeth Arden from Lilly, and it's happening everywhere. The ironic part of it is that the return of the entrepreneurs is occurring just when the cosmetics industry is moving much closer to the pharmaceutical industry.'

It is also a time when the flower pickers of Grasse are finding work harder to get. In the spring of 1988 I went to this showplace Provençal town and heard sad tales of the diminishing use of the petals of rose, jasmine and other flowers. These were once laboriously picked, sorted and crushed, their essences distilled to make the great natural perfumes. 'Today, synthetics and flowers imported more cheaply from abroad – particularly the Far East – are killing the industry here,' I was told. 'Grasse is now mostly a museum town.'

Only those older companies of blender and mixers with established contacts are said to be still thriving. In the factory of one of the great perfume manufacturing houses the Société Lautier, founded in the pre-revolutionary days of the eighteenth century, I saw chemists mixing liquids not made from petals picked in the fields outside and then crushed, but supplied ready-bottled in five-litre jars by the pharmaceutical companies of France, Germany, Switzerland and Japan.

'Only a few of our most expensive fragrance essences are based on natural products these days,' I was told. 'Everything can be synthesized, and synthetics don't go off as quickly as the natural fragrances. Nor do they possess the same problems of allergic reaction. Altogether they are safer – and of course cheaper – to use.'

Is this why Annette Green's new entrepreneurs are thriving? I wondered. In New York I put the question to Stanley Kohlenberg, who saw the dawn of American-made fragrances during his time with Revlon. 'Until the late sixties,' he told me, 'the fragrance business here belonged to the French – we didn't mess in it. But then Charles Revson introduced Norell in 1969. It was the first all-American fragrance, and it was an instant success. Suddenly the back of the whole French fragrance business here was broken.'

As soon as he and his colleagues realized that they could perfect designer fragrances, that American women would buy American fragrances, 'Why, the floodgates were open.' Others began pressing their research chemists to find, or produce, new scents to be marketed in their names.

But Charles Revson was a hard man to beat to the draw. 'While everybody else was chasing Charles' great success with Norell,' Kohlenberg recalled, 'he knocked himself off! He introduced

Charlie, which was the first moderately priced American fragrance – based on sociology, women's lib, the woman who could fend for herself and wear trousers and go out herself and do all the things a man could do – so it had a man's name.'

Kohlenberg laughed. 'Charlie was just Norell with a little more spice in it. We took Norell, which was already successful at the high end, copied it down to the middle, gave it a different twist entirely and sold it as Charlie. And of course Charlie was enormously successful. Now you had two levels where fragrance manufacturers in the US said, "Wow! I don't have to worry about the French any more. I can do moderate-priced fragrances without caring about the classics, like Poesie and Houbigant and the others. I can do my own!"

'So there was a whole series of moderate-price range fragrances made here. And then they discovered musk, and suddenly we were inundated with musk oil fragrances – God help us!'

The era of the seventies that followed was America's first 'fragrance design era'. 'That was when Calvin Klein and Ralph Lauren and Giorgio emerged,' Kohlenberg explained, 'and celebrities of all sorts came out with their own fragrances. Once again habits changed. We went from the period when a woman had her own favourite fragrance which she wore forever, to her wanting a whole family – a wardrobe – of fragrances which she wore according to her mood, or what the current fashion was. And we actually created a problem for ourselves, because we created fickle fragrance buyers!'

Annette Green's dream come true, surely? So why was this a problem, if it left in its path an increased appetite, a desire to try everything new and different? America's biggest selling fragrances today – Giorgio (owned by Avon and so powerfully scented that there's a joke about a sign in a New York restaurant banning smoking, bare feet and Giorgio), Dior's Poison, Clavin Klein's Obsession and the longest-lasting classic of them all, Chanel No. 5 – all depend on women changing from one to the other. But Kohlenberg sees another side of the fragrance coin from Green's prediction of ever-expanding sales.

'A woman of your mother's generation wore Evyan's White Shoulders, launched in 1945, all her life. That was it. Now, it would be considered heresy. She'd have to tire of anything she wore for too long to be in the fashion. So, although one or two of the great classics like Chanel No. 5 have held on, most of the big French names – Guerlain, Givenchy and others – have slipped.'

And how did the Paris houses, which could no longer depend on selling merely on their exotic labels, react to this invasion of their sacred territory? 'It was too late to react. They'd owned the market – they'd had a lock on it. And they'd never spend any money on promotion, because they didn't have to. But suddenly the Revsons and the Lauders and the Cosmair outfit [the US base of L'Oréal] realized that this was a different business, and began to compete. And they put a *lot* of money into advertising and merchandising.'

By the late sixties a goldrush-like fever was abroad, despite the fact that the cost of getting there had soared. It drove the top companies in America to adopt increasingly competitive lures, which Stanley Kohlenberg blames for the present decline. 'Because that was when Estée Lauder started the worst horror we could have inflicted on ourselves – "gift with purchase"!' he explained. 'Charles, seeing how successful it was, chased her. I created Ultima II for him, and with that we, too, started doing gifts and give-aways.'

At first, Lauder and Revlon were the only two companies offering them, because they were so expensive. But then John Revson, Charles' son who was with another perfume company, introduced 'purchase with purchase'. The trick there was that the makers could sell their free samples instead of giving them away.

'After that, anybody could do it,' Kohlenberg explained. 'And the theory now is that it costs you nothing, so long as you can cover the basic cost of the goods. But it opened the floodgates for everyone, and it has become the bane of our existence.'

His view was that these incentives 'had taken a loyal consumer and turned her into someone who'll run from counter to counter asking "Who's got the best gift? – Who's giving out the best deal? – Which umbrella is best?" We're now at a point where the fragrance industry is flat – which is partly because there are so many new fragrances, and partly because the cost of doing business has gone sky-high with these gimmicks.'

To illustrate, he pointed to Calvin Klein's costly 1985 launch of Obsession by Minnetonka, then owner of the licence for the fragrance. 'Robin Burns, president of the company, spent $15 million on its introduction. She shipped out an additional $7½ million worth of sales stock. If it hadn't taken, she would have been down not 15, but 22½ million! Quite a gamble.'

But Obsession had been a hit, surely, according to all reports?

'Yes,' Kohlenberg agreed, 'and by the end of the year they had obtained a new level, and were building. But now she's about to do it again, with yet another new fragrance. This one is called Eternity, which the press says she's going to spend something like another $20 million on for its first shipment! Another crazy crap-shot!'

In a remarkable way the size of the money at risk seems to Kohlenberg to compare with a Broadway musical. 'Producers of musicals are always being criticized for creating fantastic productions, but borrowing a little on the music side. You might say that these fragrance makers spend a lot of money on hype and maybe not so much on quality. It's the packaging, not the stuff in the bottle, that matters. That's why we call them "fad fragrances". If you can blow one into an enormously successful couple of years, then even if it starts to slide, so what? As it begins to slip, throw up another one! The only question is, how high is up?'

To hold the interest of the public for anything longer than a few years, he believes, requires a particularly unique fragrance. 'It has to be one that's destined to become a classic. I mean, Chanel No. 5 will be Chanel No. 5 for ever, and will stay a classic. It's been here since 1926, gone through all sorts of stages, and is now back again. Even Coco which Chanel brought out in 1984, cannot surpass it. The real classics, Joy and three or four others, are few and far between.'

And in an increasingly fickle market there can be no guarantee that even these will always be as successful. Kohlenberg pointed to one classic that did not make it. 'Lanvin's Arpège was marketed out of existence,' he said. 'It was run by Ritz and owned by Squibb, and I guess they tried to make it a very big fragrance without worrying about its staying power. They marketed it lower and lower, cheaper and cheaper. The stock-keeping units that were created were less and less expensive, because the company was going for a broader distribution. Eventually lack of quality, lack of caring, lack of control of franchise, killed a good fragrance. Arpège is not a factor any more. It's dead.'

He nevertheless shares Annette Green's faith in the fragrance entrepreneurs, the big gamblers who work on hunches and instinct rather than the companies which adopt a statistical approach to the game. 'When a large corporate entity gets hold of a cosmetics company, it generally fails,' Kohlenberg told me. 'For a lot of reasons. First of all, this is a business for risk-takers. Your executives have to be almost schizoid, because they must keep one foot in Madison

Avenue, where hype and the ad men are, and one in the marketplace. This is something the giant corporations don't understand. They test-market, they plan, and they have rules and regulations. It goes on for four or five years, and gets nowhere. It's just not that kind of a business.'

His two periods with Charles Revson at Revlon ('I was a recidivist – I went back after I'd lost it!') taught Kohlenberg to expect constant, incessant novelty and change. 'Charles would put out 100 to 110 new products every year. If we were successful with 40 per cent of them that was fine. We just threw them all up against the wall and saw what stuck. The ones that slipped off didn't hurt us, because we limited our losses by not making too much of the stuff in the beginning. If it didn't take, we'd get rid of the rest – send it to Europe, send it to Hong Kong – anywhere, to make it go away, so we didn't get killed. But the ones that stuck we turned round quickly and made more.'

The tempo in the company, he says, was 'near hysteria. We were running it like a giant candy store – always out of stock on everything, always on a very tight manufacturing schedule. 'I mean, you didn't sit in your office all day and have meetings. You'd run out in the hall and grab the production guy, grab the packaging guy, and get things done. Otherwise they'd run right over you. So it wasn't the orderly structure of a corporate company in the slightest. In fact, when Charles was dying and Michel Bergerac from ITT took over – well, you couldn't find a place further out.

'He came to see me and said, "Tell me, Stanley, when do you have your monthly budget meetings?" I said, "We don't have them. We don't have a budget." He couldn't believe it. "What do you mean, you don't have a budget?" I told him, "What we have is a kind of rolling actual. Whatever we've done, that's the budget." '

That may have been fine in the days before graphic warnings began to appear in the media, stirring the controversial aspects of the business, but would it still work today? I wondered. As the big companies are being forced by the FDA and other censorious bodies to recognize, the consumer is becoming increasingly worried. Nasty rumours of allergic reaction, due to new fragrances and new natural products, are circulating, making bad publicity. Surgical catastrophes are broadcast to millions on television. And the media is more than ready, always, to magnify the slightest injury caused

150

by anti-ageing 'miracle products', or by injections with strange and potent chemicals. As to the potential damage lurking in the use of untested drugs, and their effect on the body's cell structure since Thalidomide, that has been a minefield. Now, too, there is the threat of cancer from the sun.

These are the terrors facing the captains of the industry, and I see no sign that they care too deeply about them. It seems rather that they are busy fighting to be the first to bring out the next, greatest, most expensive new – ever more new – product. Who will survive, and how many will fail, are questions the shareholders may soon be asking with some force. Because today the stakes are rising, the gamble is greater, and the price of failure is higher than ever before.

15

MAKE-UP FOR MEN

In my prowls round the lavish cosmetics floors of Bloomingdales, Saks and Macys in New York, and Harrods and Selfridges in London, I seldom saw a man who was not escorting (more accurately, trailing in the wake of) a lady. The main Paris and Tokyo stores were similarly male no-go areas. Men, I was told, do not enjoy intrusion into what they see as an intimate woman's world.

As for wearing the stuff, perhaps they may be encouraged to rub something on their skins before ski-ing or sun-soaking. And after-shave lotions are no longer considered unduly effeminate. But most beauty products remain off-limits for all but the most eccentric or advanced of males.

'Why can't we sell to men?' Amelia Bassin wanted to know. 'Aren't men human? Don't they compete? Weren't they once the show-off of the species? Can it be that they don't *want* to pleasure themselves, to be attractive to others?' The answer, as she unhappily concluded, may be nothing more than old-fashioned male resistance to being thought unmanly. 'I'd say it's mostly what I call the macho mystique,' she told me. 'Men see fashion and fragrance as feminine – and nothing could be worse! A man's success symbol is his car or his woman. To be perceived as a clothes horse or fashion non-conformist is the kiss of death.'

According to US economist William J. Fitzgerald, 'Nearly three out of every four – 75 per cent – of the purchasers of male cosmetics are women.' Men themselves rarely find the nerve even to enter the cosmetics department of a major store. They are too well aware that the doll-like ladies behind the glittering counters, and the special-promotion girls who stalk the aisles looking as if they have just stepped out of *Dallas* or *Dynasty*, will either treat them with haughty disdain or – worse still – spray them mercilessly with an assortment of strong fragrances.

152

Does this bother the giants of the industry? You bet it does. The frustrating knowledge that, despite all their expensive advertising hype – seeking a tweedy, tobacco-stained and open-air image for men's toiletries – the mass of their stuff is bought by women, is just too much. Bassin, who is read at all levels of the industry, is not afraid to ask the pointed question. 'Wouldn't it be great if we could educate men in their own territory? And get men to buy 75 per cent more of their own stuff?''

Yet in March 1988 the British trade journal *Soap, Perfumery and Cosmetics* positively announced a breakthrough in this obstinate market. The magazine reported that 'Without doubt the success story of late has been the meteoric growth of the male market.' What the over-enthusiastic writer of the report omitted to emphasize was that the figures supporting this 'meteoric growth' reflected the Christmas trade. Women were then buying men's products as gifts for their men. And inflicting them on those men, whether or not they were well-received.

'Most stores report phenomenal increases in both [men's] fragrance and cosmetic business,' exulted Liz Platts. 'After all, a Christmas without seeing the Old Spice man on the surfboard [a TV commercial] would be rather like having a Christmas cake without the icing.'

Season of goodwill or not, in the USA sales of men's skin care products were not looking so good, considering the relative size of the market. Referring similarly to the Christmas sales statistics in New York, Amelia Bassin begged her cosmetics industry readers to look these less congenial facts in the face. 'Skin care for men?' she asked. 'Nowhere! Why, most men may not be averse to using women's products in the privacy of their homes, but they wouldn't be caught dead buying it in a store. *Any* store.'

Despairingly, she urged the big companies to concentrate on 'the non-macho man, the gentle man'. Her advice was based on hard research of where the actual sales were happening. 'Bloomingdales reports that over half its men's toiletries goes to gays,' Bassin wrote. 'And we know that there's something many terrific women find appealing, even sexy, in the mouse that roared. But nobody's making a real effort to reach that lucrative market. All it takes is for a major marketer to come out of the scaredy-cat closet and advertise in the gay media.' She wasn't joking. 'The straights would never know,' she slyly predicted, 'and it's a valid gap in the marketplace.'

Sounding a little like the conscience of the entire cosmetics industry, Amelia Bassin also expressed strong dissatisfaction with the type of hype being used to try and break down male resistance. 'To whom are we talking?' she demanded. 'We're so fond of using nude women [in cosmetic ads aimed at men]. But do we think nude men would encourage women to spend more? Not bloody likely!'

Perhaps the British male is less sensitive. During a ski-ing holiday in Switzerland in 1988 Euan Clarke, a young housemaster at a tough English public school, was astonished to find 'a number of chaps my own age putting stuff on their faces – eyeliner, and make-up'. Clarke, an Oxbridge rugger and cricket blue, tried not to let his surprise show. 'I asked if they did it as a protection against the cold,' he told me. ' "Oh no," they said, "we use it all the time." '

In hard financial terms, male sales in the States are roughly estimated to top a billion dollars annually, while in the UK they are only a quarter of that figure. *SPC* published a more balanced survey in July 1988, showing that most encouragement was coming from the New Man. This figment of marketing statistics was said to be 'disconcertingly young (still in his teens or twenties) – or at the other extreme'.

Since the age gap between these coincides with the years normally spent in supporting a family, it would appear that there is very little the manufacturers can do to appeal to the man who has to mow the lawn and wash the car on Sundays. He is, anyway, likely to be too economically strapped – with mortgage repayments, school fees, holidays, debts and tax bills – to be able to afford the luxury of fragrant additives.

Writing in the British daily *Independent* last spring, Robert Farago noted a more sinister effect arising from the promotion, in advertising and hype, of the New Man. 'The latest buzz-word circulating through London ad agencies is the "new man",' he wrote.

This fantasy figure is young, rich, successful, handsome and thin. Although he used to regard beauty products as mostly for a homosexual audience, the 'new man' now sells a wide range of products – razor blades, blue jeans, after-shave, breakfast cereals, high-priced sports cars and more – to the general population. Some doctors feel that this unrealistic concept of masculine beauty will lead to a dramatic rise in male anorexics and bulimics.

Whether the New Man is more myth than reality has yet to be proved by sales factors. The prestige brands seem bent on gaining greater acceptance with men. They claim more success than their downmarket contemporaries. Certainly, in this range which includes most of the big cosmetics companies, some extraordinarily costly efforts are being made. Yves St Laurent launched a male fragrance called Jazz in spring 1988 in the firm belief that Englishmen will pay £23 for 125 millilitres of toilet water – despite the knowledge that perhaps nine-tenths of the cost will have been spent on advertising, packaging and hype.

How to reach out to men – to 'touch their face' as Estée Lauder would aim to do – has always seemed an insoluble problem. Anything even faintly suggesting delicacy, weakness or effeminate traits is likely to be cold-shouldered. But then, so is a tough-guy, Rambo-style image. When a new fragrance line, Raffles, was launched in 1988 by Parfums Le Fort it was described as having 'a refreshing cologne top note and a sparkling herbaceous green character, mingling orange flower and lavender, orris and jasmine, plus rich tones of patchouli, vetiver and sandalwood'. Any bottle with that on the label would be liable to cause riotous mirth in a male sports changing-room.

Amelia Bassin again put her finger on the problem when she remembered that 'In the old days, Old Spice and Brut did fine, selling fragrance for its own sake whereas now Brut is advertising it "smells like a man". As if a man can't smell like a man – which isn't always the greatest thing – on his own!' As for Lauder's Aramis, the established top seller to men in the USA and UK, Bassin commented sharply, 'Aramis gave us *status*. A popular euphemism for high prices!'

Searching her memory for further evidence of the trait, she continued, 'I thought the early Chaz ads with a romantic man appeal were great, but then Revlon switched to the traditional, with not much more success, despite great good luck in choosing a macho model who promptly became a celebrity. Even Jordache's steamy pre-Obsession ads didn't play too well. Meanwhile, hundreds more came and went, with zillions of dollars down the drain, faster than you can knock it off.'

Yet, like the forty-niners who reached the Klondike too late to stake a claim, the big names refuse to admit defeat. At every sales conference they convince themselves that there must be untapped gold in male sales; indeed, that there is a huge seam of it buried somewhere deep in the male psyche, just waiting to be exploited. Mine it, they dream, and surely we'll find a source of wealth greater than El Dorado, richer than anything ever before seen?

'Of all the cosmetics and fragrance markets, men's preparations is [*sic*] perhaps the most exciting,' burbled British trade paper journalist Tricia Welsh last summer. She had to admit, however, that this was not because of its size (still small in the UK at £269.5 million), but because of its potential. 'Men at last are beginning to take grooming seriously,' she wrote, 'and entrenched fears and hang-ups surrounding traditional definitions of masculinity are being revised.' Wishful thinking, Amelia Bassin would say. But Welsh insisted: 'At last, men no longer view an interest in fashion and personal care as the sole prerogative of women. They may have a lot of catching up to do when it comes to emptying their wallets, but this is one resting place where the moths are unlikely to return.'

This, of course, is the sort of music the leaders of the industry could dance to all day. But the same tune has been around for so long that they may be pardoned for doubting its validity. As far back as 1981, Lauder's Clinique Skin Supplies for Men was claiming a 'successful breakthrough into the male market that began in 1976'. Only four years later Lauder was trying another approach, with its new Lauder for Men range of colognes and after-shaves. This, too, was claimed to be designed expressly for 'a new kind of man'.

Where is he? If anywhere, this potentially dynamic creature exists solely in TV commercials and in the fertile imaginations of PR executives. 'Yes, it's the market with the greatest potential,' Bassin agrees, 'but the most disappointing performance of all. For years they've been saying it's our next big boom area. Don't hold your breath. Obviously, where men are concerned (maybe that's what's wrong – they're *not* concerned!) we have *not* come a long way, baby.'

Bob Chavez, in charge of cosmetics at Macys in New York, offered me the same lacklustre picture as we traversed the perfumed aisles of his luxurious cosmetics floor. 'In 1987 we turned over $127 million from cosmetics alone,' he told me, 'and only $5 million of it was from men's toiletries.'

In Annette Green's office on West 30th Street, New York, where she presides in sovereign state over the influential Fragrance Foundation, she told me, 'I don't see that market moving up very much, or very quickly. There will be some upward movement, mostly in after-shave and soap – they now amount to about 37 to 38 per cent of all fragrances sold in the US, which means close on one and a half billion dollars.' The reason for market lethargy, she said, was that 'the cosmetics companies are a bit shy of promoting skin care products to men.'

As Maureen Barry, the London businesswoman who has run several beauty salons, confirmed, this is a stark fact of the male end of the trade, giving the lie to all the hype and PR-instilled wishful dreaming of the beauty columnists. 'I think it's appalling that men don't put stuff on their faces, and yet they've got good skins. Why don't they have to use creams?' Her husband, she explained, 'is a great big ex-Olympics rowing man who thinks it's foppish to use anything with scent in it. But he has two grown-up sons, twenty and twenty-one, who colour their hair – one week it's blond or grey, the next it's growing out. That seems perfectly normal to them, so why not to him? It is really a generation thing, and I think that in the next decade, if the industry do the right advertising, men *will* use more cosmetics.'

Paradoxically, as Anita Roddick had pointed out in her BBC radio interview with Russell Harty, the industry Barry refers to is run almost entirely by men. 'Every one of the cosmetic major giants is run by men,' Roddick commented, 'and if they put more women on the boards they'd probably say [of the emphasis on "looking beautiful"] – "Come on! this is irrelevant!"'

But if, as we are told, male face-lifts and hair transplants are a major growth industry, can anti-ageing creams, fragrances and at least some make-up and skin care be far behind? Plastic surgeons in Britain and the United States are enthusing about a new 'skin expander' they use on men. In New York, James Reardon told me how he inserts what is virtually a small inflatable balloon under the skin of their bald pates. He then blows it up until the hair on either side can be nipped together, before cutting away the hairless skin. 'Over the past five or six years I've been using it more and more,' he said. 'It has the additional advantage of lifting the sag out of the face. Men are now very prominent among our face-lifts.'

In Tokyo, my hosts at Shiseido (almost alone among the giants in having a woman director, Shizuko Yamauchi, on the board) called their men's market 'very interesting – especially the younger generation'. Japanese males use little after-shave, I was told, but their thick, dark hair needs a strong cream. 'And, strangely enough, last year one of our best-selling products was a black face-mask called Gear, which young men put on their faces to improve their skin texture,' Yasutaka Mori told me.

In Britain, the days when film star Richard Greene, with the patent-leather slick hairstyle of the thirties, could bring about a revolution in the sales of Brylcreem are long gone. But fear of premature balding, much wider use of perfumed shampoos and fixatives, and the breakdown of barriers between the sexes are thin ends of a wedge which, in time, could overcome a large part of male resistance to cosmetics in general. 'Men age better, of course,' beautician Sally Wilson told me in London, 'and they're getting over being called pansy when they use hair treatments and cosmetics – especially in our ethnic communities. For them, with skin that scars more than white skin, and with hair that needs a lot more attention, what we offer is a real boon.'

Myra Sims, who treats both men and women in her clinic, was less sure of the attraction that hair care and facials have for the male sex. 'They certainly need treatment, poor things,' she said. 'They are terribly stressed, some of them. But twice recently we've had men's wives make appointments for them and they haven't turned up. Funked it!' Men refuse to see either their skins or their bodies as in need of more attention than they already give them. But hair, crew-cut or punk-spiked, may well hold an identifiable key to men's future in the beauty jungle.

Men, though, have always been limp prey for the big cats when their hair recedes. Until July 1988, when a clinical study in Toronto found potentially dangerous side-effects in the anti-baldness drug Minoxidil, any product promising hair growth and restoration would sell like new-reg motor cars. Every wimp, it seems, believes there is a Samson in him somewhere.

The study dashed a lot of hopes. The American pharmaceutical giant Upjohn, producers of the drug, had been watching their stock rise and rise. Orders for Minoxidil had arrived from all corners of the world. The Canadian report was a setback to a universally attractive elixir of youth and good looks. But as it was run by an eminent professor of medicine and pharmacology at the University of Toronto, Dr Frans H. H. Leemen, the study was irrefutable. It concluded that Minoxidil, also sold in Europe under the name of

Rogaine, 'has effects on the heart'. Exactly what these were, the report did not specify. The mere implication that the risk of heart disease and death could be accelerated by using the drug as a baldness cure was more than enough to slam the door on rising sales.

However persistently the Upjohn company tried to counter it, to disagree with the findings, nobody but an idiot was going to risk heart failure for the sake of a possible increase in follicle growth. Today, it is still too early to say what the outcome will be. In the USA the FDA is rumoured to be considering approval of the drug as a cure for baldness. But on Wall Street the effect has been depressing in the extreme to holders of Upjohn stock. Its value has fallen like a wingless bird.

In Britain a smiling-faced businessman, Stuart Hall, continues to advertise a hair restorer containing Minoxidil. Throughout 1988 photographs of Hall appeared in national newspapers, purporting to illustrate – by the growth of his well-combed head of hair – that the treatment works. Stuart Hall offers the picture, he says, as a demonstration of what his discovery – a baldness treatment which he admits contains Minoxidil – can do for others. Hall's Transform Medical Group based in Bowdon, Cheshire, was claiming in early 1989 to be 'Britain's leading clinic in the field of hair restoration with over 15,000 patients benefiting from our treatments, which are totally monitored and controlled by top medical men'.

Hall further claimed that 'after clinical trials both here and in the USA our new product can *double* the response to regrowth'. Such careful wording suggested that his own belief in its ability to grow hair where none had grown before was cautious. Biological 'response' to any form of growth – or 'regrowth' – suggests only that the treatment will increase the patient's willingness for it to happen, not that it necessarily will.

In John Terry's private hospital it also appeared that the drug with known side-effects was being offered to those who would risk using it. 'Minoxidil certainly works,' Terry was quoted as telling James Dalrymple of the *Independent* newspaper in March 1988, several weeks after publication of the Canadian report. 'But only on certain people, and on certain types of hair loss. How it works is a total mystery.'

The mystery would seem to be that anyone is still promoting its use when there is the slightest risk to health attached to it. Minoxidil was first developed to treat hypertension. In 1985 Upjohn applied to the FDA for approval to market the drug as a baldness treatment in the USA. But following the Canadian report, chances of this being granted were said to be extremely slim.

Yet, according to Terry, Stuart Hall's company is importing the drug from Europe. 'In Italy, they are selling it for £900 a kilo,' he told me. And the attractive profit margin that this allows may be guessed at from the fact that last year Hall's Transform was offering an introductory '£25 voucher – against the cost of surgical and non-surgical treatment', either at his Wimpole Street, London, clinic or in Cheshire.

As cosmetics doyenne Hazel Bishop emphasized during our meeting, anything that can make two hairs grow on a man's bald head where only one grew before will always add 'a tremendous extension' to the pulling power of male cosmetics. She had heard, she said, 'of a Chinese doctor claiming he has a product that will do that – but it contains *no* drug at all'.

If that is so, then how long can it be before the unfulfilled dream of all who enter the cosmetics business in search of fortune comes true, and the male market at last falls to them?

16

ULTRA-VIOLENCE

Skin cancer became a holiday horror story in the early eighties. So frightening were the statistics that the threat could have dried up sales of sun tanning oils and creams like a desert wind. L'Oréal's Ambre Solaire was seriously affected. Sales of Estée Lauder's Golden Sun Pre-tan Accelerator were threatened. A host of profitable others faced setbacks.

But in a smart about-face, the companies and their chemists set to work on their menaced formulas, introducing 'sun block' and 'sun screen' ingredients to the fragrance-layered oils and emulsions. Fresh and vigorous advertising carried the message to a doubting world. 'Fear not! These products will *protect* your skin from damaging ultraviolet rays of the sun.' What had looked like an approaching disaster had actually increased the companies' earnings and created a new, even more profitable, market out of the ashes of the old.

For in spite of the risks, and oblivious of dire warnings from doctors, women – and many men – still go on clamouring to get a golden tan.

In 1988, skin care – with the exception of make-up and hair care, but including the new sun care products offering protection from harmful 'UV', or ultraviolet – was the biggest seller in the United States. It grossed close on $3 billion despite the fact that, as leading dermatologists warn, none of the 'sun-blocked' products can guarantee total safety from the injurious rays of the sun.

It was left to the irrepressible Amelia Bassin to explain why. 'Despite warnings about skin cancer and ageing and wrinkles, we gullible women still perceive an expensive tan as a status symbol. With a little much-needed help from our government, which declared sun screens to be drugs, the industry has worked out a nifty SPF – sun protection factor – rating. And so all is well between them for a change.'

161

But is all so reassuringly well? Betty York, a San Francisco hotel executive and ex-fashion model who spent many years in Florida where the sun's rays can turn the bodies of young women darker than potato crisps, has fought a costly battle against skin cancer since the early eighties. It was brought on, she believes, entirely by excessive exposure of her very fair skin to the sun's rays.

During her ordeal, York's otherwise unblemished face and the upper part of her chest have suffered disfiguring eruptions of scaly spots that could have developed into malignant melanomas. 'I was in my mid-forties,' she told me, 'when I first saw these flakes and rough spots on my face. I didn't think anything of them at first, but then a man I was dating said, "I really don't like what's happening to you."'

'So I went to see a dermatologist. He began by freezing them with something so cold it blistered. And after a while, they formed little scabs which peeled away within a fortnight.'

Others took their place. And sometimes Betty York left the visits to her dermatologist too late. 'I found that, if I didn't have them treated in the very early stages, even what seemed to be only a tiny little flake of skin on my face could eventually become malignant.'

Twice she suffered that fate. 'Then I had to undergo surgery to have them cut out, costing me hundreds of dollars and permanent scarring. Ever since, I have had to be extremely careful. I mustn't let them get too big.'

Although she can have them frozen off while they're just flakes, every one she leaves for more than a few days will develop into a malignancy. And, as the skin doctors are warning, the more violent form of malignancies, known as melanomas, can form links which transfer the cancer to other organs. Melanomas can kill.

Betty York is luckier than most. Her malignancies were not lethal. But all her life she will have to make regular, close inspections of her skin. 'I really shouldn't walk out of the door without putting on a sun block,' she confesses. 'But I sometimes do. At least, I always wear a hat.'

The experience has left her with a realistic appreciation of the current medical scare about sunbathing. She does still go occasionally to resorts where she lies on a beach to get a tan, but only with full protective armament of hat, strong sun block and dark glasses. Why, she wonders, has it taken medical science, and the cosmetics companies that have been plugging the healthy virtues of their sun tanning creams, oils and lotions so profitably, so long to draw attention to the problem?

'In my twenties and thirties I had no idea it could be so terrible. We heard that sun was drying to the skin, and that people did get cancer from it, but it was only a remote possibility. That only happened to other people! Nobody ever talked about skin *damage*, which I now have.'

She also condemns some of the accepted forms of medical treatment for topical skin problems, such as her own. 'In the early stages, I was treated by a dermatologist who had been recommended to me. He prescribed a cream called 5 FU, which I started putting on the spots. But the effect was to make them come to the surface and erupt. In some cases this caused great suppurating sores, maybe an inch in diameter. I'd wake up stuck to my pillow.'

She put up with this for as long as she could, believing that, as the doctor said, the eruptions would clear the poison out of her system. Finally, she had enough. 'I mean, I went to work bandaged! The doctor told me he was delighted. He wanted to step up the strength of the cream – "We're getting such a wonderful reaction now, we'll put you on to double strength – 10 FU." '

By chance, Betty York heard that the FU drugs were being used in chemotherapy to reduce cancerous tumours. She became seriously worried, especially when a friend introduced her to another woman who had been treated by the same dermatologist. And with the same substance. 'She'd had the most alarming results. Apparently her whole face was so badly damaged by what he had done to her that she'd had to have hospital treatment. My friend urged me to get another opinion.'

She stopped the treatment immediately, and found a new dermatologist who told her that nothing more drastic was needed than the preventative treatment she has been having ever since. Today, apart from the visits she makes to his surgery for occasional freezing off of newly formed skin flakes, and a barely noticeable blotchiness left by the surgery (which she is able to disguise with make-up), the worst of Betty York's danger is past.

For others, it is only beginning. Morris Herstein, though he works almost exclusively *for* the industry, is plainly worried. He told me, 'Sun screens are not 100 per cent effective. They're just not.'

But surely they are being advertised as 'full protection'. How could that be?

'Well,' he said warily, 'the cosmetics industry is one of the very few bodies that is studying this problem in a serious way. All I'm saying is we haven't found a complete answer to it yet.'

Nobody, he says, is even sure where the rising threat comes from. Or what has caused the sudden rise in the incidence of skin cancer. The theory that pollution has punched a hole in the protective ozone layer around the earth, with aerosols from spray cans and methane from decomposing food matter, is as likely as any other.

Whatever the cause, the cosmetics companies are fully stretched to take advantage of the ill wind blowing sales their way. When sales of aerosol hair sprays plummeted (at the same time as sun tan lotions) the manufacturers adapted and found a lively new market in products that addressed the new fears.

In Herstein's view, there is a direct link between worries about skin cancer and the recently increased emphasis on skin care. 'Anti-ageing and the greater destructive powers of the sun are one and the same thing,' he believes. 'There are several theories of ageing,' he explained to me, 'but I think they all come back to what we call the "free radical" theory of ageing. That, I believe, has become the most important and relevant issue today. And not just in cosmetics.'

Free radicals are highly charged particles of a molecule which become 'free, and dangerously radical' when released by a molecule breaking up. No scientist has a good word to say for them. Beauty journalist Amanda Cochrane calls them 'a noxious group of substances – highly unstable and reactive'. Experts on ageing, she says, 'theorize that they are largely responsible for age-related changes'. Albert Kligman in Philadelphia blames free radicals for some of the damage resulting from exposure of the skin to the UV rays of the sun. 'It can encourage an attack by these hostile elements,' he told me.

Herstein, like many of his chemist colleagues, is hoping that work now being done on free radicals at Britain's Brunel University, under Professor Robin W. Willson, will yield ways of dealing with them. Tests there have shown that the particles can be turned round by vitamins, which either destroy their potency or actually make them work for, rather than against, our skin cells. It would be comforting to believe, as laboratory tests seem to have indicated as a possibility, that a combination of vitamins C and E would rid the body of any risk from the invaders. But that has yet to be proved. 'It takes a quantum leap of the imagination', writes BBC science reporter

Teresa Hunt in her book *Growing Old, Living Longer*, 'to state that this is what is happening inside the body. Which is why scientists are becoming more and more intrigued by reports of the beneficial effects of vitamins on diseases thought to be due to the effects of free radicals.'

Amanda Cochrane, too, believes that free radicals generated by skin-penetrating ultraviolet A-rays 'may alter the nature of the collagen and elastin fibres lying in the dermis'. She has investigated Skinavenger R, another antidote to sun damage developed by the chemist of the French Rochas company, Elizabeth Papaconstantin, and found the creams 'a delight to use'. They contain, she reports, vitamins E, C, and 'the precursor of A'. 'But surely,' she asks, 'if we eat foods containing these nutrients, we should be afforded sufficient protection from within?'

Apparently not, she was told. How effective they are in preventing free radical damage, or ultraviolet injury, is also a question that could not satisfactorily be answered.

It does seem that, behind the purple smoke of the hype machine, the big companies are not going out of their way to find an ace-in-the-hole solution to sun-related skin damage. As skin cancer continues to increase everywhere in the affluent countries of the world, sun tanning and leisure activities seem to be the most obvious cause.

But, equally, there is the possibility that environmental pollution could be the main factor. Those who expose their bodies to the sun are simultaneously making themselves vulnerable to every other damaging substance in the atmosphere, and these could be a major contributing cause of serious injury to the skin.

We know, for instance, that people who (like Professor Kligman's Buddhist priests) live in darkness *and out of all contact with the outside world* are free of both skin damage and the usual signs of ageing. And it is also a known fact that, until environmental pollution hazards rose to a dangerous level in the second half of the twentieth century, fair-skinned people in South Africa, Australia and California could soak up any amount of sunshine with only the most occasional outbreak of skin disease.

Whatever its cause, the way the cosmetics companies have been tackling the problem has been characteristically defensive. It is hard to avoid a suspicion that they are governed more by fear of losing a profitable market than by a desire to find a solution. Eradication of the threat would send their mounting graphs showing the sales of the new sun block and sun screen products hurtling downwards. Selling creams and lotions that *repair* the damage, on the other hand, has provided a welcome relief.

Anita Roddick apart, no voice is heard demanding an urgent solution to the problem of environmental poisons, or offering to finance such work. I have been unable to discover a single one of the huge sums regularly donated by the companies to charity being directed towards such organizations as Greenpeace and Friends of the Earth.

There are vast and opulent charitable foundations in the beauty jungle. One much praised for its public service is operated at Revlon by Ronald Perelman, assisted by Nancy Tuck Gardiner. Others, including those devoted to funding research and the endowment of a professorial chair in dermatology, unquestionably do meritorious work. But the ill wind withering the leaves of the beauty jungle has blown too much money into the pockets of the big companies to encourage self-destruction.

As always, the Lauder company was among the first to react to the cancer scare. Intensive work by their research chemists produced a 'new' substance – Eyzone – which, the company claimed, replaces ultraviolet-ray damaged skin. Eyzone was said to be particularly effective in women's most vulnerable and sensitive area, around the eyes.

Using the customary pseudo-medical jargon of cosmetic hype, Lauder's promotion explained that the product

> not only acts as a physical support system for the epidermal cells, but also appears to influence their organisation and tell them what to produce. In young skin the basement membrane is undulating and solid, especially that which has been over-exposed to ultraviolet light, the membrane is broken in places and flattened.

And Eyzone would restore that completely.

Lauder's researchers indeed claimed that their magical substance would 'help restructure the frayed basement membrane'. But this, in dermatological opinion, is a harder feat than a successful skin graft. Nevertheless, the report concluded that 'The work has led to the formulation of Tissue Matrix Fluid, which is rich in a type of collagen found in large quantities in the basement membrane itself.' Collagen, of course, is the mystic substance that nothing can reach.

166

Here again it is being thrown into the battle as proof absolute of the magic potency of the product. No matter that it exists only *under* the impenetrable dermis layer of our skin. Or that this inner covering is immune from penetration, or even repair, by anything other than a drug applied topically (that is, to the outer surface) of it. As to the scientific probability of Tissue Matrix Fluid – or any substance with a molecule the size of collagen's – finding its way down below the dermis, both Kligman and Herstein would say that this is 'total nonsense'.

It is, however, a nonsense that sells. Eyzone is currently Estée Lauder's best-selling product in the United States. And it is likely to go on selling, the more the controversy over sun soaking heightens. 'This helps reconstruct, by filling in the gaps,' Lauder claims for the product, 'but only when used continuously.'

How long is 'continuously'? Don't ask.

One way, however, does exist for women to prevent at least the symptoms – and even more importantly, perhaps, the feeling – of growing uselessly old. Hormones, taken orally and in some cases applied vaginally, will replace what menopausal changes reduce, or completely eradicate.

Unfortunately for the cosmetics manufacturers, the use of hormones in cosmetics has been banned for some years. In Europe a directive issued by the EEC in Brussels in 1976 'forbids their use in skin creams or cosmetics', CTRA director general Marion Kelly told me. But there are exceptions, she explained. 'There are two little-used hormones which are shortly to be added to the list.'

In the main, since hormones are listed as drugs, they lie outside the province of cosmetics, and a doctor's prescription is needed to obtain them. But for a woman suffering the discomforts of 'the change', and wanting to replace the natural supply of hormones cut off by oestrogen loss, they can be a boon. Hormone Replacement Therapy, HRT, is increasingly recommended by doctors, with results that testify to its rejuvenating effects.

Properly prescribed and administered, hormones can extend a woman's normal sexual vitality. An implanted hormone pellet not only reduces osteoporosis or bone brittleness – one of the most common effects of oestrogen lack – but helps her to enjoy sexual relationships to the full. The fact that it will only do so during the length of time of the treatment is a major disadvantage, but this

167

deters few of the women who discover renewed vitality and sexual satisfaction while taking it.

One London doctor, Stuart Ungar, prescribes hormones to many of his middle-aged women patients. He implants a special 'hormone cocktail' into those who complain of having lost their normal sex drive due to, or during, the menopause. The drying-up of vaginal fluids is what many women find the most distressing and ageing of all menopausal symptoms. Ungar tells them he is going to install his cocktail in the form of a pellet which will include both oestrogen, to replace the lost hormone, and testosterone, the male hormone. As he explained to me, 'I find that the combination of the two tends to restore a woman's appetite for and enjoyment of sex, where she has lost all desire for it due to the loss of the fluids. It also, of course, reverses many other damaging changes which happen in her body at this time.'

In her book, science broadcaster Teresa Hunt agrees with Dr Ungar. HRT, she writes, comes remarkably close to providing at least a temporary immersion in the waters of the fountain of youth. 'Full-blown rejuvenation is hard to verify, but there have been reports of improved complexion and a reversal of osteoporosis. As well as relieving the uncomfortable side-effects of oestrogen loss, like joint pain, breast pain and swelling, some women say it makes them feel rejuvenated.'

Those who experience this find it hard to believe that *any* woman would not use this apparently harmless addition to the enjoyment of – and prolongation of – a full life. 'Of course I take them,' Betty York, the sun cancer victim, told me. 'My doctors would think me crazy not to, and so would I. Aside from helping to keep vaginal juices flowing, they guard against osteoporosis, which seems to afflict women more than men.'

Do they stimulate her sexual appetite?

She was unable to say. Instead, she pointed to recent reports that the same rays of the sun which have brought cancerous injury to her skin can do this equally well.

There is some scientific basis for this. A founding member of the British Society for Nutritional Medicine, Dr Damien Downing, was quoted in a United Press dispatch during July 1988 as saying that 'after a week in the sun we feel more relaxed and, therefore, less inhibited. Our sex hormones have been given a boost and our whole bodies are tuned for reproduction.'

Downing claims that experimental studies have demonstrated convincingly that 'the level of sex hormones in the body doubles when the back is exposed to sunshine, and triples after the whole body is exposed'. Betty York, despite her injuries, agrees with him. She commented cheerfully. 'He's right! Take me to a warm beach with the right man, and I'll prove it!'

Nor does she deny Dr Downing's assertion that 'We were designed to feed on sunlight, and we suffer if starved of it.' His belief is hardly what the big companies, with their expensively promoted new sun block and sun screen products, want to hear. Downing brazenly advises that 'The secretary who slips out of the office at lunchtime and sunbathes in the park for forty minutes has the right idea. As well as gorgeous brown legs, she is giving herself protection *against* cancer' (my italics).

Whatever we do to make life easier, to make us feel and look better, it seems there are always snags. Nine years ago a distinguished British doctor, a Fellow of the Royal Society of Medicine, was warning women that 'female hormones make the epidermis thinner, more delicate and consequently more likely to wrinkle and age, while they also influence the deposition of fat to make thighs, bottoms and breasts more noticeable'.

In his book *Face Values*, the author of this gloomy prediction, Dr Vernon Coleman, accused 'hormonal changes' of worse things. 'It is also established,' he wrote, 'that the use of steroid injections and creams may be associated with the development of stretch marks (striae). It seems possible that the hormones weaken and rupture the elastic fibres in the dermis while mechanical forces subsequently decide the extent, length, site and direction of the striae.'

Strong words. But Dr Dev Basra, a Fellow of the equally distinguished Royal College of Surgeons, argues the exact opposite today. 'Oestrogen creams, applied externally, give the skin a wonderfully youthful appearance,' he told me. 'These hormones increase the water content in the epidermis and bring about a decrease in the ageing process. The collagen fibre bundles become less fragmented and new elastic fibrils (branches) are formed.'

It seemed reasonable to ask, then, how he could account for the wide gap between these two expert opinions.

'Dr Coleman hasn't done his homework,' Dr Basra told me. 'He's talking about steroids, not oestrogen, isn't he? Oestrogen is not a steroid. And it does put more moisture into the collagen, which gives the body a healthy glow.'

In fact, *Collins Dictionary* includes some hormones under its definition of a steroid. And Dr Coleman specifically refers to 'the hormone oestrogen' in his highly critical conclusion:

The female hormone can cause serious skin problems if used in excessive quantities. There are other disadvantages, too. For example, the skin can become a hormone junkie, needing its daily fix to stay healthy. In addition, there is no proof that I have been able to find to show that female hormones in skin creams relieve dryness, retain moisture or do anything useful to the skin.

So who is to be believed? At about the same time, 1980, that Coleman was writing his book, the then features editor of the London *Times*, Margaret Allen, was researching another book which she called *Selling Dreams*. Of hormone cream containing female hormones of the oestrogen type, she wrote that 'There is no evidence that [they] reach the second layer of the skin, the dermis. So the implication is as with any other skin creams: they cannot restore skin to its youthful appearance, but they may slow down the ageing process.'

More recently still, a wave of fresh excitement in the anti-wrinkling, anti-ageing properties of hormones has arisen with the discovery that one of them, acronymically known as DHEA, appears to increase the maximum lifespan of mice and rats. Regrettably, it was later found that long-term use of it could also lead to tumours. As Teresa Hunt reported: 'It is unlikely to find its way on to the shelves for at least another ten years.'

It does seem that the rising clamour for eternal youth, for an elixir to banish all lines, wrinkles and the cancerous risks of sun tanning, will continue for quite a while yet. Nobody on the manufacturing side is likely to be upset about that – without doubt, the big companies will carry on making hay while the sun shines, UV-induced cancer or not.

Perhaps the outspoken Dr Miriam Stoppard best sums up the dilemma forcing this conclusion. In an introduction to Dr Coleman's book, she wrote, 'I love cosmetics . . . it's the cosmetics industry I can't stand.' Dr Stoppard, of course, was not facing multi-billion dollar stakes in a game that, as it grows hotter and fiercer and more competitive by the year, keeps adding to an ever-lengthening list of victims the players who lose their shirts. But, as she knows, there is a price for everything, and we consumers are usually the simpletons who have to pay it.

17

DRUGS IN DREAMLAND

It is now, in 1989, more than two years since the big cats of the beauty jungle received official notice that their lairs were under serious threat. The authorities were breathing down their necks and ready to force a change in their now close to 'miraculous' claims and puffs. Since it was a change that could cost the industry millions, it is hardly surprising that the FDA in America described the reaction as one of 'astonishment and dismay'.

When, in the spring of 1987, uncompromising regulatory letters from the FDA went to twenty-three of the major cosmetics companies, it was the start of a war that may still ruin more than one of the combatants, if only in lawyers' fees. As the nation's watchdog, the Agency was requesting them to account for claims that they were flagrantly making in magazines, films and every possible area of hype and sizzle – claims that they had added 'magical' anti-ageing and cellular replacement ingredients to their products.

The list of the accused reads like a *Who's Who* of the cosmetics hierarchy. The twenty-three chief executives of Christian Dior, Charles of the Ritz, Prince Matchabelli, Almay, Coty, Rachel Perry, Jason, Frances Denny, Biotherm, 'Jacqueline Cochran La Prairie' – (as the fast-changing company was addressed), – Princess Matchabelli, Borghese, Chanel, Elizabeth Arden, Germaine Monteil, Orlane, Caron, Max Huber, Clarins, Estée Lauder, Avon, Adrien Arpel, Cosmair and Shiseido were flatly challenged. No British company was involved, nor any of the popular, low-priced brands such as Oil of Olay (Beecham's Oil of Ulay in the UK) and Unilever's Vaseline Intensive Care and Ponds creams. It was an attack on the richest and most prestigious in the trade.

For eight years they had successfully been holding the under-staffed and tightly budgeted FDA in Washington at bay with complex arguments put up by their lawyers. It had given them the

172

comfortable illusion of being able to satisfy the law, if not exactly to remain within it. It had even led them to think that such a terrible thing as this crackdown could never happen, that they were free to add more and more glitter to the blandishments and hyperbole of their ads. And, rashly, they had been tempted by this false sense of security to gamble on 'discoveries' that they claimed could do what only drugs could do. (Under the strict definition of the US statutory ruling a cosmetic can only make physical, that is superficial, differences; while anything altering the physiology of the human body must be a drug, and subject to official sanction.)

That was going too far. If these things were drugs, then they must be so defined, and immediately submitted for rigorous clinical testing and approval. Furthermore, should they be approved as such, they would then only be available on a doctor's prescription.

All that the letters, signed by FDA director Daniel L. Michels, initially requested was either immediate withdrawal of the claims or submission for testing as drugs. As Michels pointed out to Leonard Lauder, 'This letter is in reference to a representative selection of your Estée Lauder skin treatment products.'

'In reference to' was a pregnant euphemism. No fewer than seven of Lauder's leading products – Night Repair Cellular Recovery Complex; Eyzone Repair Gel; Skin Perfecting Creme Firming Nourisher; Prescriptives Line Preventor; and the popular Estée Lauder nourishers Swiss Eye Creme, Swiss Neck Creme and Age Controlling Creme – were held to be 'in serious violation of the Federal Food, Drugs, and Cosmetic Act of 1938'.

In his summary, Michels stated that these (and a number of other equally assertively labelled products) 'suggest that the articles are intended to affect the structure and function of the human body'. Because of this, 'The products are regarded as drugs as defined in section 201(g) of the Federal Food, Drug, and Cosmetic Act.' He added conclusively: 'Also, we are unaware of any substantial scientific evidence that demonstrates the safety and effectiveness of these articles. Nor are we aware that these drugs are generally recognized as safe and effective for their intended uses. Therefore, the products are new drugs within the meaning of . . . the Act.'

A similar letter reached Hicks B. Waldron, chairman of the board of directors of Avon Products. Avon's eulogistic claims on behalf of four of their top-selling products – Bioadvance Beauty Recovery System, Momentum Cell Energising Formula, Night Support Skin

Revitalizing Formula and Collagen Booster Line Controlling Lotion – were all questioned.

As with Estée Lauder, Michels demanded submission for testing as drugs, or retraction of Avon's claims that 'the products are adequate and effective for cell renewal, reversal of signs of facial ageing, increased collagen production, cell repair and other claims'. By way of a *coup-de-grâce*, his letter again spelled out the damning fact that: 'We are also unaware . . . that these drugs are generally recognized as safe and effective for their intended uses.' If they were indeed drugs, then, as the director pointed out, 'these products are in serious violation of the Act'.

Michels spared none of the suspects. In each individual case he detailed his reasons why the scores of products listed, and possibly others not under review, were allegedly illegal. He was signalling that the fat cats and their games were no longer to be tolerated. They must justify their claims, or admit that they were promising more than their products were capable of. Either way, it was a savage blow.

It took the cosmetics companies three months to build a defence against his attack. After a stalling meeting with the Agency on 11 September 1987 a fifty-five-page document was delivered to the desk of the associate commissioner for regulatory affairs at the FDA, John M. Taylor, in Washington. It was signed by the legal counsels representing twelve of the twenty-three companies under review (Avon, Lauder, Clarins USA, Shiseido, Dior, Chanel, Arden, La Prairie, Jacqueline Cochran, Arpel, Orlane and Denny), and their assembled legal brains set out to 'resolve this matter fairly, expeditiously, and in a cooperative manner'.

Their way of doing so was to argue, point by point, that the distinction between cosmetics and drugs should be left largely to common sense. With healthy and no doubt expensive optimism, the lawyers offered a 'conceptual framework' for consideration. It had not, they said, been easy to formulate, but 'we believe that we have found a way to harmonize the various and sometimes conflicting legal, scientific, commercial, and practical realities of marketing cosmetic products that is workable for both FDA and industry.'

They had believed wrong. The outcome, at the time of writing in early 1989, is still to be delivered. But by late 1988 the first shots were being fired, the first casualties listed. Estée Lauder had filed suit against the FDA, alleging harassment and restriction of trade. The FDA, it was widely believed, was preparing to seize 'mislabeled product', and to institute litigation in the US District Court against the companies responsible. Then, in a dramatic front-page announcement in his *Cosmetic World* on 5 December, John Ledes reported the confiscation of a 'shipment of cosmetic and skin-care products' belonging to one of the threatened companies.

In May 1988 Ledes had gone to press protesting that 'the reasoning and logic used in the decisional process of the FDA seems irrational'. By this latest action, and perhaps provoked by Lauder's legal counter-attack, the Agency seemed conclusively to be demonstrating that there was nothing irrational in the way it was prepared to deal with the situation.

Signs of edginess were beginning to show. Would the FDA accept the companies' basic refutation of all its main accusations? Ledes had asked. Would the companies be allowed to carry on as before, but with even more freedom to offer tempting illusions of everlasting youth? The editor had consistently trailed this provocative cloak in his columns, inviting the FDA to charge or admit defeat. Now he had his answer.

But John Ledes is not a quitter. Under what he caustically labelled the FDA's 'skincare scam', the campaigning editor claimed that 'the threat to seize skincare products . . . has left an impression with the public – and even some retailers in the trade – that there is an element of danger . . . There is no danger to the public.'

In other words, the FDA had been wasting its time and the nation's money. That is not quite what Amelia Bassin, another well-informed watcher of the game, had warned in her popular newsletter to the trade. 'So here we are,' she wrote, 'face to face with the future. If we keep on doing what we're doing, our future is bleak; we'll self-destruct.'

Bassin's logical appreciation of the situation was not what the big manufacturers wanted to hear but after twenty years with Fabergé in New York this expert knows as well as anyone alive what would happen if the authorities really got tough and began impounding the products under threat. An already scared retail trade would dive under its counter and rip out pages from its order books as if a second Flood was heralded.

Sitting in her Manhattan office-apartment in February 1988, Bassin hinted to me of trends already pointing in that direction.

175

'If Shiseido is marketing their new product (BH 24) in a way that suggests it is a drug, or is close to being a drug, then I think they are quite wrong to do so. The FDA investigation is in the claims, which in many cases are in the names. So you have a product like Night Repair or Cellular Recovery Complex and it's right there, on the label, clear as day. Or even something as fantastic as Moon Drops – that's a line-preventer by Estée Lauder. They may get around it, but the FDA are threatening to sue, the companies are threatening to sue back, and so I don't think Shiseido's new product will sell.'

In Tokyo, concern showed on the faces of Shiseido's top management when I raised the question. 'It could,' one of the senior executives on the commercial side told me warily, 'make a big, a very big difference. Yes. Very costly for us if we should have, for any reason, to adjust our marketing technique, which is based on the valuable research we are doing.'

Shiseido know, from high-tech research into the needs of women in every country they go into, that their revolutionary 'cellular improvement' techniques are among the most attractive in cosmetics today. But they are also extremely costly. And the drain on their resources has shown in recent poor financial results. If the FDA ruling goes against them, the question of how they would cope with the situation is acutely worrying. But like the other twenty-two they must wait and see.

In Britain another formidable critic of misleading claims, senior professor of dermatology Malcolm Greaves, has been constantly badgering the industry over the years. It has a commitment, he maintains, to distinguish in its claims between those products that can only be drugs and those that are cosmetics. Having recently been persuaded to carry the fight further, by writing a book which will clearly define the British attitude to all claims, Grieves is due to add unwelcome weight to the attack.

Thus John Ledes' conviction that there is no danger to the public from the present situation looks increasingly naïve. The danger is that all those alluring assurances and promises may soon have to be withdrawn, or strenuously modified. At whose cost? Ultimately, of course, the customer will pay. But if that means that what goes into the products will then measure up to what is claimed for them, then perhaps it will be worth it. The FDA believes it will. Slow though it is to act, its determination is unquestionably in the public interest.

Asserting that 'time has run out for the cosmetic industry',

Deborah Blumenthal, an experienced journalist writing in the *New York Times* in May 1988, predicted that the Agency, 'fed up with a profusion of therapeutic-sounding claims in labeling and promotion', had 'put cosmetic companies on notice to watch their language'. This, she believed, could very well mean that it would 'shortly act by seizing the offending lines'. Failure by the companies to comply with the new directive on working 'could result in the forced removal of products from the marketplace', Blumenthal wrote. The products, she maintained, would remain the same, but the surrealist nature of some of the claims would disappear. It had taken the FDA nearly twenty years (as the lawyers representing the defendants pointed out) to bring these guns to bear. How long would it now take to find the range, and make the shots effective?

In November 1987 John M. Taylor, associate commissioner for regulatory affairs, gave the Agency's reply to the lawyers who had prepared the defence on behalf of the twelve protesting companies. 'After fully considering your letter, we feel that the principles you suggest would permit manufacturers to make drug claims on products that would be regulated as cosmetics. Therefore, we cannot accept the great majority of these principles.' There was to be no deal.

'Most of the anti-ageing and skin physiology claims that you outline,' Taylor explained,

> are drug claims, because they can fairly be understood as claims that a function of the body, or that the structure of the body, will be affected by the product. For this reason also, all of the examples that you use to allege an effect within the epidermis as the basis for a temporary beneficial effect on wrinkles, lines, or fine lines are unacceptable.

At the same time the commissioner rejected the companies' claims for comparison with a number of their leading sun screen and skin care products. 'Products that affect the structure and the function of the body in the ways that you describe, or that prevent or mitigate disease, are drugs and must be scrutinized by FDA in the manner prescribed by the Act,' he wrote.

It was left to each company individually to respond within thirty days 'as to the measures that it will take to correct the violations cited'. Failure to do so, he said, would mean that 'the Agency will take such action as it deems necessary to resolve its regulatory concerns.'

Yet nothing more drastic followed. And the accused were still on remand. As we looked out over Tokyo bay from the panoramic windows of Shiseido's offices in the Ginza district, I asked Yasutaka Mori, deputy general manager of the company's international operations division, how they hoped to meet the threat.

He laughed, uneasily I thought. 'It is a rather touchy area. We do not yet know exactly what they will permit, and what they will not. Which is very restrictive for us, seeking to expand at the present time.'

At the beginning of December 1987, he told me, the FDA had agreed to let each of the twelve companies negotiate individually. 'Then on 18 December they asked each of us to make a proposal. We sent ours, but so far we have not received any reaction from the FDA.' Mori added that he did not know exactly what Shiseido's proposal was, 'but we are ready to negotiate'. In Japan, as he explained, things are very different. 'Regulations are strict. The activities of all cosmetics companies are under the direction of the Ministry of Health and Welfare.'

For this reason, and the fact that his company, according to their director in London, 'Sam' Sugiyama, spends so much on research, Mori and his colleagues feel 'very confident of the outcome'. But I was also told, by one of his senior colleagues, that the cost to them should they be forced to make major changes would be 'colossal'.

Remembering how the mere hint of an impending crackdown by the FDA on earlier wild claims made for Dr Christiaan Barnard's 'miracle' product, Glycel, had forced its withdrawal and the loss of millions of dollars for its backers in America, Alfin Fragrances, one wonders if any of the other threatened companies would share Shiseido's confidence.

In 1986 Barnard, world-renowned as South Africa's surgical heart transplant originator, entered the beauty jungle with every hope of making a killing. His product promised miracles of skin care and age reversal, and was backed in an $11 million launch by America's shrewd and tenacious Irwin Alfin. Glycel was an immediate hot seller.

Unfortunately, Alfin's lore deserted him before the product could recoup more than a fraction of his outlay. The backer had either read the writing on the wall more diligently than the others under review, or he had recognized that in his case the stakes were too high to make possible any reasonable defence of Glycel. As soon as the FDA seriously indicated that the claims being made for the stuff needed substantiation or alteration he pulled out, losing the millions he had put into the launch and very nearly sacrificing his whole business.

Why he did so in such haste remains something of a mystery. While doing research in Switzerland, Barnard had claimed to have discovered an entirely new and secret ingredient, which, he said, was the basis for the preparation. The surgeon, whose chemistry and scientific skills are not the best recognized of his qualities, no doubt believed it had both curative and anti-ageing properties when applied to the skin. When severe arthritis in his hands prevented Barnard from carrying on with the delicate transplant operations that had made him famous, he sought a sideline to compensate for his lost and profitable professional career. It was then that he decided to bring his discovery to the market.

Barnard also seems to have been influenced by the course of cellular rejuvenating treatment, as we know, he had recently taken in Switzerland, at La Prairie, the clinic founded by the imaginative Dr Niehans. According to its director, Dr Eddé, Barnard became a patient in the hope that the injections would restore the use of his hands. While there, he no doubt studied reports of dramatic new work being done in Mexico, where implanted cellular tissue in the brains of patients suffering from Alzheimer's and Parkinson's diseases was producing remarkable results.

Eddé told me, during my visit to the clinic, that Dr Barnard was so impressed by the Swiss techniques that they must have influenced his decision to launch his discovery on the world. Whatever prompted him, there was no doubt that, with his fame and scientific reputation, Barnard would have no difficulty in finding a backer for his dream; or that it would be an initial success on the market.

The fact that Glycel contained – as the doctor vouched with professional authority – an astonishingly effective and new (to cosmetics) if unpronounceable substance, 'glycosphingolipid', lent it immediate and massive appeal. When he and Irwin Alfin formed an alliance to market the product, the latter's excitement at being able to announce the great surgeon's own discovery (Barnard was fully prepared to authorize claims to the effect that Glycel possessed an ingredient

179

with 'the ability to cause the rejuvenation of cells') was more than understandable.

Neither had any reason to suspect that the product, launched in January 1986, would be among the first victims – or indeed become the catalyst of – a new and totally unheralded FDA purge. Alfin was horrified when asked to account for the claims made on Glycel's behalf, especially as similarly miraculous-sounding products were being advertised by several of Alfin Fragrances' biggest rivals.

As always when threatened by a dangerous novelty, the big lions had turned copycat. Alarmed by the attraction of Alfin's bid – the strength of claims backed by such an eminent and highly respected medical expert as Dr Christiaan Barnard – they had rushed out a variety of similar anti-ageing miracle creams and potions. Avon's contribution was Bio-advance, billed as an 'anti-ageing cream'. Estée Lauder increased its promotion of Night Repair Cellular Recovery Complex. Clarins, not to be outdone, was trumpeting the marvels of its Anti-Ageing Total Skin Supplement. All were ready to stand firm against any FDA inquisition if it should happen, and were relying on their lawyers to prevent the Agency from forcing them to make costly changes in their advertising copy and labelling.

Then, to their horror, Irwin Alfin raised the white flag. After only sixteen months, in May 1987, he pulled Glycel off the market without a writ being served. Barnard's product was dead almost before it had drawn breath, and the illustrious heart transplant surgeon was being regarded by many as little more than a publicity-seeking commercial adventurer. His first and to date only bid to enter the beauty business had left him with few friends there.

Irwin Alfin was less bothered about friends than about trying to save his whole corporate structure from collapse. As John Ledes reported, 'pulling Glycel back [which had been furiously denounced by some industry critics] stopped the bleeding from legal fees and other costs and set up the company to refile prior year tax returns.' By this ruse Alfin later managed to recoup $11 million and, as Ledes cheerfully concluded, 'set the company firmly back from red to black at the bottom lines'.

A happy ending? Not quite. As Ledes also confirmed, there were still several of Irwin Alfin's competitors and colleagues in the cosmetics industry who seriously believed that it was only his hasty scupper that had brought the wrath of the FDA down on them all. They blamed Alfin for lack of confidence in Barnard's product, and for an act of bad faith 'that would mark the end of his ambitious plans for the company'. In fact, his decision and prompt action may have saved the day for his shareholders, his retailers and himself.

But just why did Irwin Alfin take such an immediate and precipitous dive at the cost of his entire launch budget and production costs? Until now the full reason has been kept a closely guarded secret in the industry, which offers nearly as many theories about it as there are shades of lipstick.

To John Ledes, the answer is simply that Alfin's and Barnard's claims were too incredible. The editor of *Cosmetic World* told me that in his mind there is no room for doubt that Alfin's claims were the problem. 'They were a circus! I predicted when he brought Glycel out that this would happen. I called it a circus then, in print. So what could he do? When he had to face up to it, he just ran. They had a patent, but it was never processed through. And as for Barnard's "magic ingredient" he's supposed to have found, don't listen to that hogwash! He didn't find anything!'

Yet since the scandal Ledes has constantly published supportive comments about Alfin and his return to prosperity. So which is it?

In the reduced offices of Alfin Fragrances, Micheline Mas denied that FDA pressure had forced her company's hand. 'Our competitors put it around that Glycel could cause cancer,' this young executive told me. 'That was what really killed it.' A sad story, very sad, and in her opinion completely unnecessary. 'The product was, and is, remarkable.'

Did she use it herself?

'Oh sure,' she said, laughing. 'I'm seventy-two!'

A far more sinister version of what caused the FDA to take the action it did was told me by a man who held a top position in the New York cosmetics world at the time. 'It was an industry conspiracy. Glycel had to be stopped, even if it meant informing the FDA that the claims being made for it were insupportable. So somebody put it to the Agency that if they did not act to pull the product off the shelves, the industry would see to it that the FDA's name was dragged through the mire for allowing it to go unchallenged.'

This executive laughs now at the way he believes the assassination attempt boomeranged. 'It was a panic move, based on fear and jealousy of Barnard's reputation,' he explained. 'Nobody thought it through and realized that the FDA would not just go after Glycel if they had to act – they'd go for the industry as a whole. Because we were all doing it, making wild claims. Glycel was just the pebble that launched an avalanche.'

According to Catherine Stott, who interviewed Christiaan Barnard for the London *Sunday Telegraph* in June 1986, the surgeon's only profits from Glycel were to come from the Swiss research company, the Schaefer Institute in Basle, which had developed the product. His royalties amounted to 3 per cent of 5 per cent. He told Stott: 'I didn't even know what was in Glycel apart from my ingredient. All I know is that it works. I use it myself, and people keep telling me how well I look.'

If Irwin Alfin had any serious doubts, he kept them to himself. One of his henchmen at the time told me: 'We believed the product was as good as we said it was. But somebody in the industry, maybe more than one, complained to the FDA that we were making false and untrue claims. They just wanted us out of the way.'

Nasty, but then as Elizabeth Arden once unguardedly said, cosmetics can be a nasty business. No lioness defends her cubs more fiercely than the big cats of that industry when fighting for a product.

Stanley Kohlenberg, while still president of Sanofi Products, assured me that he had actual evidence that information was laid with the FDA against Glycel by forces inside the industry. As head of an important and rising cosmetics and fragrance group, and someone who had worked with Irwin Alfin at Revlon, Kohlenberg watched every move. He told me he has no doubt that Irwin was 'shopped' by people from his own side.

Two things contributed to the fiasco, in his opinion. 'First, Irwin basically is a fragrance maker – he used to work for Chanel – and skin treatment is an entirely different business. It takes much more time to hype a treatment product into orbit. This is a business you have to build a door at a time, a store at a time. You create a network of distributors, sampling, building card-files of customers, creating confidence. You don't expect a huge explosion. All you can hope for is a steady growth over a period of years, up to a kind of plateau which, if you're lucky, you stay on.

'Irwin went for what you can get in the fragrance business – quick results. Right now, it is a kind of a boom-and-bust cycle. You get a Giorgio that shoots all the way up, to as high as it's ever gone – $140 million or whatever – then starts to slide. But that doesn't happen in skin care. So, to begin with, I don't think Irwin was prepared for the treatment business. He didn't fully understand it.

'And number two, the claims were outrageous. Not only were they outrageous, but this was the first time in history that we can recall a physician putting his name to a cosmetic line. We've had linkage, sure. There was some kind of suggestion that Lauder's Clinique line, when it appeared, was backed by the medical profession. But that was only a whispering campaign. This was hype. In terms of hype, you've got to say that it was well done. But too well done.

'Dr Barnard went on national TV talking about "cells with a memory". Here he was, a very colourful man talking about how this product triggered the memory of our body cells. And then having the entire medical community come back at him, when no doctor had ever endorsed a treatment line before!

'As a result of that, the initial selling was enormous. But there were problems. Expectations were raised higher than you might expect. And then the products themselves were not necessarily the most elegant. Just from an aesthetic point of view, they didn't feel as good as some of the other creams that had been around for a long time.

'So, first, you bought this thing and used it, and you still weren't young overnight. Then, second, the products didn't feel as good as what you'd been using before. And third, suddenly the entire industry is up in arms about the undue advantage that a physician would have! That was what really killed it for Irwin. Someone from the industry blew the whistle to the FDA. Two men. We know who they are.'

Would he say? Stanley Kohlenberg is an unusually frank man. He has a great many friends and a shrewd inside knowledge of the business.

He told me, 'The initial complaint came from the attorney at Cosmair, the American end of L'Oréal. That's the one I definitely know about. But John Ledes had been printing a lot of attacks on Irwin, virtually every week in *Cosmetic World*. And I know they don't get along. So I believe that the combination of press pressure and the letter from the lawyers forced the FDA to act.'

Kohlenberg continued, 'When they did act they overacted perhaps, and attacked the entire industry. I've lived through three FDA reviews – one in 1959, one in the early seventies, and now this one. So it had to be expected, after all. I was just sitting here waiting for it to happen, for someone suddenly to say "That's enough! You can't talk about cell penetration and all of the things you're talking about now, because these are drug claims!" We knew, we all knew, that at some point the FDA would step in.'

It was no accident, he says, that his own company's skin care brand, Stendhal, was not on the FDA's blacklist. 'We were being a little more careful in terms of knowing. And we didn't have the kind of miracle products – *supposed* miracle products – that were being offered. Also I'd been through it before, so I was aware of what would happen.'

Kohlenberg had been with Helena Rubinstein in 1959 when one of her skin care creams, The Tree of Life, was outlawed by the FDA. 'She was eighty-nine then, and boasting that this cream had special rejuvenatory powers, on account of the fact that it contained placental liquid, the womb's natural protective element. Lots of others came out with the same thing, and the FDA stepped in and finally banned the stuff in American products.'

Rubinstein's product was renamed Essence and Kohlenberg, working on the advertising side of the business, was forced to drop his miracle rejuvenation claims. 'We started all over again, using herbs in place of placenta. It cost us a lot of money.' And claims which were being made widely by other cosmetics companies for the magical use of 'living cells' from placentas disappeared faster than the wrinkles they were supposed to eliminate.

As usual in the skin game, as soon as one major player threw in his hand the others folded with him. The FDA threatened all users. Placentas were out, finished, though whether because they were held to be drugs or for reasons of ethical taste Kohlenberg never discovered.

'In the early seventies Coty and Revlon got involved in a serum, a product called Lineaway. It wasn't really a drug, and we made no claims for it being a drug. But we did say that it eliminated wrinkles, while what we should have said was that it only took away the *visible appearance* of wrinkles. The FDA came in again and seized the product right off the shelves of both Coty and Revlon.'

The product, he says, was not a good one. 'So it would have died anyway. It used to flake on your face if you smiled. Lineaway was an albumen product which dried like egg, and stretched the wrinkles. It also reflected the light so you couldn't see them. Nice, so long as you didn't move your face.'

He agreed that today's crisis could cost millions in relabelling, changing advertising copy, reshooting television commercials and even, in some cases, forcing the withdrawal or seizure of whole batches of product around the world. Claims aside, if an ingredient were outlawed the effect on even the biggest manufacturer would be close to crippling.

'The period we're in right now is very touchy,' Stanley Kohlenberg explained. 'We don't know how far back we have to go. And the problem is that some of the large individual companies will fight the various rules. And those of us who are not necessarily in the position to fight, or who do not want to fight, may be at an unfair disadvantage for a while.'

Kohlenberg's dilemma is shared by many of the lesser lights. On the day we talked the *New York Times* was forecasting – with what read like chauvinist glee – that

makers of anti-ageing creams now must either prove drug-like claims to be literally true, or abandon the strange vocabulary of 'cellular effects' and 'microsomes', which the FDA insists must have specific meaning. But that's not so terrible an imposition. All the FDA is asking is that fantasy and reality be kept separate. The cosmetic companies need only retreat back to fantasy, and their customers will live happily as before.

In fact, on what Amelia Bassin called 'a bloody battlefield surrounded by marshmallow fudge swamplands and glittering, cottoncandy jungles' the whole beauty business was tilting, with lawyers' lances, at the FDA enemy, and falling back on all fronts.

'Our most recent chart would show something that to me is absolutely horrifying,' she told me. 'In three of our major categories, sales are down. In skin care, hair care and fragrance: *down* – despite steadily increasing prices and golden bulls running rampant on Wall Street. Down – even though we keep introducing, year after year, dozens upon dozens of socko fragrances, and all kinds of wonderful, breakthrough, never-before, visibly different, new-technology clones for ageing skin and hair and everything else we can think of. Down for the very first time in my memory, and that's long!'

Was all this due to Irwin Alfin and Dr Christiaan Barnard's little escapade? Did the disaster stem entirely from Alfin's decision to pull the Glycel magic off the world's shelves with such feverish haste?

The FDA is not prepared to say. Like every government agency there has ever been since the signing of the Magna Carta, the Agency will make only general if-and-but statements. 'The anti-ageing products cited have never been considered as cosmetics,' I was told. 'They are new drugs. If the companies want to market them, then they must accept the regulations governing drugs.'

No matter that grave professional questions are being asked in Britain, and in the great French houses that sell in the USA where 50 per cent of the European cosmetics market is. The FDA concerns itself only with the safety of the public. It is not its business if withdrawal of the ads, and repackaging of the products, ruins an industry.

Amelia Bassin is disgusted by the whole thing. She understands and supports the need to protect the safety of the cosmetic-using public. But it upsets her that it took Dr Barnard's Glycel fiasco to twitch the dragon's tail, to awaken the FDA to what had been going on for years. 'I'm right at the point now,' she said, 'where I suspect that the motivation behind many of the lawsuits is not only punishment deserved or justice earned. It is vengeance, vindication and plain old jealousy!

'Glycel got off to a terrific start. It made a splash, mostly because Dr Barnard was associated with it. But the claims made for it were certainly no worse than those made for many of the skin care products around.'

Then were those who complained to the FDA not acting in the public interest?

'I'm guessing,' Bassin admitted, 'but I'd say the FDA was fearful that they were going to be shown up as not watching out for the consumer. So they had to take action – and not only against Glycel – to protect themselves. That is how the industry has hanged itself.'

Amelia Bassin's guesswork may be closer to the truth than the government agency would like to admit – or ever would admit. It leaves unanswered the question of where the US cosmetics industry stands now.

18

FULFILMENT

In his medical school office in Philadelphia, with pictures of unbelievably terrible skin diseases – deep corrugations, rashes and ferocious disfigurements of all kinds – on its walls, Professor Albert Kligman stands on the far edge of the beauty business, a respecter of all that's good and a harsh critic of everything bad in it. Let the last word come from him.

Kligman sees appearance as a vital part of health. But he also knows the sins of the entire sprawling, multi-billion dollar cosmetics industry. He has seen its leaders in all their guises and, scientifically, he has assessed the value of their dreams. If there is any doubt about the merits of appearance, or of the cosmetics that offer to improve us in the eyes of the world, this man should share it.

He does no such thing. To him, cosmetics are valuable aids, however infamously they are ballyhooed and hyped. He refuses to accept that ageing should push people on to shelves and leave them with nothing but their memories. He will not listen to those who see appearance as mere vanity or wimpish conceit.

'That's one of the biggest goddam illusions of all Western society!' he said, tapping my knee to emphasize his point. 'We declare that we judge each other by internal criteria – by character, compassion etc. It ain't true! Almost all our judgements are based on personal appearance. Getting a new job, dates . . . every study that has been done shows that it is the good-looking, the beautiful, who have the advantage. They get the first chance!'

He sighed, leaning back in his chair. The man whom many regard as the free world's greatest expert on cosmetic disorders and the care of skin seems to have the cares of an ageing world on his shoulders. 'Otherwise, why do those who are disfigured get sicker more often? Why don't they live as long? I'll tell you why. People who don't meet tne norm are physically handicapped. That is why I take appearance to be a medical problem.'

Not all Professor Kligman's colleagues, I learned, agree with this humane diagnosis. 'They think I've gone bonkers in my old age,' he told me, grinning mischievously. 'They say I'm getting away from science. But I have a clinic for ageing skin, and I see a lot of women.

'When I used to see someone of twenty-five with a little wrinkle, I'd say, "It's nothing, forget it – that's not serious." Well, I don't do that any more. I do my best to help them at any age.

'I've learnt that the penalty for being unhandsome – especially with age – is severe. And it's no longer a matter of personal judgement. We've done enough studies to know that it's true. Let me assure you, a little old lady who's ugly is in a bad situation. I'll tell you. If you are unhandsome and you come into any hospital, intending to stay for two weeks, you'd be better off signing out the day you get there! Hospital is a dangerous place for people who look prematurely old!'

Can Professor Kligman really mean dangerous? Is it not the proud boast of every hospital that the rate of curing is as high as it is possible to be?

Kligman tossed aside the query. 'If you come in looking like an old, beat-up person – as if you're going to die whatever happens . . . well, I have to tell you that nobody is going to hold your hand. They've got too many post-surgical crises threatening death every minute to worry about a poor old lady who is *not* dying, who just looks awful and who scares the shit out of everybody.'

Professor Kligman's warning was confirmed by doctors, nurses and patients everywhere. A retired senior radiographer in London told me, 'I'm afraid he's perfectly right. It's very sad, but if somebody really does look past it, they aren't likely to be moved to the head of the queue. More likely they'll be pushed aside by some seemingly more urgent case. As Dr Kligman says, it doesn't do to look too bad.'

And Albert Kligman does not just talk. He crusades against this attitude to the ugly, the old and the unsightly. Anything that can help them has his approval, provided it does not promise more than it can deliver. 'Losing youth, losing appearance through the ageing process, is one of the most distressing things that happens to a human being,' he said.

'Older people frighten young people. We've done tests, showing pictures of a really old-looking woman – who in fact was only in her early fifties – to young students, then asking if they think she'd make a nice granny. The answer? Always negative. "Christ!" they say, "If I have to look like that, get me out of here!" That's why I am very serious about ageing.'

It is also the reason why his work identifies so closely with the beauty business. Cosmetics, inescapably, have become the chief tools of his dermatological trade. A lipstick and mirror are often better therapy than a whole slab of painkillers.

Albert Kligman's words stayed in my mind while writing this book. 'We have added thirty years on to the human lifespan,' he told me. 'We celebrate that as an achievement, but you have to ask – is it such a gift?'

In Tokyo I had perhaps come closest to finding an answer to the question. Dr Ozawa's chilling prediction of cosmetics being vital to our future offered hope. Shiseido's chief scientific director's forecast – that cosmetics would cover up the worst effects of genetic engineering and 'spare parts' surgery, to keep pace with our greatly extended lifespan – made a sort of sci-fi, if horrific, sense.

It was easy to share Professor Kligman's worries, but Ozawa seemed to be offering an altogether more inspiring vision. 'It has been man's aspiration since the dawn of history to seek longevity and perpetual youthfulness,' he pointed out. 'Now that molecular biology has taken a major step in the direction of progress, there is the promise of untold blessings for the human race.'

Blessings? Well, certainly in this cosmetics chemist's view, undreamed of advantages would fall to his own industry. 'Despite warning voices,' Ozawa had said, 'all future scientific approach routes to the phenomenon of life have been placed on solid foundations. The continuing search for the secrets of life will see us into the twenty-first century, with immense consequences for our particular field of interest, the science of cosmetics.'

And 'spare parts' – replacing limbs and organs worn out by time and use – must play a crucial part in this. His work with the Mitsubishi company's research centre had recently offered an appendix to Dr Ozawa's visionary assessment of man's future. 'The main innovations in life science that will shape our future are revolutions in biology, new materials, the data revolution, robotics and fibre optics technology,' the company forecast had stated. It went on:

> In 1993 the structure of the antigen will be unveiled, allowing safe artificial vaccines to be produced by synthesis. A year later it will be possible to synthesize a variety of substances under near-constant temperature and pressure.
>
> 1995 will bring the final clarification of the mechanism of immune response, thereby creating the possibility of adjusting immunological phenomena by the use of drugs [and thus, presumably, leading to an antidote for AIDS, and other attacks on the body's immune system].
>
> As history passes over the threshold of the year 2000 and enters the twenty-first century, new insights will be made into the mechanism of cell generation. Cancer prevention will be brought within the bounds of possibility. By the year 2003 mankind will have come close to understanding the mechanism of artificial manipulative applications.

Even more important to the industry, further progress, as Dr Ozawa maintains, will have to provide an increased understanding of the behaviour of ageing, along with techniques to delay its effect on our skins. 'It is my considered view,' he told me, 'that a great contribution can be expected from "added values" generated by our cosmetics industry. Progress in cosmetic science in the twenty-first century will move further towards unveiling the internal mechanism of skin ageing, creating the possibility of reducing this by controlling cell division.'

Ozawa himself forecasts revolutionary achievements in make-up and fragrances. 'The current trend is to reinforce the moisturizing ability of the skin with a foundation designed to beautify,' he explains. 'We will see the development of new, highly sophisticated foundations, using volatile silicones and new types of silicone resins.'

Wrinkles will be made to appear less prominent. Novel pearl materials will produce fresh colours through the skilful use of light interference phenomena. 'And the psychological effect of fragrances now being highlighted is another interesting new field,' Dr Ozawa says. 'I feel that the science of fragrance holds the key to much greater development.'

But he warns that these goals are not going to drop neatly into the cosmetics companies' laps. 'Our survival will critically depend on our ongoing ability to react sensitively to these developments. This means a very tough challenge, where the reality makes the effort worthwhile. For these thoughts make it clear that the twenty-first century can bring the resurrection of man.'

With spare parts for our bodies as readily available as for our fridges and cars, Ozawa believes that only cosmetics can offer the skills and products needed to cover over the cracks. Already there are reports that today's teenagers regard transplant surgery as a fact of life. And it now seems that every single part of the human body except the central nervous system could theoretically be replaced.

In July 1987 a Thai surgeon claimed the world's first penis transplant. And testicles – capable of permitting fatherhood – are available for as little as £80 a pair. Such possibilities of genetic engineering are limitless and – to some – terrifying.

So the ultimate question of the value of cosmetics, irrespective of how much we pay for them or how many risks are involved, becomes more and more bewildering with each passing year. One thing we know. Good, bad or bunkum, the use of them does a power of good for the ego.

Professor Kligman is not alone in believing that appearance is an underestimated part of human equipment. The actor Walter Matthau recently explained in a BBC broadcast why he and Barbra Streisand were not speaking to each other during the making of a film. 'She is very insecure,' the famous joker said. 'She thinks she is not good-looking. I, on the other hand . . .'

And thirty-five years ago Joseph Hansen, leader of the Socialist Workers' Party in the United States, found that deriding the value of cosmetics as an aid to spiritual wellbeing can be politically as well as socially disastrous. One day when he was short of material to fill his Marxist magazine, *Militant*, Hansen composed an attack on all cosmetics and high fashion. They were symptoms, he sneered, of 'the oppression of working women' in the class system. He then published his diatribe as a letter, under a pen-name.

To his astonishment and dismay, it resulted in one of the largest and most heatedly hostile postbags the magazine had ever received from its readers. The editor had reviled the owners of the big cosmetics companies who, he said, 'manipulate women's insecurities and fears to . . . rake in massive profits'. One of the angry letters protested that 'the writer is challenging the right of working-class women to strive for some loveliness and beauty in their lives'. Another complained that

> Beauty is predominantly monopolized by the wealthy. The wealthy are beautiful because the workers are wretched. Of course the standards are bourgeois, but they are the norms that women have to meet. If women want these things, they should have them. It is part of the struggle of women to emancipate themselves from the status of household drudges and to acquire an individuality of their own.

Hansen, keeping up his alias, retorted that 'the customs and norms of capitalist society are ridiculous and even vicious, including the customs and norms of wealthy, bourgeois women'. It was no good. His women readers refused to be denied the balm and uplift of cosmetics.

So strong were the feelings expressed that in October 1954 the political committee of the SWP published a *Discussion Bulletin* containing seriously debated arguments on both sides of the issue. It was intended to settle the question one way or the other. Had Marx preached against cosmetics? Were they merely the evil tools of bourgeois oppression?

A leading contributor, Marjorie McGowan of Los Angeles, wrote: 'There is nothing beautiful in dishpan hands, premature wrinkles, scraggly hair, and dumpy figures in dumpy housedresses. It is an inherent part of every normal female ego to strive towards the preservation of beauty, a proper female goal.'

Hansen was not to be quelled. In a further article, entitled 'Sagging Cosmetic Lines Try a Facelift', he deplored the 'billion dollar market' and quoted a report in the *Wall Street Journal* of 16 July 1954 claiming that Hazel Bishop Inc., the Revlon corporation and the Toni division of the Gillette company were 'spending $33 million on advertising' during the coming year to counter a 30 per cent slump in sales. That was proof, he said, that working women were being outrageously exploited. Among other cosmetics companies he smeared with the same brush were Warner-Hudnut Inc., Lehn & Fink, Procter & Gamble, Helena Rubinstein, Helene Curtis Industries, Harriet Hubbard Ayer, Elizabeth Arden and General Beauty Products corporation, a subsidiary of Coty. All these, he maintained, were ruthlessly adding to the crushing poverty of working-class women. 'The emphasis on cosmetics in our miserable, superficial society is one of the signs of the barbarism of the times,' he wrote. 'Lovers of beauty in the new society will feel no need, I believe, to decorate lilies.'

Equally convinced of the opposite view, McGowan (who later tore up her party card in disgust) argued that 'the cosmetic industry and their hucksters do not thrive on natural beauty which is the birthright of youth of whatever class. It thrives on the lilies who have begun to fade, a phenomenon of nature which strikes every woman in her thirties.'

A leading member of the party hierarchy, author Evelyn Reed, published a damning indictment in reply:

There are three main gangs of profiteers who batten off the mass of women they dragoon or wheedle into their sex-commodity market in search of beauty:

1. Those who profit by the manipulation of female flesh into the current standardized fashion mold.

2. Those who paint and emulsify this manipulated flesh with cosmetics, dyes, lotions, emulsions, perfumes, etc.

3. Those who decorate the manipulated and painted flesh with fashionable clothes, jewelry, etc. . . .

Accompanying them are the face-lifters, the nose-bobbers, and other surgical rescuers of female beauty.

Through Hollywood stars and beauty contests of all kinds, these fleshly standards are maintained and ballyhooed. As 'beauties' they are paraded before the eyes of the hypnotized mass of women through every available means; in the movies, on television, in the slick and pulp magazines. But the monotonous uniformity of these 'beauties' is appalling. Every vestige of *variety*, the keynote of real beauty, has been erased. They might as well be so many sugar cookies stamped out of the same dough with the same mold.

So fierce was the debate that it took a seminar and several deeply felt articles and papers (later published as *Fashions and the Exploitation of Women* by Pathfinder Press) to contain the bitter feelings on both sides. Against the big cosmetics companies, the big cats of the beauty jungle who in her opinion were the arch-villains of the piece, Reed had written: 'Perhaps only the workers in the factories of the cosmetic dealers, perfumers, dyers, and emulsifiers of this manipulated flesh know that the same cheap raw materials that go into the ten-dollar jar or bottle also go into the fifty-cent bottle or jar.'

And those workers in the factories, as Dr Brauer and Dr Ozawa and everyone else in the business knows, are wrapped in a conspiracy of silence. They are only too happy to be able to keep their jobs, to buy their own supplies of make-up, skin care, scent and cosmetics at a heavy discount.

'To the naïve and innocent,' Reed concluded, 'it seems that the ten-dollar jar must contain some special magic. The propaganda machine says so, so it must be true. These poor women strain their financial resources to get the magic jar, hoping it will transform them from miners' daughters into Rockefeller heiresses.'

It is thirty-five years since that was written, but who would argue that the dream has faded? The ten-dollar jar is now the £50 or $100 designer pot, but the naïve and the innocent still cherish hope that what is inside will be worthwhile.

And while there's hype there's hope.